PRAISE FOR *WHAT STICKS*

"If there is one book you want to have read about advertising, it's What Sticks. *It is the most comprehensive review of how to succeed at developing advertising campaigns that I've ever seen."*
BOB LIODICE, PRESIDENT AND CHIEF EXECUTIVE OFFICER
ASSOCIATION OF NATIONAL ADVERTISERS, INC.

*"*What Sticks *is a must-read manual for the modern marketer. Briggs and Stuart have captured in one fascinating volume all you need to know to make a dramatic improvement in the effectiveness of your marketing budget.* What Sticks *is a blueprint for change and a gold mine for smart marketers."*
DAVID VERKLIN, CEO *CARAT AMERICAS*
CHAIRMAN *CARAT ASIA PACIFIC*

"Nothing gets the attention of our CMO clients today like the issue of marketing accountability. What Sticks *has a clear and innovative solution for marketers of all levels and budgets to get more Bang! for the buck."*
LINDA KAPLAN THALER, CEO AND CHIEF CREATIVE OFFICER
THE KAPLAN THALER GROUP
AUTHOR OF *BANG! GETTING YOUR MESSAGE HEARD IN A NOISY WORLD*

"This book will be to marketers what Six Sigma was to GE's Jack Welch. Everyone knows that marketing is broken. Briggs and Stuart have the data-proven fix. A must read."
MICHELLE CONLIN, ASSOCIATE EDITOR
BUSINESSWEEK

"The marketing communications industry has undergone dramatic change over the past few decades: new technologies, increasing consumer control and the proliferation of media channels have created a marketing landscape with many potential potholes and wrong turns. Rex Briggs and Greg Stuart have created a smart road map for navigating this rough terrain, providing the do's and don'ts of maximizing ROI."
O. BURTCH DRAKE, PRESIDENT AND CEO
AMERICAN ASSOCIATION OF ADVERTISING AGENCIES

What Sticks

WHY MOST ADVERTISING FAILS AND HOW TO GUARANTEE YOURS SUCCEEDS

Rex Briggs and Greg Stuart

KAPLAN PUBLISHING

This publication is designed to provide accurate and authoritative information in regard to the subject matter covered. It is sold with the understanding that the publisher is not engaged in rendering legal, accounting, or other professional service. If legal advice or other expert assistance is required, the services of a competent professional should be sought.

President, Kaplan Publishing: Roy Lipner
Vice President and Publisher: Maureen McMahon
Acquisitions Editor: Karen Murphy
Development Editor: Trey Thoelcke
Production Editor: Karen Goodfriend
Typesetter: Todd Bowman
Cover Designer: Design Solutions

Published by Kaplan Publishing,
a division of Kaplan, Inc.

Printed in the United States of America

06 07 08 10 9 8 7 6 5 4 3 2 1

Library of Congress Cataloging-in-Publication Data

Briggs, Rex, 1971-
  What sticks / Rex Briggs, Greg Stuart.
    p. cm.
  ISBN-13: 978-1-4195-8433-6
  ISBN-10: 1-4195-8433-2
  1. Marketing 2. Advertising. I. Stuart, Greg, 1959- II. Title.
  HF5415.B666 2006
  658.8'4--dc22
                                    2006015680

Kaplan Publishing books are available at special quantity discounts to use for sales promotions, employee premiums, or educational purposes. Please call our Special Sales Department to order or for more information at 800-621-9621, ext. 4444, e-mail *kaplanpubsales@kaplan.com,* or write to Kaplan Publishing, 30 South Wacker Drive, Suite 2500, Chicago, IL 60606-7481.

DEDICATION

To Carmel, my wife, partner, and friend,
and our twin boys Caleb and Jared.

REX

To my wife Pamela, the twins Amanda and Sofia,
and son Morgan, you make every day worthwhile.

GREG

Contents

PART III

Guaranteeing Your Advertising Works

Actions You Can Take Today to Fix Your Own Advertising—
Insights from Research on $1 Billion in Ad Spending

Foreword

Two kinds of problems exist in business: messy ones and neat ones. Inventory forecasting is an example of a neat problem. You can go in and count the inventory in the morning, then count it again in the evening and calculate the depletion and replenishment needs, model inventory and data, and become more efficient. It might not be easy to develop the tools for optimal control of inventory, but at least the problem is well defined and everything is easy to measure.

Then there are the kinds of problems I like: The messy ones, the ones where it is hard to even know what the right questions are to ask. And once you ask the right question, figuring out how to answer it isn't easy either. These are the kinds of problems that people tend to fall back on conventional wisdom to answer, but these are also precisely the problems where conventional wisdom is most likely to be wrong.

Marketing falls into the messy category. It is messy because there are lots of variables such as competitive spending, unobserved fluctuations in demand, and a complex array of intersecting media. It is messy because people generally do not spend their marketing budget at random. For instance, big electronics firms advertise more before Christmas. Are their sales high at that time of year because they advertise more, or do they advertise more because their sales are high at that time of year? It is hard to know for sure.

Marketing is messy, but not impossible. In particular, as the authors of this book so convincingly show, the key to solving the thorny problem of measuring and managing marketing expenditure is experimentation. Randomization, so long the gold standard in scientific research, has the power to cut through the Gordian knot of advertising and marketing complexity. *What Sticks* will show you how to use these tools—remarkably simple ones it turns out—to show you what works and what doesn't in your own marketing campaigns.

The book pinpoints where marketers waste billions of dollars and how anyone in marketing can put in place processes and measurements to significantly improve the return on investment (ROI).

The fact that the book is built on a foundation of data rather than speculation and hype makes *What Sticks* a rarity among advertising and marketing books. This book offers a fundamental challenge to existing marketing conventional wisdom. It is going to rile a lot of feathers. It may get messy—just the way I like it.

Steven D. Levitt, author of *Freakonomics*
Professor, Economics, University of Chicago
April 2006

Acknowledgments

What Sticks exists because marketers were willing to explore, in a public study, the role of the marketing media mix in the hope of learning how to achieve better results for the same budget. Without their thirst for an understanding of marketing return on investment (ROI), the research and this book would never have been possible. This book measures over $1 billion in advertising spending, and spans over 30 marketers, plus their agencies, and their media partners. We deeply appreciate the contribution of each, and, at the risk of missing some, we'd like start off by thanking Heidi O'Connell and Doug Weaver who first raised the issue of integrating Internet marketing into the overall marketing media mix. Thanks go to Unilever, Tony Romeo, Charles Newman, and the Dove team who pushed forward the idea of cross-media analysis and the first study to put our design of experiments measurement approach to real-world use. Thanks to the Advertising Research Foundation (ARF), Jim Spaeth, Bill Cook, and Scott McDonald, for checking our work and providing valuable recommendations in the development of the return-on-marketing-objective (ROMO) methodology.

After we released the research on the Dove Nutrium bar soap, that research captured the imagination of the marketing industry. Thanks to the companies and marketers who jumped to the front of the line to participate, specifically the following: McDonald's Neil Perry and Richard Guest; Colgate's Jack Haber and Vicki Hugh; Tom Lynch of ING; David Adelman of Johnson & Johnson; the entire team at Universal Studios Home Video; Melanie Branon of Veri-Sign; and the team at AstraZeneca, particularly Marc White, Jean Pundiak, and Heather Coda. Their desire to get to the right answer, regardless of what it might show, was an inspiration for the authors of this book. This round of research revealed broader patterns in marketing ROI and the media mix. It also was the genesis for our Communication Optimization Process (COP), an approach that is certainly a key to improving marketing effectiveness and making it stick.

Ford, Kraft, Procter & Gamble, Nestlé, Johnson & Johnson, Target, Motorola, Warner Bros., Philips, and Volkswagen pushed even further and sought to connect branding and sales to precisely calculate the contribution-to-bottom-line profits from marketing.

The following people who made this research happen also deserve acknowledgment: Richard Stoddart, Jeff Voight, Tom Green, Kathy Riordan, Seth Diamond, Carole Walker, Tim Kopp, Joe Auriemma, Tom Brehm, Joe Schroder, John Stichweh, Todd Manion, Kimberly Peddle, Kimberly Sauceda, Jan Hall, Salini Bowen, Rebecca Seerveld, Kathy Risch, Luis Garrido, Mike Brown, Richard Del Belso, Lewis Oberlander, Don Buckley, Kerry Carroll, Elwin de Valk, John Carter, Karen Marderosian, Tesa Argones, Todd Riley, Rachel Benore, and many, many others. Thanks to their agencies and the many, many talented people that make up the agencies for their support, including Arnold, Avenue A, Carat, DDB, Digital Edge, JWT, McElroy, Media Contacts, Mediaedge: CIA, MediaVest, MindShare, Modem Media, Ogilvy, OMD, Saatchi, Haworth Media, IMC2, SF Interactive, Starcom, Team One, Tribal DDB, Weiden & Kennedy, Young & Rubicam (Y&R), Zenith, and Zubi.

A major thanks to the ARF and the Association of National Advertisers (ANA) for their support and guidance along the way, especially to Bob Barocci, Joe Plummer, Bill Cook, and Taddy Hall of the ARF and Bob Liodice and Barbara Bacci-Mirque of the ANA, who understood that there was something significant going on with our research and chose to put their time and names behind it. Thanks also goes to the Interactive Advertising Bureau (IAB) for all their hard work and dedication to ensuring Internet marketing was measured within the marketing mix and promoting the idea of public research, and the Newspaper Association of America (NAA), particularly Jim Conaghan and Melinda Gipson, for their active participation. And thanks to Mike Donahue at the American Association of Advertsing Agencies (AAAA) for your moral support along the way.

Thanks to the media companies that had the courage to share the cost with the marketers with no guarantee that the results would be favorable, and, for the sake of research integrity, agreed to the stipulations that they couldn't have any input in the research design and couldn't even see the results until after the ARF and marketer had reviewed and approved them. An especially big thanks goes out to Joanne Bradford for the leadership of MSN around the research, having the foresight to adopt an open approach that involved the broader media owners. Thanks to Wenda Harris Millard of Yahoo! who not only embraced the research but also suggested increasing the funding level, and that was before there were any results. Thanks to Stephen Kim, Piya Panyavetchawat, Michele Madansky, and Van Riley for their consistently strong support of time, money, and insight behind the project, and thanks to 24/7 RealMedia, ABC, Advertising.com, Ask.com, Autobytel, BusinessWeek, Cars.com, CBS Marketwatch, CNET, DoubleClick, Edmunds.com, ESPN, Forbes.com, Google, iVillage, Meredith, Newspaper Association of America, New York Times Digital, Oddcast, Real Networks, Revenue Science, Terra Lycos, The Excite Network, The Wall Street Journal, The Weather Channel, Univision, Uproar, USATODAY.com, Walt Disney Internet Group, and Washingtonpost.com.

Thanks to the Marketing Evolution team who strives every day to help marketers achieve better results from their marketing. A special thanks to Dave Gantman and Adam Coleman for their feedback on the manuscript, to Dyana Fitzmorris who worked weekends deciphering pages of notes and edits, and to Christine Jensen, Mike Merrill, Nicole Hart, and Adam Martin, who culled through the Marketing Evolution archives for materials.

Thanks to our friend Myles Thompson who gave us a dream team in Jim Levine and Ruth Mills to really ensure a quality book. And thanks to Karen Murphy at Kaplan, who saw that our material met the test of any good book—the opportunity to change the world (we only hope it lives up to that). Thanks to Brooke Campbell for her expert legal review, and to Bruce MacEvoy and Gail McPherson for their reviews and feedback on various versions of the manuscript. A special thanks to the team at InsightExpress. Remaining true to the principles of this book, they offered their help in testing potential titles to identify the best options from our list. Using their IdeaGauge research solution, we were able to assess consumers' reactions to 12 potential titles. *What Sticks* scored at the top, giving us the confidence that this title would be more appealing than the others considered. Will this title ensure success? It's hard to say, given that we are unable to release the book isolating all other variables except for title. However, by conducting the research and staying true to the principles of this book, we not only prevented ourselves from choosing a title that would not appeal to our audience, but we also eliminated "title" as a potential negative factor impacting the success of the book.

Finally, we applaud any marketers who choose to respond to the uneasy feeling in their guts confirming that there has to be more reliability in the work they as professional marketers and an industry do. And we especially applaud those marketers who love this business as much as we do and who on the strength of their convictions will fight for change.

Introduction

READ THIS FIRST IF YOU WANT YOUR ADVERTISING TO SUCCEED

Marketing is failing: CEOs sense it; top marketers know it; and our research proves it. That's a strong statement—but we can back it up, from our experience and from our research.

We've conducted enormously extensive research over the past 5 years, with over 30 major marketers—blue-chip companies such as Ford, ESPN, Procter & Gamble (P&G), Colgate, Kraft Foods, Inc., VeriSign, Johnson & Johnson, Volkswagen, and Philips to name just a few. They hired us to measure the impact of more than $1 billion in advertising spending in a revolutionary new way that shone a light on some very serious problems and opportunities. For those of you who are cynical about marketing research in general (as we might be if we were coming upon new research-based insights), it is worth noting our efforts to guarantee accurate, objective, and independent insights. We therefore put in place certain independent checks on our work. Specifically, every marketer that agreed to conduct a public study needed to agree to the following four requirements prior to our execution of the research:

1. The advertiser *must* be identified. The ads must be available and shown so that the public can evaluate the advertising and the brand.
2. The advertiser must be identified to the Advertising Research Foundation (ARF) *before* the campaign and data collection so that the ARF can independently referee Marketing Evolution's analysis and ensure that all public data is released.

3. The ARF will have complete, open access to the data, media costs, and other relevant inputs in the model.
4. The ARF will review the report and analysis *before* the client sees it. In that way the ARF can ensure that the public version reflects an accurate view of the analysis.

The ARF was an important partner in this research. The principal mission of the ARF is to improve the practice of advertising, marketing, and media research in pursuit of more effective marketing and advertising communications. Founded in 1936 by the Association of National Advertisers (ANA) and the American Association of Advertising Agencies (AAAA), the ARF leads key industry learning initiatives that increase the contribution of research to better marketing, more effective advertising, and profitable organic growth.[1] The ARF reviewed every study we released. In addition, the underlying research methodology was reviewed by the 30+ marketers and often their advertising agencies thoroughly before they agreed to fund the research. The methodology won international awards from the European Society for Opinion and Marketing Research (ESOMAR) and a nomination for best international research. It's been referred to as a best practice by independent companies such as the Corporate Executive Board and Forrester Research. In the process of conducting the research, we analyzed the buying behavior and attitudes of more than 1 million consumers using Marketing Evolution's methodology based on design of experiments, certainly a large and robust enough group to glean some new insights.

What we found was staggering: Our research *proves* that of nearly $300 billion spent per year on advertising in the United States alone,[2] as much as *$112 billion is wasted.* That's horrifying, right? No one wants to know their money is being wasted. Our goal is not to *damn* the advertising or marketing industry for this waste—or any particular company or any person working hard to make their marketing successful. The marketers in this book who chose to do this research could be considered heroes who are trying to improve marketing return on investment (ROI). Our goal is to *help* marketing and advertising professionals understand and improve marketing productivity with the use of new approaches, new thinking, some science, and quite a few ideas based on what we've learned from our research with leading marketing departments in Fortune 200 companies.

If you've ever felt that some of your company's marketing or advertising budget has been wasted or not spent in the best possible way to get the most bang for your buck, then this book is for you. If you want to know *what really sticks* when marketing and advertising your product or service, then this book is for you. If you really want to turn your marketing and advertising into a predictable, competitive weapon, then this book is for you.

WHO WE ARE

For those of you who are wondering how we were able to conduct this research, here's a bit of background on the authors. Rex has more than 15 years' experience specifically in marketing research. He started his career at the strategic market research consulting firm Yankelovich Partners, where his clients included McKinsey & Company, IBM, Toyota, Nissan, AT&T, Hearst Magazines, Fox Studios, Disney, and Microsoft. Before he was 30 years old, his marketing theories were being taught at Harvard and published in multiple books.[3] The *Industry Standard* called him a "wunderkind." Rex was named one of the dozen "Best and Brightest" in Media and Technology by *Ad Week*, and one of the people to "watch and learn from" according to *BrandWeek*. He has been honored with the Atticus Award for his work in direct marketing, the Tenagra Award for outstanding contribution to branding, and the Fernanda Monti award for his work in customer relation marketing (CRM). Rex pioneered the leading methodologies for cross-media marketing measurement, tracking television, magazine, radio, interactive advertising, CRM, events marketing, and the effectiveness of Web sites. Rex is also the founder of Marketing Evolution, a marketing research consulting firm with offices in New York and California and with clients in more than 20 countries around the world. His company helps clients measure their marketing to improve effectiveness of their advertising and increase ROI—in other words, to get more for their money.

Greg brings to the table 25 years' experience in advertising and marketing. During his first 10 years in traditional advertising, he worked for Wells Rich Greene, Grey's LHV&B, and Young & Rubicam's WCJ, where he helped develop brand advertising and direct marketing campaigns for such major marketers as Procter & Gamble (for Zest, Bounty, Spic & Span, Safeguard, and other brands), American Express, AT&T, Quaker Oats (Gatorade), Pepsi's Frito-Lay, Panasonic, Ethan Allen furniture, Sears, and many others. During the next 10 years of his career, he helped build or launch several Internet advertising businesses, some of which became number one in their category and others that went public on the NASDAQ, including Sony Online Ventures' The Station, Young & Rubicam's WCJ Interactive Communications Group, Flycast Network,

Venture-backed DeltaClick, and the newspaper industry's Cars.com. Greg now serves as CEO of the Interactive Advertising Bureau (IAB), over a period when the industry grew from $6 billion to $16 billion in the United States. The IAB is the leading global association (there are over 25 IABs in the world) for the interactive advertising and marketing industry and includes AOL, CNET, Disney, Forbes.com, Google, MSN, New York Times.com, Yahoo!, and more than 275 other leading interactive companies.

Over the past five years, given our front-row seat to some of the most radical changes in advertising and media to date, we wanted to do some research exploring the old quote that says, "I know half my advertising is wasted; I just don't know which half." Of course, to describe our work as "some research" is an understatement. Here's what we really did.

A BRIEF BACKGROUND ON OUR RESEARCH

As mentioned, we conducted research with over 30 top marketers. Following are more than a dozen of the top[4] companies who participated in the public studies and their specific brands whose advertising and marketing we measured, analyzed, and evaluated:

1. AstraZeneca (Nexium, "the little purple pill" for heartburn)
2. Colgate (Total toothpaste, the #1 toothpaste in America)
3. Ford (F-150 Truck—the #1 selling vehicle in America)
4. ING Financial Services
5. Johnson & Johnson (Neutrogena)
6. Kimberly Clark Corp. (Kleenex)
7. Kraft (Jell-O)
8. McDonald's
9. Philips (Norelco)
10. Nestlé's (Coffee-Mate)
11. Procter & Gamble (Olay)
12. Unilever (Dove soap)
13. Universal Studios Home Video (*ET the Extra-Terrestrial*)
14. VeriSign
15. Volkswagen (Jetta)

The research we conducted for these and other companies is likely the largest research effort ever conducted regarding advertising's real impact. Our research applied proven marketing research methods in a way that had never been done before. The Marketing Evolution proprietary methodology combines two approaches: *design of experiments* and *continuous tracking.*

Two-thirds of marketers today use *continuous tracking* which involves the measurement of consumer brand attitudes over time and in response to advertising. And although applying *design of experiments* is generally new for marketers, this approach is in essence what governments require of drug companies to do when they test the effects of new drugs by giving the drug to one group (the test group), while giving a placebo to another similarly matched group (the control group). We were able to create perfect (or near-perfect) test and control cells, enabling us to examine the impact of advertising versus no advertising, as well as the impact that many combinations of advertising creative, media mix, spending levels, etc., had at a very fine level.

For the first time ever, we really determined what the next dollar of advertising spending would accomplish at different levels, in different media or media combinations, and sometimes against different segments of consumers. We measured $500,000 campaigns and $200 million campaigns. We measured what happens when a company targets its advertising over a single weekend versus what happens when it spreads it out over a six-month span. More on the research itself can be found in Appendix A. The more than 30 brands we worked with have signed off on the validity of this measurement. And so have more than 30+ advertising agencies, 20+ media company researchers, the ARF, and quite a few PhDs lending their support as well. But what's most important is that the results of our research should concern all marketers, CFOs, CEOs, shareholders, and even consumers.

HOW THIS BOOK CAN HELP YOU

The focus of *What Sticks* is to be prescriptive and to lay out what we've learned from working with the big marketers to guarantee that their advertising works. And the book might have arrived just in the nick of time because the world of advertising and media is not getting any simpler. In fact, quite the opposite is true, and the rate of accelerated change in the media landscape combined with the pressure of increased accountability of marketing by management are making achieving success that much harder.

It used to be that advertisers could buy time on the three TV networks and space in *Life* magazine and reasonably expect they would reach the majority of the consumers. Today, most homes have over 100 TV channel options and multiple TVs per household in addition to remotes, TiVo, and other TV options on the Internet or on the go with video iPods.

Increasingly, consumers get their news, information, shopping, and entertainment online, as well as manage their friendships online, connected to their laptops with wireless broadband access throughout the house. The internet extends to mobile phones, and maybe soon broadband wifi will be ubiquitous. And it's not like the other media are sitting still: There is already a magazine for every niche interest and a couple hundred new magazines are launched every year; radio has gone satellite and digital, and so have out-of-home billboards and posters in malls; and there are new mobile devices and new networked media channels such as Games. Most disturbing, however, is that consumers are willing to pay for media and aggressively take action to avoid ads. How on earth is a marketer to know what sticks? And importantly, how do we give companies management the confidence that we know what sticks?

First, can we make you a guarantee? That guarantee is that you will improve the results of your advertising if you start to do what we suggest in *What Sticks*. Of the 30+ brands we have worked with so far, every one of them got better results with the same budget. And remember, we worked with some of the best marketing companies in the world. We've seen gains from 8 percent to over 100 percent in advertising or sales performance.

Second, our approach can be relatively simple, or as sophisticated as needed; and you can use as little of it as you like or you can use all of it to truly optimize and maximize your entire communications platform in an extraordinarily scientific way. One word of caution, though; strengthening marketing ROI requires action: Just like a gym membership, the more you push yourself and your brand's marketing, the stronger it will get.

Third, this book will likely make it easier to get more marketing funds (or to protect the funds you have) from your CFO. No more having to make the oblique and convoluted "you gotta believe marketing is working" arguments to try to get marketing funding. Using our strategies, you'll be in a position to make a solid return on investment argument that will let CFOs (and even CEOs and CMOs) sleep at night.

Fourth, and probably best, we'll do our best to give you real nuggets of wisdom on how advertising really works, wisdom that you can apply today to your business. This book provides clear "take it to the bank" insights. And unlike so many other books in this field, these are not based on someone's random opinions. Instead, these insights are based on real data grounded in real-world situations for real brands.

Fifth, you could start tomorrow—really, tomorrow (or at least the day after you finish reading through Parts I and II). At the end of a long workday, marketers and their ad agencies want to know what sticks, but most don't have any processes or systems for gathering that knowledge in a systematic way and using it to make marketing work better. Our Communication Optimization Process (COP) and 4Ms of marketing can be applied tomorrow to help evolve your marketing approach and improve bottom-line results.

So we ask you to join in on a transformation of an industry, your marketing, your business, and even possibly your career. And once you have finished the book, come join the evolution of marketing at *www.whatsticks.NET.*

Marketing Is Broken

(But It Can Be Fixed)

CHAPTER ONE

Making It Stick

The New Marketing

Marketing is failing: CEOs sense it; top marketers know it; and our research proves it. Businesses spend nearly $300 billion per year on advertising in the United States alone,[1] and our research analyzing more than $1 billion in worldwide ad spending *proves* that as much as *$112 billion is wasted*.

The purpose of *What Sticks* is not to damn the advertising or marketing industry—that would miss the opportunity for capturing the competitive advantage that we have observed the best marketers achieve. Instead, our goal is to *help* marketing and advertising professionals understand the scope of this marketing malaise—and then *solve* it with the use of new approaches, new thinking, some hard data, and quite a few ideas based on what we've learned from our research with leading marketing departments in Fortune 200 companies.

This chapter takes an insider's look at the problems facing marketing and then points the direction to some of the solutions.

THE PROBLEMS FACING MARKETING TODAY— AND THEIR DISASTROUS EFFECT ON A BUSINESS'S BOTTOM LINE

Leading marketers are realizing that their time-honored methods aren't working—consider just the following three warning calls, out of many we could cite:

1. One of the world's most respected consultancies—McKinsey & Co.—observes: "Today's chief marketing officers confront a painful reality: Their traditional marketing model is being challenged, and they can foresee a day when it will no longer work."[2]
2. Jim Stengel, the CMO of Procter & Gamble (P&G)—one of the world's most respected marketers—declares: "I believe today's marketing model is broken. We're applying antiquated thinking and work systems to a new world of possibilities."[3]
3. A 2005 Association of National Advertisers (ANA) survey of senior-level marketers found that the vast majority (73 percent) said they didn't see the sales impact of their marketing campaigns. And although approximately 60 percent said that defining, measuring, and taking action on ROI is important, only about 20 percent reported being satisfied with their ability to do so.[4]

> *Today's marketing model is broken. We're applying antiquated thinking and work systems to a new world of possibilities.*
>
> Jim Stengel, CMO, Procter & Gamble

The ANA's own senior vice president, Barbara Bacci-Mirque, gave a provocative presentation once in which she presented a program for marketing accountability modeled on the 12-step program for Alcoholics Anonymous.[5] Marketers, she pointed out, have been living in denial regarding the severity of the problem. Therefore, she suggested that the first step for marketers was to admit that their current approach to marketing renders them *powerless* and that achieving marketing success with their current tools is *unmanageable*.

The problem isn't lack of brain power or diligence (marketers and agencies have very bright people who work very had to do the best job possible). The problem is a rapidly changing marketing landscape that has made the old approaches and research tools obsolete. A new approach is clearly necessary.

The most important causes for the waste include a lack of solid business processes to deal with the complexity of marketing, lack of objective measurements of each campaign element's performance, and a lack of a predictable means to improve results.

It is a lack of really knowing what works or "what sticks." The industry calls it a *lack of accountability*—it means that budgets cannot be rationally spent and returns cannot be evaluated against investment and that produces waste. *Waste* is a chronic problem in marketing departments. Compounding the lack of accountability are outdated approaches to communication planning, project management, and teamwork arrangements among marketing departments and their advertising agencies and media suppliers. These old-world approaches stymie the ability to react to changes in the marketplace and respond to consumers' changing attitudes, behaviors, and media habits. The old-world marketing measurement that's used in most companies today was developed decades ago under different conditions. Most measurement systems don't measure the complexity of today's media landscape, and, compounding the problem, most measurement systems deliver results *long after* the campaign is over. How helpful is that? Not very.

. . . .

BACKGROUND ON OUR RESEARCH
WITH 30+ MAJOR MARKETERS

The foundation of this book is the gold-standard, expert-endorsed research we conducted over five years among more than 30 of the bluest blue-chip companies, including McDonald's, Ford, Procter & Gamble (P&G), Unilever, Kraft, Johnson & Johnson, GlaxoSmith-Kline (GSK), Colgate, Philips, Volkswagen, ESPN, Motorola, and Carlsberg, in the United States, Europe, and Asia. We measured more than $1 billion in advertising spending and analyzed the buying behaviors and attitudinal shifts of more than 1 million consumers. Many of the marketers cited in this book conducted the research as part of

(Continued)

public studies—agreeing to release the results whether they were good, bad, or indifferent. They did so for the betterment of their own marketing and to contribute to the knowledge base of the marketing industry.

Ours was likely the largest and most comprehensive research project ever conducted to quantify and understand advertising's real impact. This research applied proven marketing research methods (*continuous tracking* with *design of experiments*) in a way that had never been done before. Although applying design of experiments is new for marketers, this method is in essence what governments require drug companies to do to quantify the precise effects of new drugs by giving the drug to one group (the test group) while giving a placebo to another similarly matched group (the control group). We were therefore able to create perfect (or near-perfect) test and control groups that enabled us to examine the impact of advertising versus no advertising, or the impact that many combinations of advertising creative, media mix, spending levels, etc., had at a very fine level.

For the first time ever, we really determined what the next dollar of advertising spending would accomplish at different levels, in different media or media combinations, and sometimes among different segments of consumers. We measured $500,000 campaigns and $200 million campaigns, a weekend and a six-month span of advertising. More on the research itself can be found in Appendix A and online at *www.whatsticks.NET*. Suffice it to say here that the 30+ brands, more than that number in major advertising agencies, 25 media company researchers, the Advertising Research Foundation (ARF), the European Society for Opinion and Marketing Research (ESOMAR), and quite a few PhDs have signed off on the validity of this measurement. And the results should concern all marketers, CFOs, CEOs, shareholders, and every consumer. They provide rich insight on what sticks.

. . . .

THE ILLOGICAL WORLD OF ADVERTISING

Welcome to the illogical world of advertising. Our research calls attention to the battle between the old magical *faith-based* approach to marketing and the ascendance of a *scientific-process* approach to marketing. Our research shows the growing divide between companies that are changing their marketing cultures and processes to improve ROI and those that are clinging to the outworn mythologies and lore of marketing's alchemist past.

Consider the illogical world marketers find themselves in today. For example, look at the way some marketers set their budgets: In Detroit, the big spenders are General Motors, Ford, and Chrysler—"The Big 3" as they are known in Motown. The media director of a major Detroit agency told us that when he was working on one of the Big 3 accounts, they set the level of TV spending based on the reported TV spending of the big guy across town, assuming they must have the magic formula for determining spending. A few years later, he went to work the very competitor across town and asked the ad agency how they set their TV budgets. You'll never guess: They said they look at the other Big 3 auto brand's TV spending and set it at that! Billions spent, with the seemingly blind leading the blind. He thought that was funny; we'd bet that the Big 3 would think it's *outrageous*. Finding a new path may very well determine survival, let alone success.

Or consider how ad agencies discuss the success of a marketing campaign for the marketers who are paying their bills: Advertising man turned TV Host Donny Deutsch[6] said recently to 500 marketers:

> We did a wonderful . . . commercial on the Super Bowl . . . for Mitsubishi Gallant . . . that stops at the end and [says] go to *seewhathappens.com*. We got about 600,000 clicks. Was that great or was that not great? We told the client it was great, so it was great [nervous laughter]. [7]

The audience responded with a nervous laugh, perhaps because many of them realized that they themselves lacked a clear understanding of what constitutes success. Because most marketers don't define a precise definition of success (and a means to measure it) prior to a campaign start, they are prone to wait for the campaign to run and then latch onto any metric that suggests something good might have happened as a result of marketing and advertising. Lack of a precise definition for success is undoubtedly a recipe for heartache. It's not a recipe for better ROI and continuous improvement in marketing.

Or, consider the conflict of interest between ad agencies and their clients. Two recent *Wall Street Journal* articles pointed out the increasing pressure from marketers to see ROI and results from advertising. The articles cited how the three largest advertising agency holding companies have set up analytic groups to measure advertising effectiveness and media selection, often within the very agencies that buy the media. But how can this measurement be objective?[8]

We think it's *problematic* to have the advertising agency's own performance, which is worth hundreds of millions of dollars, measured by *itself*! One of the agency CEO's summed up the conflict of interest nicely when he said, "If you can show the value of what you are doing with analytics, advertisers will be more responsive." That's probably true—and what he's recommending is good for the *advertising agency*, but that strategy may or may not necessarily be good for its *client's* marketing efforts! Of course, most ad agencies work hard to serve their clients well because they benefit if the client is happy and the advertising works; still, isn't there a potential conflict of interest in having the agency measure itself? And, in a worst-case scenario, might these dysfunctions in advertising have direct consequences on a business's bottom line?

> *It's* problematic *to have the advertising agency's own performance, which is worth hundreds of millions of dollars, measured by* itself!

Or, consider the disconnect in measurement within an advertising agency. While the more progressive advertising agencies see opportunity from embracing independent measurement because it addresses the pressure to make marketing accountable, many other advertising agencies, and the rank and file who work day-to-day on client accounts, see scientific measurement as an inconvenience and a threat.

Scientific measurement is seen as a threat to the standard operating procedure—the status quo. Consider the way many marketing campaigns are created. The business identifies a need for marketing. Marketing engages the agency, and together they throw a bunch of ideas out there against the wall in hope that one of the ideas will stick. The "let's see what sticks" approach is fine, except that most marketers are not scientifically analyzing if the marketing concept sticks or falls to the ground as waste. Stopping to measure what sticks adds cost, threatens control of the strategic direction, and introduces an unknown to the marketing timing (because if the idea doesn't stick, it's back to the drawing board, a deadline might be missed, and someone else might seize leadership of the project). But the value of measuring what sticks is undeniable. Measuring what sticks and adapting accordingly can be worth significant increases in sales and profits.

Instead of measuring what sticks, there is a guru mentality that suggests: "Marketing is magic, and because I know what sticks, there is no need to measure it."

The image of the all-knowing advertising guru who uses gut instinct to determine what will be effective is as phony as the wizard in *The Wizard of Oz*: a lot of smoke but no real substance. This is not to take anything away from the importance of creative brilliance—that is still at the heart of the marketing world. But the core problem is that traditional attitudes and old methods of advertising measurement are not able to create true accountability. The significant changes brought about by new media have pulled back the curtain to reveal that there is no wizard, it is just a regular person struggling to figure out how to connect a consumer with a brand to build greater value for the business and the consumer alike. There is hope. We've found in our research that any person can achieve extraordinary results with a little help from a Communication Optimization Process, which we've termed COP, and gold-standard measurement.

We know that a few marketers may want to put this book down at this point. The idea of scientific measurement clashes with the "I know it in my gut"–style of decision making. The suggestion of measuring what sticks, and adapting accordingly, is sacrilegious to them. Keep an open mind. Remember, we were able to compare the effects of advertising using powerful measurement tools never available before. Research independently reviewed and validated by the leading minds and organizations in the industry and the insights reveal hundreds of billions of dollars in increased marketing productivity.

> *The image of the all-knowing advertising guru who uses gut instinct to determine what will be effective is as phony as the wizard in* The Wizard of Oz.

OPPORTUNITY KNOCKS: THE NEW MEDIA

The changes to the media landscape in the past decade have rendered many old approaches to marketing obsolete, ineffective, and counterproductive. For example, consider the expansion of the average number of TV stations in each home; the proliferation of TiVo-type digital video recorder (DVR) devices; iPods and video iPods; satellite radio; mobile media via cell phones; and, of course, the Internet. Media planning has become so much more complex and, in our experience, most marketers' methods are ill-equipped to optimize the success of their marketing campaigns in the face of this change. The significance of each new technology and media could be discussed at length, but let's just look at one—the Internet.

The Internet is completely reshaping consumers' media habits and buying preferences and has been nothing short of the catalyst for a reorientation of marketing. Taking stock of the changes over this past decade is breathtaking.

Reflect for a moment on how much your life and the life of your friends or children have changed as a result of the Internet. For example, in the past year alone, we (the authors) have each been to two weddings—and both couples met through Internet dating. We have friends whose main source of play is managing fantasy sports teams online, and others who love online poker. Neither of us has called a travel agent in years; instead, we book on the Internet. We've purchased books, toys, a vacuum cleaner, furniture, even a car (sight unseen), and countless other items online. News and research is gathered online. Packages are sent and their progress to destination tracked online. E-mail communication is now far more common a mode of communication than telephone. Sales, support, and management now keep in constant communication around the world through e-mail, instant messenger, and wireless connectivity. And, one of the authors considers his eBay rating to be more important than his credit rating.

These changes are not in what we do, but how we do it and how we think about it. They represent a fundamental shift in our *modus vivendi*—the way we live our personal and professional lives. Internet dating, for example, changes the dynamics of search and selection of a significant other. If the Internet can change the search and selection process for something as significant as a spouse, is it at all surprising that it changes the search process for a new car? Buying a vacuum cleaner online allowed me to quickly compare models based on price. We could have bought the same vacuum cleaner from a neighborhood store but instead bought from another country because the price was so much lower (even after shipping charges were added). Consider the cases where new pricing transparency has changed your buying decisions, and then consider how pricing transparency alone is changing the playing field for brands.

With such a profound influence on various aspects of life, it's no wonder the Internet can have an equally profound effect on our marketing *modus operandi* also. For example, the Internet allowed Pepsi to redesign its promotions and move them online. Pepsi's marketers discovered the move not only saved them money, but it gave them a direct relationship with their consumers.[9]

And Pepsi is not the only consumer company to rethink the nature of its products and marketing through the use of the new Internet channel: banks and financial institutions, auto dealers and auto manufacturers, pharmaceutical brands, diet services, package shippers, service brands, and many more companies are working backwards from the goal of Internet-based consumer interactivity to redefine their product concepts. They use the Internet to build a service component into the product, and that represents a new dimension to many brands.

The Internet has brought about a re-evaluation of marketing and rendered some older approaches obsolete, ineffective, and counterproductive. The reevaluation of marketing has led many to ask, "How can I know if Internet marketing works?" Sophisticated measurement systems have emerged to answer this question. The Internet has brought transparency to marketing success measurement. Internet advertising is one of the catalysts for broader marketing accountability.

THE TOPIC OF THE DAY: MARKETING ACCOUNTABILITY

The Internet promised to be the "most measurable media ever"—and it delivered on that promise. We're not talking about the fact that marketers get a count of how many people clicked on an advertisement (that's just a tiny piece of the measurement); instead, we're talking about the ability to quantify the attitude and purchase behavior shift caused by advertising. The fact that online, by its nature, has gold-standard design of experiments research integrated into the ad delivery systems, along with having better media measurement for ad exposure, ad response, branding impact, and product sales (online and offline), means marketers can more precisely measure the true incremental impact on consumers' attitudes and behaviors caused by online advertising. Marketers' ability to measure marketing success with Internet advertising sets a new benchmark.

But the superiority of online ad measurement is not the story. The story is how savvy marketers used the measurement and data to push organizations to change and to encourage *broader* marketing accountability from *all* marketing elements. The measurability of the Internet captured the imagination of marketers. They asked: "If the Internet can deliver this level of accountability, why can't we get this from other marketing elements?" And the marketers included in this book achieved marketing measurement and accountability from their offline marketing elements too. As these marketers looked more closely, they found room to boost marketing ROI.

There's an old quote in advertising, usually attributed to retailer John Wanamaker: "I know half my advertising is wasted; I'm just not sure which half." In our own research based on careful quantitative analysis, we found that the actual waste is about one-third of the nearly $300 billion spend in the United States. More startling is that 19 percent of advertising fails outright, and another 67 percent could achieve significant improvement that would require *no additional spending*.[10] Take a look at the following specifics of marketing inefficiency that could be easily fixed (and we'll tell the full story on each of these later in the book):

- Is your advertising helping or hurting a good product? Kimberly-Clark had to grapple with this question after they spent millions of dollars introducing a new product line extension for Kleenex called Soft Pack. Near as we can tell, there was nothing wrong with the product. We know through our measurement that the advertising for it did not work as well as was needed. As we understand it, the product failed to meet sales projections and was in danger of being withdrawn.
- Are your campaigns successful, but your media allocations suboptimal— or do you even know? McDonald's found this inefficiency when it launched a new menu item. After the launch, the company learned it could have influenced *6 million more people* without spending a penny more—if it had simply reallocated its media mix.
- Are you underspending on advertising? ING Financial Services had this problem. We found ING still had plenty of upside to its spending and could have spent 50 percent *more* on its advertising, with the bulk going to TV.
- Is a single element of your advertising masking the underperformance in other aspects of the campaign? VeriSign (a B2B advertiser) learned that 10 percent of its budget drove 98 percent of the actions its marketing team wanted.

The above examples are not the exceptions; they are the *rule* under the current regime of marketing.

TIME FOR A NEW APPROACH

Our experience is that CFOs and the increasing number of CEOs, especially those with a financial background, are no longer comfortable with advertising's "loosey-goosey" approach. Neither are shareholders. Not to mention, there is a major competitive opportunity for those brands and marketers who make the leap to greater marketing certainty.

CFOs and the increasing number of CEOs, especially those with a financial background, are no longer comfortable with advertising's "loosey-goosey" approach.

WHAT MARKETERS CAN LEARN
FROM ROCKET SCIENTISTS

Because our research found that over $112 billion out of nearly $300 billion is wasted due to suboptimal advertising, and because most marketers we researched had no systematic way of defining and managing the facets of effective advertising, we began to look into other complex business fields for guidance on a new approach. We found a very interesting parallel in a most unlikely source: The National Aeronautics and Space Administration (NASA).

Richard Grammier of the Jet Propulsion Laboratory (JPL) is a decorated hero of American space exploration; many NASA missions owe their success in part to his dedicated project management. His latest project, called *Deep Impact*, was extremely complex: Its goal was to fire two space probes 83 million miles into space to intercept a comet—one probe to hit the comet hard, creating a deep impact (hence the name); the second probe to fly by the comet, observe the impact, and collect science data to determine the chemical composition of the materials excavated by the impact. Grammier described the challenge of this project as "shooting a flying bullet at another flying bullet, while having a third flying bullet observe the impact and collect science data." It was no easy feat, to be sure.

Moreover, Grammier inherited a mess of a project. He summarized his management challenges in terms of the following four fundamental problems:

1. Rigorous processes either not understood or not followed
2. Inability to perform a project validation and verification (V&V) program
3. Incomplete or insufficient project progress reporting
4. Inadequate flight operations concept and contingency plans

So we asked the marketers attending this conference at which we invited Grammier to speak—representatives of ABC, Colgate, Disney, Procter & Gamble, Microsoft, ESPN, Hallmark, Volkswagen, Williams-Sonoma, and the Association of National Advertisers (ANA)—to consider whether they had faced these four problems in their recent marketing campaigns. Everyone, even P&G (who we would consider one of the best marketers in the world), agreed that they faced many of the same problems, and they were inspired by Grammier's solutions, which could be applied to marketing.

Deep Impact, however, was a complete success because of how Grammier addressed the four problems, as follows:

1. First, he ensured that the team understood and was working with *the proper process.* The process we suggest in this book is a Communication Optimization Process (a COP), and as with NASA, working with a COP can make the difference between success and failure.

2. Next, Grammier and his team fixed the inability to perform adequate *validation and verification tests.* For marketers, this is the core of measurement—it translates to testing different consumer motivations or alternative advertising messages to see which work better, or testing different consumer targeting strategies or different media mixes. Just as it was critical to the success of Deep Impact, using verification tests to ensure each element is right is critical to marketers' success.

3. Next, Grammier fixed the incomplete and insufficient *progress reports* that failed to provide a clear, overall picture of performance of key project elements. This is similar to the way marketing needs to fix its measurement and data reporting in order to provide a clear overall picture of the success of individual marketing elements. We introduce a way to organize this information—called the *4Ms*—that provides a clear, overall picture for marketers.

4. And finally, Grammier addressed the inadequate flight operations concept and *contingency plans* in the same way that marketers will need to develop a clear definition of success and contingency plans of what action to take if certain elements of the campaign are off base (we call it *scenario planning*).

Now, you might be thinking that for a project like Deep Impact, *of course* extensive process and measurement need to be central to the way things are done. After all, there's a lot of money at stake and a very narrow window to get it right; otherwise, it might be years and years before another opportunity presents itself. What we found fascinating, though, is that the total annual cost of Deep Impact is *less*—*a lot less*—than most big marketers spend: It's somewhere around $87 million a year (for a grand total of $350 million over four years). In stark contrast, Ford alone spends $1 billion in a single year on advertising. And, don't marketers have a similarly narrow window for success?

After hearing Grammier describe overcoming the challenges at NASA, Barbara Bacci-Mirque from the ANA commented: "It is absolutely amazing how similar the core challenges he faced are to marketers' core challenges. Hearing the management tools Jet Propulsion Lab's Grammier used to fix essentially process problems gives hope that the marketing process can be fixed too."

In the Q&A session, Grammier expressed surprise that marketers would spend so much more than NASA does on a mission such as Deep Impact and yet have so few tools and so little process in place to manage that spending. He quipped that maybe that's because "if things go wrong in a NASA project, he'd get hauled in front of Congress, and no one wants to be seated in that chair."[12]

Then again, if boards of directors are analogous to Congress, then the comment of Philips's CEO should be a clarion call to sort out marketing. As he said, marketing ROI is now the second-highest priority on his board's agenda. If marketing continues to underperform, or simply fails to document its value and performance, marketers will soon find themselves in the hot seat. Maybe there will come a day when company boards of directors begin to demand accountability for the millions of dollars spent, the way Congress does of NASA.

> *Maybe there will come a day when boards begin to demand accountability for the millions spent, the way Congress does of NASA.*

WHAT'S NEXT?

In Parts II and III of *What Sticks*, we'll show you how to apply a little rocket-science thinking to marketing. But first, to take advantage of the changes in the marketing landscape, and to ensure your marketing is successful, let's understand the problems and malaise advertising and marketing face. There are lots of problems but, in our experience, the root of the problems can be grouped into the following three major areas:

1. Knowledge storehouses for learning how advertising really works are often nonexistent.
2. The traditional marketing culture resists true commitment to scientific marketing and process improvement.
3. Organizational structures inhibit change.

These three factors contribute significantly to the waste. At the end of the day, marketers and their ad agencies want to know what sticks, but most don't have any processes or systems for gathering that knowledge in a systematic way and using it to make marketing work better. The next three chapters show why.

CHAPTER TWO

Overcoming Lack of
Knowledge Storehouses

Our experience is that marketers don't really have the adequate storehouse of information, knowledge, and insight they need about the consumers they're trying to reach or how to effectively communicate with those consumers. This lack of knowledge is compounded by a *mistrust of research* and a *maverick mentality* that demands that rules (even when they generate proven results) should be broken. So let's look at these problems in a little more detail.

PROBLEM #1: NO STOREHOUSE
OF WHAT MAKES ADVERTISING WORK

Most marketers don't know the dynamics that drive the success of their brands. In the cases where it is known, the insight is trapped in the skull of one or a few people, and when that person leaves, often so does the knowledge.

Most marketers don't know the dynamics that drive the success of their brands.

A knowledge storehouse is a collection of continuously updated best practices stored and harvested from ad campaign to ad campaign. It is not only available to others in the company, it is actively distributed and used. Only a few companies we studied do this well. Most companies suffer from the lack of a good knowledge storehouse.

A good example is McDonald's. Consider the learning from the Grilled Chicken Flatbread sandwich campaign. Its core goal for launching the campaign was to build awareness for this new menu item. The company hoped this new product would draw in customers who previously viewed McDonald's only as a place that sells plain old burgers. Going into this, McDonald's did not know there was any vehicle besides TV that could accomplish the goal of building rapid awareness. McDonald's is a very smart and successful company and, to its credit, the company was willing to explore. And when McDonald's changed the media mix in TV and online—without spending a single dollar more, just changing its media allocation—it found that *6 million more people* could be made aware of that new flatbread sandwich.

Another thing McDonald's learned through the research we conducted is what a big difference the time of day targeting makes: When you're trying to sell people food, it's best to advertise to them when they're *hungry*. Our research found that there's a four-hour window around lunchtime to show very appetizing images of food that can lead to a ten-point gain (from 36 percent to 46 percent!) on their intent-to-purchase measure than if advertised outside that lunchtime timeband. Because many media carry lower costs during the day, this is a real high-value insight.

> *When you're trying to sell people food, it's best to advertise to them when they're hungry.*

So, is McDonald's using this insight? We don't know. Less than a year after our report was delivered to McDonald's, the champion of the research, Neil Perry, left McDonald's, and with him, we suspect, left many of the insights.

On the operations side of businesses, it is not uncommon for individuals to stay within the same functional group while being promoted through the years. Not so in marketing, where turnover is higher than in other fields and promotions within the company generally mean working in a new brand group. As a result, finding ways to store and access insights becomes all the more important.

The fact that most big marketers who spend hundreds of millions of dollars don't have those engraved-in-stone rules and instead launch every campaign without this institutionalized learning is a great example of the cost of what we would label "information rot."

What is *information rot?* Think of marketing insights like a valuable crop of grain planted in the field, ready to be harvested. If left unharvested, it rots. But if harvested and properly stored in an information storehouse, it can feed the organization for years.

Consider the many facts that marketers can and should know about their marketing—but don't have a place to store insights for easy access. For example, everyone knows about the 4Ps of marketing (product, price, place/distribution, and promotion). But to solve this lack of a storage facility for what makes marketing work, we think what's equally important is to complement the 4Ps with the *4Ms* of marketing: Motivations, Message, Media mix, and Maximization.

Remember, $112 billion is wasted each year by ineffectiveness and inefficiency in various aspects of the 4Ms. Part III of this book provides detail on why this waste occurs and how to avoid it to achieve superior marketing ROI. Right now, however, let's take a brief look at the 4Ms and the waste we've measured.

The 4Ms are a framework that every marketer should know cold about its consumers and consumer communications. If a marketing team is not perfecting its knowledge within the framework of the 4Ms, then we are sure it is operating with a basic lack of knowledge. Fixing your advertising is hard; building improvement with your 4Ms is easy. Here's an overview of the 4Ms:

1. *Motivations:* Why do consumers buy your brand or your product? It's amazing how many times we talk to marketers where we get equivocation on this: They don't fully know the answer to this question. And if a marketer misses the mark here, every dollar they spend will produce dramatically lower ROI than it should. Out of the marketers we studied, 36 percent missed motivations and $53.5 billion is lost here alone. And, if you miss here, you're guaranteed to miss the next M.

2. *Message:* How do you communicate with consumers based on their motivations in a way that they hear what you are saying? The key here

is that what you think you're *saying* is not necessarily what consumers are really *hearing*. It's important to measure what the consumer is hearing. Of the marketers we researched, 31 percent missed the mark, resulting in $35.8 billion in waste.

3. *Media:* What is the real role of each media in contributing to a marketer's success, and what is their cost and effectiveness? Does the media match with the goals and does the media combination add to the brand? Clearly, if you don't know the value of different media, you're not going to allocate appropriately, and we can guarantee you'll have suboptimal advertising results. The waste here is $23.1 billion. There is also an upside. By rebalancing a media mix to reflect the best ROI, we've observed that most marketers (83 percent) can get at least 5 percent better results for the same budget—a majority can get 10 to 20 percent better results. The upside is $19.8 billion in extra media effectiveness without spending a dollar more.

4. *Maximization:* Whereas getting the media mix right is important, we found only 2 out of 36 marketers were systematically maximizing the effectiveness of their marketing and building knowledge storehouses to share the learning organization-wide. These ongoing programs to truly assess new media and marketing channels for inclusion in future plans produce significant competitive advantage. If we ask marketers what they have tried and what else hasn't worked, most marketers often don't know. They often have no systemic way of maximizing their results and trying new things and new approaches. Several have ad hoc efforts to figure out marketing effectiveness, but maximization (as you'll see in Chapters 16 and 17) isn't about a single effort to analyze a particular program.

Maximization is about continuous improvement in marketing ROI through ongoing innovation and research paired with information storehouses to ensure the learning doesn't rot in the field. We calculate the upside on maximization at $59 billion in marketing savings through the elimination of waste and $43.8 billion in additional profit. The upside comes from finding new ways to reach consumers and generate sales more profitably. In the increasingly dynamic and ever-changing marketing landscape, every marketer should be aggressively pursuing marketing maximization.

PROBLEM #2: A GENERAL MISTRUST (AND MISUNDERSTANDING) OF DATA AND RESEARCH

In general, the broad mistrust of data and research in advertising agencies and among marketers is borne out of misuse and abuse of data. Many people use research the way a drunkard uses a lamppost: more for *support* than *illumination*. This has led advertising agencies and marketers to rightly question research.

> *Many people use research the way a drunkard uses a lamppost: more for* support *than* illumination.

But this data abuse and mistrust is a pernicious cycle that must be broken because good data and insight is vital to learning and improvement in business. Ask anyone in operations about the role of data in generating millions and billions of dollars in productivity. Ask a six-sigma black belt about the importance of good measurement to achieve continuous improvement on the factory floor. But ask a marketer, and you are likely to get a different answer, or, more likely, no answer.

And the problem may only get worse. With the rapidly changing media landscape and the increasing speed of business and the expectation for success, marketers need research approaches worthy of their trust and a culture that embraces good quality data.

Here's an example from a major automotive company

From the headquarters of this automotive company came an edict to improve marketing that went roughly like this:

> Every part of the company—production, operations, and the supply chain—has gotten more efficient over time and improved productivity significantly over the years, so we would like to see marketing productivity increase by 10 percent this year: Tell us how you're going to do that.

With that as a backdrop, the marketers' ad agency saw an opportunity to help. The advertising agency brought us in to conduct extensive research on a new campaign launch. When we came back to present our results and analysis, it was very clear that productivity gains could be achieved: The auto brand's TV ads worked well, its magazine ads worked well, and even its online ads worked well—but the *spending* on the TV ads was way past the point of diminishing returns.[1]

During a 6-week period, the ads stopped producing incremental gains after 10 to 15 impressions. On average, the consumer was seeing the TV ads 20 to 30 times in six weeks, and that was overkill. Yet, in magazines and online, the brand had not yet hit a point of diminishing returns. Now, the agency and the marketer could not have known the point of diminishing returns prior to the research, so kudos to the advertising agency for having the foresight to gather this information for its client in an effort to help them improve marketing productivity.

The research showed that the brand could increase its efficiency pretty substantially—on the order of 15 percent to 20 percent—by simply reallocating its budget to increase magazine and online ads in the marketing mix. The company could have a more optimal plan, where TV would still be the majority of the advertising mix and the main driver, but magazine and online advertising would be about 15 percent each, instead of 5 percent each, of the ad spending.

To the *ad agency*, this was great news: Because of its proactive work to set aside agendas, the agency was able to help answer a key corporate mandate to improve efficiency. But to the *marketer*, there was a sense of shock that it had so much room for improvement. There was a lot of resistance to this whole idea of reallocating the media mix, illustrating perhaps the company's general mistrust of data and research.

When we finally met with the auto company's marketing team, we hoped they would ask us something like: "What *other* research can we do to validate this data or understand it or act on it?" But no such luck. Instead, one of the company's marketing research people pulled us aside and said, "We don't believe anything our ad agency brings to us, this study included."

As a completely independent firm, we were stunned: This person's disbelief and distrust was such a surprise because we had received so much validation by this point in our research studies, as follows:

- We had already completed research with Unilever that lent credence to our new research method for disentangling the effects of different media through gold-standard design of experiments.

- The methodology design was receiving wide praise as a major innovation in advertising measurement from a range of independent organizations from Jim Nail, Forrester's senior advertising analyst,[2] to the European Society for Opinion and Marketing Research (ESOMAR) that had nominated the methodology for a prestigious excellence in international research award.[3]

- Dr. Jim Spaeth, president of the Advertising Research Foundation (ARF), had personally reviewed all results for this company's study and referred to the best-practice nature of the measurement.

Instead of at least saying, "Let's try to confirm this data," the company left the insights to rot in the field, unharvested. The company probably missed an opportunity to improve its bottom-line profitability.

In our experience, this mistrust of data and lack of knowledge storehouses about how advertising really works is pervasive and is at the root of many of advertising's current challenges. That tendency coupled with a lack of appreciation, comprehension, or application of research learning and insights really limits advertising's ability to ascend to a leadership role for companies. A poor knowledge base and no agreed-to systematic plans for how to build the knowledge base leads to stagnation.

> *Mistrust of data and lack of knowledge storehouses about how advertising really works is pervasive and is at the root of many of advertising's current challenges.*

Now that we've described two of the key problems associated with *lack of knowledge* of how marketing can be improved, let's explore the problems related to the *culture* of many marketing departments.

CHAPTER THREE

Overcoming A Marketing Culture That Resists Change

Culture is a term generally defined as "the predominating attitudes and behavior that characterize the functioning of a group or organization."[1] The chairman of Insight Express, Bill Lipner, is fond of saying, "In a business competition, culture will eat strategy for lunch. If you have a great strategy but a bad culture, you'll lose." So in addition to the two problems described in Chapter 2—which together constitute the overall problem of a lack of *knowledge*—the next root problem with marketing is its culture. The marketing culture can be problematic in one (or more!) of the following four ways:

1. The culture may be afflicted with the "knowing-versus-doing gap."
2. The culture can produce *a distorted view* of the consumer's relationship with advertising.
3. The culture has a fear of failure.
4. The culture believes that *marketing is "magic"* and buys into the myth that *"you can't measure branding,"* with a major resistance to research.

Let's look at each of these problems in a little more detail.

PROBLEM #1:
THE KNOWING-VERSUS-DOING GAP

Here's an example from Unilever

Unilever is a great company with smart marketers, and as a testament to their innovativeness, one of our very first studies was for Unilever's Dove brand of bar soap. Here, the marketer was involved and the research department was involved. We met at Unilever's headquarters called the Lever House, which owns the distinction as the first glass skyscraper in Manhattan. One of the company's 30-year veterans of market research is Charles Newman (who began and ended his career at Unilever and was a well-respected researcher in the industry). He said that the type of research we proposed was exactly what he'd been wanting to do: Looking across media and figuring out where the diminishing returns were—in essence, answering the critical question, "What is the value of the next dollar spent and where should we put it?"

We started the research in the summer of 2001, but after 9/11, Newman decided he'd finish the research study and retire. At that point, we still believed that the marketers' ability to apply the research successfully was simply about getting them the numbers. We believed that if the marketer had the data based on good research (backed by the expertise of Marketing Evolution and the independent review of both Forrester Research and the Advertising Research Foundation [ARF]), then the truth of the information would enable companies to execute based on the results of our research.

Knowing what to do based on the data is a world apart from *doing* it. Facts alone don't change action. And, when the champion of a research initiative leaves, most organizations do not have an institutionalized way to ensure that the findings are implemented. Most organizations are overly dependent on the leadership of the individual to see that the results are acted upon.

> Knowing *what to do based on the data is a world apart from* doing *it. Facts alone don't change action.*

Our research showed that there was a significant opportunity to boost results without spending a single dollar more. For Dove Nutrium Bar (a premium bar soap product), a 14 percent gain in consumer purchase intent (which Unilever said has a strong correlation to actual sales) could be achieved simply through rebalancing the advertising mix among television, magazine, and online advertising.[2] In parallel to our study, Unilever was also testing eight other brands with another independent research firm, Information Resources Inc. (IRI). Similarly, IRI was doing sophisticated sales experiments to see not only if online advertising had an influence on branding, but whether it actually would move sales volume in grocery stores.

As Sunny Garga of IRI put it, "The work we do in conjunction with Marketing Evolution provides clear proof of advertising impact on actual sales in grocery stores and other outlets." All the studies converged on a common finding: The brands were spending 1 percent of their budget in online ads even though their target consumers had shifted their media behavior (at that time, 14 percent of consumers' media time was devoted to online media versus TV, radio, magazines, and other media). As a result, Unilever could seize a big opportunity for improving results using the same budget by remixing their media to optimize sales and profits.

Although Unilever later presented these findings proudly at the annual ARF conference in New York,[3] somehow the findings didn't seem to become common practice throughout Unilever. While there were brands (such as Dove) within Unilever that took advantage of the learning, there were many others that didn't. We suspect we've all seen occasions in business where the findings may not turn into action. Failure to convert insight into action can come from a lack of institutionalized systems for ensuring that research is acted on. It can come from misalignment in the agency partners and conflicts of interest. And it can come from a host of other cultural and structural reasons we will touch on. Clearly, a knowing-versus-doing gap exists in most marketing departments and can cost millions of dollars in marketing efficiency and competitive advantage.

Why do so many companies find it difficult to convert insights into actions? It has become a common enough problem that Stanford's MBA program now includes a course called "Knowing versus Doing: Problems in Implementation." Watching a number of organizations with clear-cut marketing results and clear upside (to sell more products without spending more) fall squarely between the "knowing-versus-doing gap" led us to develop a business process that would parallel our research. The cornerstone of the business process uses scenario planning, which is a subset of Marketing Evolution's proprietary Communication Optimization Process (COP). Scenario planning builds a bridge between knowing and doing. We found the COP with the scenario planning process to be the decisive difference in helping companies to profit from our marketing measurement insights.

The marketers who have done studies since the implementation of the COP have closed the gap between knowing and doing and improved marketing ROI as a result. We'll describe the COP and its application in detail in Part II.

PROBLEM #2:
THE DISTORTED LENS OF MARKETERS

Another central problem with the *culture* of marketing is its *distorted lens*—our term for how marketers see their advertising very differently than consumers do. To understand the distorted lens problem, one need look no further than the advertising agency's conference room. This is where an agency brings its client to show them "the creative" (the ads themselves). These rooms typically have beautiful paneled walls, impressive conference tables, comfy leather chairs, and other fine furnishings, as well as tens of thousands of dollars' worth of electronics (including sophisticated video and sound systems)— all of which are used to "sell" the agency's creative to the client—as part of winning them over in a new business pitch.

During a presentation, the lights fade, creating a different tone to the room, and the largest plasma screen ever created (maybe even multiple screens) often descends from the ceiling as if it were divinely sent. As the commercial begins, a booming THX surround-sound system heightens the experience, and the clients watch the 30-second TV commercial in rapt attention—while the agency raptly watches the client.

Typically at the end there is applause (often started on cue by employees of the advertising agency). By the end of the presentation, everyone present is staring through this *distorted lens* at the advertising message, and the ad agency and its client are holding up the ad like an idol on a pedestal, worshipped by the people who created it and those who are asked to pay for it. Is this far fetched? Maybe a little, but there is still a valid point—agencies and marketers are unable to see the advertising in the same way the consumer does.

Have you, as a consumer, ever sat and watched a TV commercial and applauded at the end of it? We doubt it. Have you spent 30 minutes focused on which breed of dog would look better in a candy bar commercial? Have you sat and counted the number of women, men, Hispanics, and others in a commercial backdrop? Probably not. That's the marketer's experience, not the consumer's experience: The *consumer's* lens is different.

> *Have you, as a consumer, ever sat and watched a TV commercial and applauded at the end of it?*

Unlike the ad agency and the marketers, *consumers* are watching TV in their cluttered living rooms, at the end of a long, hard day; they're vegged out on the couch, and they're not watching TV commercials with the same reverence that marketers watched them. For the most part, consumers are absorbing the ads with *low attention*.[4] In fact, because so many TV commercial products either have no relevance to that individual (or worse, because they don't even try to *establish* any relevance), consumers have learned to *avoid* TV commercials. In fact, as we all know, your consumers might not even be *in the room* when your commercial is on; they might be getting a beer, or putting their kids to bed, or not paying attention because they're answering e-mail or reading a magazine—or trying to do all four tasks at once.

But marketers seldom stop to think about how *consumers* interact with their advertising; they only see it through *their own eyes—through the distorted lens*. If you (as a marketer) are intently watching your ad, perhaps in an uncluttered company conference room, then you're viewing the ad in *high-attention* mode, meaning you're no longer seeing and processing the ad in the same way that consumers will. Again, consumers mentally process the vast majority of ads in low-attention mode—they're barely paying attention to your ad! Instead, they're looking for the remote control between the couch cushions so they can switch the channel.

The same is true of print ads; consumers are not sitting in a conference room in front of a magazine ad blown up ten times its size and sitting on an easel to be carefully studied. As a consumer, have you ever scrutinized a print ad to check the Pantone shade of blue used for the brand logo? Instead, consumers flip through a magazine in a doctor's office, anxiously waiting for their appointments. Or they're zooming past a billboard on a highway. Or they're leaning against your out-of-home ad while waiting for a bus—and they may not even recall looking at the ad at all! Consumers will spend, on average, only three seconds looking at a magazine ad,[5] in contrast to marketers or advertisers, who spend *days* studying and evaluating that same ad.

Consumers will spend, on average, only three seconds looking at a magazine ad, in contrast to marketers or advertisers, who spend days studying and evaluating that same ad.

Now, just because consumers are processing the ads with low attention and potentially without even recalling that they've seen your ad doesn't mean that your ad doesn't work. In fact, quantitative proof demonstrates that advertising can be effective in impacting brand attitudes and sales for the advertised product.[6] Most marketers' mental models for how advertising works is locked into a distorted lens of high-attention mode, while consumers are actually processing advertising in a low-attention mode.

Moreover, many ad agencies and marketers filter what they know about their products and brands through *their own* life experiences—but the life experiences of marketers rarely match that of their consumers! So when you combine that distorted lens with the problem of viewing the ads in a distorted, high-involvement environment, it's no wonder that we marketers have no idea how consumers will experience the ads or how the ad will influence consumer's behavior. And that distorted lens is ingrained in the very culture of marketing.

To overcome it, marketers first need to be conscious that our guts are unreliable indicators, that our eyesight is not 20/20. We see things differently from our customers. We need to be humbled by the challenge of understanding how advertising works in low-attention processing. We need a set of glasses to correct our imperfect visions so we can see in "low-attention processing mode." We need objective research systems to overcome this distorted lens, to develop an *accurate* view of how our advertising really works. And we'll tell you later in the book how some of the best companies are applying research that acts as corrective vision systems to offset the distorted lens.

PROBLEM #3: FEAR OF FAILURE

There's high stakes in admitting that a marketing campaign is *wrong*. Think about this for a moment: If you were measuring your own marketing program, would you be happy to learn a campaign or an aspect of a campaign failed?

When the Japanese find a defect in the manufacturing process, they call it a *treasure*. Finding it, dissecting it, and figuring out how to eliminate it is the path to improved productivity (translation: higher profits). But there isn't this idea in marketing, where you find what's not working, where you seek it out, where it would be considered a treasure. Instead, too many marketers view the opportunity to analyze advertising, figure it out, and improve it as a huge *burden* to the organization. A problem discovered in marketing is *not* a treasure—quite the opposite is true. It's the f-word: *failure*. And one f-word can lead to another f-word: *fired*. The f-word *fired* leads to another pernicious f-word: *fear*. The greatest fear of the advertising agency and perhaps the marketer too is failure. The average tenure of a CMO is only 22.9 months—and that is less than half the tenure of a CEO.[7] It is a very narrow window in which to achieve success.

> *When the Japanese find a defect in the manufacturing process, they call it a treasure. Finding it, dissecting it, and figuring out how to eliminate it is the path to improved productivity (translation: higher profits).*

The tendency of marketers is to spin, so every campaign is portrayed as a success. It doesn't take a marketing insider to notice the spin. There is no premium given to knowing through validation, and there is little downside to misuse of data to support a point of view rather than to provide objective insight. *This attitude must change.* Marketers must overcome their fear of failure and embrace the value of knowing and improving. We've seen the benefit of applying research *throughout* the marketing process. If you compare production and operations management to marketing, there have been lots of statistical approaches in production and operations and huge advances in these areas, but the approach to data and objective analysis hasn't made its way over to marketing in most companies. But it will.

PROBLEM #4:
MARKETING AS "MAGIC" AND THE MYTH THAT
"YOU CAN'T MEASURE BRANDING"

Some people really do think of marketing as magic. They use the "spray and pray" method of advertising, that is, you spray your message out there, and then pray that it resonates and works. And when it does, something *magical* must have happened. Because it's hard to repeat that magic or to formulate it into rules and principles, that belief structure of marketing as magic means that you believe marketing success is more like a lightning strike. And if this is true, you're not going to spend time trying to find out what works and what doesn't and *why*. If it's magic, how can you even begin to refine it and systematically improve it?

Similarly, some marketers talk about their advertising as if it were a religious belief that they must have *faith* in. They search for divine inspiration for their next "big idea" that will "magically" transform their business (and maybe even make them famous). They look at advertising success as somehow unseeable and unknowable. They tell their CEOs, "You just have to *believe* that advertising works." Nonsense.

"You can't measure branding" is a statement that you'll hear from some marketers when they're challenged about whether their advertising worked or didn't work. In general, those making this statement are *completely unaware* that they can in fact measure branding—though in a few instances, the statement stems from an *adversarial defense* against measurement. The marketer or ad agency uses this defense as a dodge against being held accountable to specific outcomes. Ultimately, this attempt to dodge accountability fails.

Here's an example from a major brand-name shoe company

We met with the former CMO of this company, who had been asked to make marketing more accountable. Unfortunately, she resisted our emphasis on research. She said her company's brand advertising couldn't be reduced to numbers because it was based on "*emotions* and what we do here is *branding*, and you can't measure branding."

This mind-set shows a fundamental misunderstanding of where research is at today. Evidence shows you *can* measure whether advertising is influencing people's attitudes and emotions toward your brand. Sure, attitudes are hard to see and touch, they're not like direct mail response rates that you can count to see how many people sent back their business reply cards. Measuring attitudes and emotions is a bit more like measuring the wind: You can't directly see the wind (usually), but you *can* see the *effects* of wind—like a swaying tree or a fluttering flag. And with the correct tools, you can accurately measure the wind.

> *Measuring attitudes and emotions is like measuring the wind: You can't directly see the wind, but you can see the effects of wind.*

Good advertising research shows you which way the wind is blowing and the strength of the wind. Good research is like a sophisticated wind sock. Good research tracks *changes* in consumers' attitudes, the *direction* of the changes, and the *magnitude* of the changes. By doing research, marketers can directly see the effects of advertising on attitudes and emotions. You don't have to just "spray and pray," with your message.

If the motivation for arguing that branding can't be measured is to avoid oversight and accountability, then the argument that branding can't be measured ultimately backfires—because eventually the CEO and the CFO look to the *sales numbers*. And if sales fail to improve, the marketer and advertising agency are sent packing. Quantifying the influence of advertising on branding is enormously helpful because advertising doesn't always produce the sales the organization counts on—and when it fails, diagnosing why sales failed to materialize allows marketers to make adjustments and achieve better results

When you combine a business function that doesn't necessarily hold a storehouse of knowledge on how its area works with a culture that doesn't believe in research and the application of that learning, then you have what many would call a "challenging" situation. Is all lost? We don't think so because we have found a path that is now proven effective in breaking through those challenges.

Unfortunately, the challenges don't end there. The next chapter looks at problems related to the *organizational structures* that inhibit changes that would help improve marketing.

CHAPTER FOUR

Overcoming Organizational Challenges for Advertising

Many marketing organizations we studied are working to sort out the incentive structure to reward learning and continuous improvement in marketing. Currently many, if not most, marketing organizations suffer from the very way in which incentives are structured and the way in which the people working in marketing, at advertising agencies, and as media suppliers are incentivised. Look at most incentive programs and few have a reward for demonstrated continuous improvement. Worse still, may incentive programs for marketers are tied to goals beyond the control or influence of marketing. Adding to the structural problems are outdated advertising effectiveness reports that offer little or no help in providing results of marketing campaigns in sufficient detail to know in time what to adjust to improve marketing performance. In fact, some organizations lack objective, detailed reports altogether. Success is defined by the agency rather than the marketers, and that sets up a structural conflict.

To better understand these problems (and therefore solve them), let's look at each in more detail.

PROBLEM #1: DIFFERING INCENTIVES BETWEEN MARKETERS AND ADVERTISING AGENCIES

Remember the Donny Deutsch comment in Chapter 1, when he said his agency didn't know whether its Super Bowl ad for Mitsubishi had worked? "We told the client it was great, so it was great [followed by nervous laughter]" was Deutsch's statement.[1] That represents one aspect of the inherent conflict that arises when there is a failure to define success prior to the campaign and a lack of objective, independent reporting. Advertising agencies want their clients to succeed, on that point there is no doubt. But success is often ill-defined, and measurement and reporting are either nonexistent or lag behind the actual campaign in such a way that they simply aren't useful. This lack of measurement causes the focus to shift from objective data to whether the agency has *pleased* the client. There's really an inherent conflict of interest in the way marketers work with their ad agencies because the ad agency is often put in the position of being too sycophantic. Deutsch is a good guy and a well-respected advertising pro. The problem here isn't Deutsch; the problem is the incentive structure between agency and marketer. It appears to us that the desire to please the client and support the agency's worth may undermine a frank and direct assessment of what's truly best for the client.

Marketers need to take a hard look in the mirror to appreciate this structural problem. How are marketers contributing to an environment within the advertising agency where fear of failure (and fear of firing) is propagated? Agencies read every week about which marketers have put their accounts up for review. The length of agency tenure for clients is shrinking. The revolving door that pushes one agency out while another comes in can result in the losing agency being forced to lay off a lot of people, and some small agencies can be forced to shut down altogether. So this fear spreads. Ask your agency team next time you're in a casual setting how many of them have ever been let go or had a good friend or very competent colleague let go due to an agency losing a key account?

This fear isn't abstract, it's tangible. This fear can lead to the agency feeling that it constantly needs to prove itself. In general, agencies prove themselves on subjective qualities such as creativity and relationship management. These are not bad qualities per se, but they are not necessarily aligned to the client's business success and profitability. Add the fact that agencies have sold in "the big idea," perhaps without a lot of research, and agencies understandably want to show that the risk the marketer took on the agency's big idea paid off. The best agencies strive for independent research, realizing that marketer and agency are in business together for the marketer's success. But some start off with "we want to *prove* ABC," rather than "we want to *understand* XYZ." And that strategy spells trouble.

Yes, it's tough in an environment where jobs and millions of dollars are at stake, CMOs last less than two years on average, and a new CMO often wants to get rid of the old agency and bring in a new one. So how do you create a culture where advertising really can systematically improve—improvement that will extend beyond the tenure of each CMO? And perhaps through quantifiable continuous improvement of advertising effect and ROI the CMO and the agency can stick around and build success that endures.

To achieve systematic improvement requires looking at marketing as a process. But many see marketing success as something magical. What if success isn't magic? What if success is a discipline? What if an agency keeps the business with its clients based on real, objective (and improving) *results*? Think about it: What if the relationship is built on systematic, continuous improvement of the results and could weather a few failures if the failures contributed to learning and growth. We've seen advertising agencies take this tactic with great success. Managing toward business success is a more powerful approach than simply managing the relationship and hoping for lightning to strike and set sales on fire. There is little doubt that agencies want their marketers to succeed. But managing for marketer's success may require a new orientation.

> *What if success isn't magic? What if success is a discipline?*

Ad agencies increasingly want to provide consulting to the client—about what the client's strategy should be, which consumers the client should target, and what media they should buy. Some go further and also want to evaluate and measure themselves. But ultimately, measurement, like accounting, is probably best done by an independent, objective third party (as Enron taught us). We have found that pairing independent measurement with a perspective that research is not a report card, it is a tool for continuing improvement, and finding elements of the marketing mix that underperformed can teach lessons that across-the-board success can't. There is an inherent conflict of interest in an agency measuring its own work. The best agencies understand the conflict of interest issue and insist upon independent measurement of their campaigns and media mix. In addition, an increasing number of marketers understand the value of independent measurement and are writing independent measurement of marketing results into their contracts with agencies. The trend toward independent measurement appears to be the lynchpin in overcoming the conflict of interest between marketer and agency because it requires defining success up front and, when structured properly, encourages continuous improvement. But many marketers lack adequate marketing ROI measurement altogether. Many marketers don't have an effective measurement system that is equipped to analyze the increasingly complex marketing landscape of today.

PROBLEM #2: RESISTANCE
TO COLLABORATION

Most parts of a business have applied value-chain thinking to improve results in operations. The analysis of how value is created in the production of manufactured products is called *supply chain* and each step in the process has been mapped and analyzed to determine how more value can be created. Collaboration among companies in the supply chain has allowed greater value to be created for suppliers, manufacturers, and retailers alike.

To illustrate the value unlocked in the supply chain, consider what industry leaders have achieved at various links in the chain. For example, one link in the supply chain is where raw materials get delivered to the factory. Toyota found that shifting to "just-in-time" inventory delivery was more profitable then the large batch delivery of raw materials. Executing against this insight generated billions in savings. The next link in the supply chain is manufacturing something from those raw materials to increase the value of the inputs and make a profit for the manufacturer. Different approaches to manufacturing create different levels of profitability. These approaches can be analyzed and improved to optimize profit. Dell is one company that has demonstrated the tremendous power (and profit) in getting this part of the supply chain right. The next link in the supply chain is where the manufacturer delivers its product to the retailer, and the retailer's expertise in merchandising creates more value (the retailer can sell it for more than the manufacturer). The retailer, as Wal-Mart has brilliantly demonstrated, can analyze and improve this link in the supply chain to create more value (profit). In sum, a company can analyze how it can be more efficient and effective at creating value at each step along the chain from raw material, to production, to distribution, to retailer sale. Collaboration that cuts across silos of raw material producer, manufacturer, and retailer is often the key to success.

But if you look at the marketing function, marketing really has not yet even begun to map out the marketing supply chain. Few have analyzed the value marketing creates and how each link fits together. There are huge disconnects: The classic one is the relationship between the marketer, the media company, and the ad agency. Our analysis has found that just as in the supply chain, collaboration across marketing silos within an organization and, more broadly, collaboration across marketer, advertising agency, and media owner, is key to success.[2] But that collaboration, particularly between media owners and advertising agencies, is rare. Historically, the ad agency was given the charge by the marketer to buy all media and act as a gatekeeper between all the media salespeople and the marketer. In this role as gatekeeper, the agency is intermediary to such a degree that there are dialogues that aren't allowed to happen directly between media owners and marketers. This gatekeeper role is a powerful position, and given the importance of collaboration between media owner and marketer, this gatekeeper role creates a structural rift that may undercut partnering to improve profitability.

Here's an example from Procter & Gamble (P & G)

P&G is one of the best companies we've analyzed in terms of marketing organization structure and process; however, that didn't make it immune to the structural challenges inherent in the agency gatekeeper role, which by definition do not provide incentives to the agency to collaborate but rather encourage a classic supplier/vendor relationship with media owners. In addition, because of the way in which risk is distributed, agencies don't have incentive to take any risk at all. In fact, the agency carries more risk by recommending a new idea, because if it fails, the agency is blamed for wasting the marketer's money. On the other hand, marketers expect their agency to be experts on new marketing trends, so agencies tend to hire a new media expert, but then hedge their risk by not doing much beyond narrow pilots here and there. Therefore, media owners with new ideas, which by their nature hold greater risk, are not likely to find receptive ears within the agency, so the media owner often tries to work around the agency and go directly to the marketer. That's what happened with the idea of advertising in doctors' offices.

P&G was approached with a new idea of advertising its products in doctors' offices to promote a variety of P&G products, such as Zest, Bounty, Pantene, and Tide. It was a pretty good idea, but the media company that pitched the idea went around the ad agencies and went *directly* to the marketer, perhaps upsetting P&G's ad agencies (all seven of them) because they had been cut out of the discussion, so they opposed the idea and barred the gates. Ultimately, the idea did not get executed.

What was unfortunate for P&G was that advertising in doctors' offices was probably a good idea, but it would have been better if the agencies had worked with the media partner to develop it. What seems to be lacking to overcome this structural rift is the ability to manage risk with good metrics or systems for really seeing if this new approach had value. Instead, the filters used to access new marketing programs were subjective, not objective.

This experience, which one of the authors witnessed firsthand, transpired a little more than 20 years ago. A lot has changed since then. Three things that haven't changed, though, are the agencies' gatekeeper role, incentives around risk, and the lack of objective measurement to determine if a new marketing program has merit. These three problems undercut collaboration and ultimately undercut the profitability of marketing.

We met with a senior executive at a major media company who compared his experience working in a manufacturing company with his experience now working in a media company. In manufacturing, his company supplied plastics to General Motors (GM). Plastics, like media, are often sold on a rather undifferentiated price-per-unit basis. Through collaboration, his team identified ways of providing plastic to help GM improve profitability. For example, if plastics could be molded to work as a bumper, GM could reduce overall costs even while paying his company more for the development of the plastic molding technology. It's a classic win/win through collaboration that any good businessperson who understands the supply chain looks for. His team understood that their success in selling plastics rested on their ability to make their customer successful. When the same executive moved from selling plastics to GM to selling media, however, he found that the same win/win through collaboration was not easy to achieve. In part, this is because many marketers lack adequate measurement systems to quantify value. In the plastics division, he knew that GM aimed to cut costs on producing vehicles, and he could run scenarios and calculate the cost per vehicle over time of making bumpers out of plastic versus metal. Looking at investment costs, analyzing the value and break-even points is second nature. Collaboration means that these calculations of value are transparent to both buyer and seller and both could proceed with business deals accordingly.

With the lack of transparent data, agencies are hesitant to take a risk with their client's money. But with media it's less transparent because, until recently, there haven't been measurement tools to isolate the impact of advertising in a particular media, and analyzing cost per impact, ROI, and break-even points isn't second nature to most marketers. It's not that the agency is blocking collaboration; it's that the agencies have seen enough bad ideas that they are rightly protective and err on the side of conservatism—saying "no"—rather than putting their necks out on a new concept. The solution isn't to go around the agency. The solution is to first recognize that the media owner must help the marketer be successful, and the marketer should provide incentives to the agency for trying new programs. Most importantly, the marketer and media owner must adopt objective measurement to ensure everyone has visibility as to the value that the new marketing program creates. We've worked with marketers and media owners to apply new measurement systems to quantify the effect of individual marketing programs, and it is a powerful success model, but without good measurement systems, both parties are blind to what sticks and what doesn't.

There's a saying that "in the land of the blind, the one-eyed man is king." The lack of system measurement has allowed those with an agenda and a little more visibility to assert themselves as king of the hill, with statements such as "the program had less value than it cost," without proof. Or sometimes you'll hear the assertion that "a program has tons of value," but again without evidence. Objective measurement gives everyone equal visibility and shifts the focus onto what works for the marketer, and this transparency is the basis of collaboration and growth.

As we look at the changing marketing landscape today, product placement, major cross-media deals, and online media options are encouraging agencies to work more closely with their media partners. However, one might wonder if innovative new programs will be challenged and adoption will be determined by politics rather than merits. The protection against politics is greater collaboration and for those programs to be measured for their ability to generate change in the hearts and wallets of consumers.

One might wonder if innovative new programs will be challenged and adoption will be determined by politics rather than merits.

PROBLEM #3: LACK OF SYSTEMS
FOR MEASUREMENT AND ACTION

We've contended that because many companies distrust data and research, they fail to establish and use systems for measuring marketing. Lack of measurement undercuts collaboration among marketer, agency, and media owner, which in turn means an inefficient *marketing supply chain*. Our experience is that fixing the measurement problem moves the company significantly forward in achieving better marketing results and helps to overcome many of the structural and covert conflict-of-interest problems.

Here's an example from Johnson & Johnson

Johnson & Johnson became the first brand we saw to really create a new system for measurement. Johnson & Johnson's top management think about things very quantitatively. A few years ago, one top executive asked his corporate marketing person about what research had been done on media testing. He asked, "How many advertising tests are we doing right now?" He found that they were doing 43 *test and learns,* as Johnson & Johnson calls these tests. "Wow: 43 across the company! How many of those have *action standards?*" he asked. With a six sigma culture and an extensive application of process excellence in production, action standards are a part of the fabric of Johnson & Johnson. Action standards are practically built into Johnson & Johnson's credo. Action standards define what steps will be taken depending on if the results come in below goal, at goal, or above goal.

The marketing person says: "Action standards aren't an automatic in market research, and none of the test and learns have formal action standards."

What an opportunity!

Johnson & Johnson's Dawn Jacobs was doing lots of test and learns in media, but without systematic action standards, these test and learns were nothing more than experiences. "There was no guarantee that our experiences would translate to better business results, and we set out to fix that."[3] The corporate marketing team embraced the idea of action standards and rolled out a company-wide ten-step marketing *process*, under the heading "Test, Learn, and Deploy," to ensure that the marketing research testing and learning translates to knowing and doing. Furthermore, action standards directly translate into subsequent marketing efforts.

The concept had promise to transform research from dusty reports that sit atop the bookshelf of research managers to living sources of data-driven decision making.

Johnson & Johnson's leadership around action standards provided fertile ground in which we refined our Communication Optimization Process, or COP for short. We applied the approach to Johnson & Johnson's Neutrogena brand with great success and became convinced that this critical business process, this COP, could single-handedly deliver significantly improved marketing ROI and overcome many of the challenges marketing faces by bringing teams together around a common definition of success and a detailed measurement of what sticks and what doesn't. We saw it in action, and we witnessed the benefits Johnson & Johnson reaped from the approach.

Perhaps the solution to the organizational structures that inhibit change is to find a way to overcome the structural rifts that exist with agencies, marketers, and media owners by improving everyone's visibility with objective data in terms of the effectiveness and cost efficiency of marketing programs. Our experience is that the best media agencies are striving for collaboration with media owners and seeking objective measurement to help their clients try new things and pursue ideas that work. Johnson & Johnson's David Adelman reported to us that central to their success in the Test, Learn, and Deploy action standards rollout was their agencies who embraced the concept and took leadership positions in supporting independent measurement. Johnson & Johnson's agencies shared this process with media owners who were pitching the idea of trying something new. Johnson & Johnson had to develop new incentive programs for its agencies to reward innovation. This transformed the agencies' focus from gatekeepers blocking innovation to gateways to innovation.

It should be clear by now that there are *a lot* of challenges to advertising and marketing. From a lack of knowledge to a mistrust of research to a culture and systems (or lack of systems) to effectively know what sticks to a lack of systematic approaches to transform insights into action, marketing is in real trouble. As marketing people ourselves, this situation pains us. The marketing and advertising industry is filled with some of the brightest and most creative minds in business, and we believe that marketers are searching for a solution—

one that delivers profit to businesses and raises the importance of advertising and its role to business and thus marketing people's role to the company.

We believe the COP, which combines measurement and process, is the solution. But before we get to our solution, let's address the reason why you should save your marketing. Then we'll go on to show you how to ensure you're making effective, impactful, profitable, business-altering marketing decisions with the COP.

CHAPTER FIVE

Can the Marriage between Advertising and Marketing Be Saved?

How do you make the problems of advertising and marketing that we've highlighted go away? Well, you could make them go away by dramatically cutting back on your marketing expense—but that's a bad idea, as we'll explain in this chapter.

Or, you can acknowledge what you're up against and find your way *around* the problems—and we'll show you the path. We've found that you don't *have* to rewrite the DNA of marketing/agency structures and try to fix each and every one of the many challenges we outlined in previous chapters. Instead, you can reframe the way you think about your marketing and advertising that will permit marketers to *work around* these problems with a new and fresh approach.

TRUTH BE TOLD—MARKETING IS HARD

Many marketers rely on intuition and gut to guide their decisions and, worse, many CEOs think marketing is easy. But consider what you're up against: No marketer is perfect—and you shouldn't have to be to achieve success. How could you be perfect and select the one marketing plan out of the vast array of possible plans? First, let's make sure we understand what we are up against.

Suppose you're developing a simple ad campaign and you have

- 6 ways to position a brand;
- 6 audience segments from which you could choose one for the focus of the message;
- 6 creative message concepts;
- 6 TV schedules (i.e., the times of day and channels you choose);
- 6 magazine combinations (the magazines you choose, as well as whether you do spreads, full pages, or half pages, etc.); and
- 6 online advertising sites.

In actuality, that's not *nearly* the number of choices you typically have to make—and yet that alone is 46,656 unique combinations ($6 \times 6 \times 6 \times 6 \times 6 \times 6$). Heaven forbid you have 10 possible decisions to make, and 10 options within each of those: That's 1 billion unique marketing plans! These different plans array themselves like a bell-shaped distribution. At the tails are two extremes, on one end are really good and profitable plans and at the other end are money-losing wastes of corporate resources. Most marketing plans that see the light of day fall in what has been called the mediocre middle. These plans generally have some really strong elements but are saddled with the baggage of some underperforming elements. These plans leave ample room for boosting marketing return on investment (ROI).

What happens when a company is developing a marketing plan? Instead of recognizing *all* the different possible marketing options, with all the decisions that have to be made, either 1 person is delegated to figure this out on his or her own, or there's a committee of 3, 4, or 5 people involved in the process. In that case, that group rarely considers more than 3, 4, or 5 possible ways of marketing a brand, even though there are several thousand, even a billion or more, different combinations—and certainly some plans will work better than others. So the odds that they will have actually picked *right* on *each* of the key decisions that need to be made is actually pretty slim. Frankly, you'd be better off taking your money to Las Vegas because the odds are better there.

The odds that you'll actually pick right on each of the key decisions that need to be made is pretty slim. Frankly, you'd be better off taking your money to Las Vegas because the odds are better there.

So there's really no way that anyone could get everything right. Let's just admit that it would be impossible. You can't humanly do it, so let yourself off the hook if an ad campaign or a marketing plan isn't performing as well as it could (or perhaps should). It's not your fault; the odds are against you. Still, the problem of how to develop successful advertising exists. So how do we deal with it? As you consider what you're up against, you might be tempted to cut bait on advertising and focus instead on direct marketing or some other more immediately quantifiable marketing programs such as coupons. Or maybe you just focus on new products or packaging, or stunts that get media coverage for the brand.

Even Al Ries, who wrote the seminal advertising book titled *Positioning: The Battle for Your Mind,* which set the stage for positioned-based advertising, more recently wrote a book called *The Fall of Advertising and the Rise of PR,* which champions PR over advertising. Some in the press had portrayed Ries's book as if Brutus himself had stabbed advertising in the heart.

So yes, there are a number of smart marketers out there who wonder whether or not we even *need* advertising as we know it. Therefore, we must ask: Should this marriage—of marketing and advertising—be saved?

WHY ADVERTISING IS STILL IMPORTANT

Given the seemingly dysfunctional nature of advertising, the complexity of getting advertising right, and the amount of documented waste in advertising, why shouldn't CEOs, CFOs, and even CMOs pack up their ad budgets and move on? Why shouldn't they kill the monster that devoured billions of their dollars without returning profit for the investment? Why is it important to save advertising?

> *Why shouldn't CEOs, CFOs, and CMOs pack up their ad budgets and move on?*

Because advertising, done right, has too much potential for tremendous long-term and short-term impact on business to simply walk away without making some effort to revise our approaches. When it works, advertising generates awareness, meaningful psychological connections with the brand, premium value, sales, profits, and shareholder value (higher stock prices). We've seen the benefits of advertising in our research enough times that we believe advertising should be saved. When it's managed with the right measurement systems, it can be improved. In our experience, it can be leveraged beyond a brand's wildest expectations. In our opinion, it's way too early to abandon advertising; it simply needs a major makeover. Here are two big reasons to save advertising:

Reason #1: Advertising Increases the Value of the Brand and the Company

Over the past three decades, the total value put on brands as a capital asset of a company has grown to where intangible assets are now around 80 percent of the total stock price of a company. Brand value is often the biggest component of intangible stock value. It used to be that the value of a company (in the 1970s) was based on plant, equipment, and *tangible* assets; now the stock market places more value on the *intangible* value.

For many Fortune 1000 companies, *the brand* is the biggest component of intangible value because investors think the brand has the power to command a higher product price, better margins, and more sales. Advertising clearly contributes to the overall development and differentiation of a brand, and, if done right, it should accelerate the value.

If you doubt the value of brand and think branding is all puffery, consider this fact: The Coca-Cola brand (the most valuable brand in the world over the past decade) is worth $67 billion.[1] Note that the market cap of Coke (Symbol: KO) is worth $100 billion as of March 2006. In other words, even if you knew the formula for Coca-Cola and could make your own jug and call it something else, it wouldn't be worth as much as the real Coca-Cola because of the value of that brand.

Coke's stock has gone down from its high in the past five years. The fix for the stock price is unlikely to come from more efficient office management or some other tangible asset being used more efficiently. It will come from reinvigoration and leverage of its brand. That's what Coke's top management is focused on, and, in the end, advertising plays such an incredibly important role in developing shareholder wealth that it shouldn't be divorced from marketing.[2]

Reason #2: Advertising Expands Number of Customers

Most of the other tools that businesses have to attract consumers only really influence consumers when they are *actively looking* for the brand. But many companies need something to speak to consumers when they're not actually seeking your brand. In economics, this is called *demand creation*.

If you want to get more sales and have more consumers knock on your door saying, "Hello, we want to buy from you," you have to bring the message to consumers, and advertising has been that delivery mechanism. Could you imagine arguing that you don't need advertising to sell a new car, you just need a really good salesperson, good distribution, and good location (so people drive by and stop and talk to the salesperson). If you followed this logic, then you're only going to get people who are in your market and who have *already* decided that they want to buy your car. This approach works in the short run, but it doesn't take long for sales to evaporate. If you're not advertising and communicating relevance to consumers, if you're not advertising and linking your brand with the motivations for selecting one vehicle over another, if you're not advertising and reinforcing preference, eventually you'll find fewer consumers including your brand in their consideration set. This might seem like "Advertising 101," but you'd be amazed at how many CEOs and CFOs (and even some marketers) forget this basic fact and run a promotion, take the short-term sales, and wonder months later: "Where did our buyers go?" Without advertising to support long-term demand creation, businesses literally sell themselves short.

But the question remains, how much does advertising sell? CFOs really want to see their marketing departments answer this question. They want to know, "If the company invests in marketing, how many sales are generated by advertising and how much intangible value is built?" And when advertising managers can't answer these questions, there is a redistribution of budget to promotions or other quantifiable approaches. A company can offer consumer promotions—such as dropping rebates, temporary price reductions, coupons offering 2-for-1, or other deals—instead of advertising, and these do produce *short-term* sales and provide easy sales measurement. However, they come at a cost of undermining the *long-term profitability* by selling the product at a discount.

For example, consider the market for breakfast cereals, which have undermined profitability through price promotions and 2-for-1 deals: If you condition consumers to wait for price discounts, or for a 2-for-1 deal, then you're also conditioning them to switch from your brand to a very similar competitive brand that may be offering a price deal this week. That undermines brand loyalty and takes billions of dollars of profitability out of the hands of companies because they focus overly on *promotional* strategies at the expense of advertising and brand-equity-building strategies. Analysis of actual scanner data from grocery stores has indicated the following: "Advertising drives 85 percent of the trial [purchasing] and 15 percent of repeat [purchasing] while consumer promotions drive 34 percent of trial purchasing and 66 percent of repeat purchasing. This clashes with the conventional wisdom that coupons develop trial purchasing."[3]

If you condition consumers to wait for price discounts . . . then you're also conditioning them to switch from your brand to a very similar competitive brand that may be offering a price deal this week.

If we want to encourage consumers to buy our product for the first time and to get full price, rather than having to discount it, advertising is a superior tool. Again and again in our research for the brands that had consumer promotions, those activities often generated the *lowest ROI* for the brands versus the other advertising options. Brands have seemingly gotten themselves hooked on the measurability and predictability of those programs, even though they have a lower return. Therefore, if we can increase the measurability and the predictability of advertising, perhaps it can regain its role as a lead tool in driving marketing profitability and shareholder value.

Advertising is worth saving because, when done right, it generates more profit and more shareholder value than other promotional tactics to move product. In the Ford F-150 launch we measured, advertising played an instrumental role in growing market share. Did Ford accomplish this by putting more cash on the hood through rebates and other incentives? No. It was a great product and great advertising that allowed Ford to sell more while cutting incentives from an average of $3,250 prior to the launch of advertising to $1,250 six months later.[4] This equates to hundreds millions in increased profit for Ford—thanks to their great advertising.

Sure, lots of people say they don't pay attention to advertising or vehemently contend that "advertising doesn't influence my behavior." We find, however, through scientific study that consumers are not *aware* of how advertising truly does influence them. They are not aware at a conscious level what impact it has, and the research supports that they can't always articulate the associations and other attitudes they have because of advertising's impact. Consumers are not video recorders. They don't record everything exactly as presented to them and hit rewind to "see" what happened that led them to buy brand X over brand Y.

Yet, as consumers ourselves, we all know that Snickers "satisfies" (hunger), Coke is "The Real Thing," Maytag appliances never break, Ford is "Built to Last," Head & Shoulders stops dandruff, AT&T helps us "reach out and touch someone," DeBeers proves "a diamond is forever," Olay helps you to "love the skin you're in," and if Cialis (the medication for erectile dysfunction) is still working after four hours, you should see a doctor.

Advertising connects a brand with meaning and can often do so on a much larger scale and at lower cost than other marketing methods. Much of our research shows that the cost to create change in consumers is *relatively low* per each person. Advertising can be very economical. This, of course, assumes that marketers create advertising that works.

> *It costs only 0.25¢ per person to make consumers aware of the new McDonald's flatbread sandwiches.*

For example, for a new menu item we measured for McDonald's, the stated objective was to generate awareness of that new product, and they did so with advertising at a cost of only 0.25¢ per person. McDonald's made 42 percent of 18–49 year olds aware of its new flatbread sandwiches in a matter of only 14 days. Again, the company's key strategy in that case was to make a large number of people aware that it offers something other than burgers. McDonald's could not have made 67 million people aware of the new product in a 2-week time span with PR, or simply with great packaging, or with any other marketing strategy, tool, or channel.

In fact, McDonald's actually pulled its ads after only two weeks because the campaign was so successful that they actually *sold out* of the new product! Try *that* with guerilla marketing! A conversation with Al Ries or careful reading of his book, *The Fall of Advertising and Rise of PR*, points out that PR is critical to establish credible meaning of the brand. And there is little doubt in our minds that PR is often under-leveraged and should play a more prominent role in marketing. But great PR doesn't negate the value of advertising. Advertising is critical as an "afterburner," in Al's words, "that keeps brands in orbit after PR gets them off the ground."[5]

Our research shows that advertising is powerful enough and cost efficient enough when done right that it's well worth saving. The challenge, of course, is that advertising has not kept pace with modern business practices in other areas where quantifiable continuous improvement has unlocked billions in business value. Marketing needs to change. So while we have to move from the old ways of doing things to a new approach, it is a lot less work than you might suspect.

In the end, what we figured out while working with some of the world's best marketers is that we don't need to reengineer all of marketing. We can simply get around the problems and ensure that marketing and advertising achieve results by adding modern measurement systems and making some changes to the marketing process. Part II describes this new process in detail.

Marketing Is Broken, But It Can Be Fixed

1. Over one-third of the nearly $300 billion spent in advertising each year in the United States alone is wasted, and marketers and CEOs are demanding marketing accountability. The root problems in marketing stem from (a) a lack of knowledge storehouses for learning how advertising really works, (b) a traditional marketing culture that resists commitment to scientific marketing and process improvements, and (c) organizational structures that inhibit change. But marketers can be successful by working around these challenges.

2. Never forget just how hard marketing really is. Suppose you're developing a simple ad campaign, and you're considering 6 ways to position a brand, 6 different segments, one of which you can choose to focus your marketing on, 6 creative concepts, 6 TV schedules, 6 magazine combinations, and 6 online advertising sites. That's 46,656 possible combinations ($6 \times 6 \times 6 \times 6 \times 6 \times 6$). The odds that you'll actually pick *right* on *each* of the key decisions is pretty slim. You're better off taking your money to Las Vegas because the odds are better there.

3. Why shouldn't company managers pack up their ad budgets and move on? Why shouldn't they kill the monster that devoured billions of their dollars without returning profit for the investment? They should not walk away from advertising because advertising has too much potential for impact on business and profits to simply walk away without fighting to save the marriage between advertising and marketing.

4. Advertising clearly contributes to the overall differentiation of a brand. And over the past three decades, the total value put on brands as a capital asset of a company has grown to where it's now 80 percent of the total stock price of a company. Advertising plays a critical role in differentiating the brand, generating demand, supporting premium pricing, developing brand loyalty through a psychological connection to the brand, and producing higher shareholder value.

PART TWO

The Advertising Fix

Improve Your Marketing

and Advertising—*Now*

6

Get a "COP"
to Direct Your
Marketing Campaign

Part I described nine core problems in traditional marketing and advertising; Part II introduces our *solution*. Our solution is based not only on our research with the 30+ major marketers examining the impact of $1 billion in ad spending, but what that research revealed about how to create change. As we are fond of saying, accountability is not measurement; accountability is doing something with the measurement.

The lack of knowledge storehouses for learning how advertising really works, the traditional marketing culture that resists true commitment to scientific marketing and process improvement, and the organizational structures that inhibit change may seem insurmountable. We would concede that these are serious challenges. But our solution is proven to work around them to help companies profit from marketing.

You don't need a title that begins with a C—as in CEO, COO, or CMO—to make change happen. *Anyone* working in marketing—at any level—can make a significant difference in their organization simply by working *around* these problems, using the approach we outline here.

Our solution helps to *reorient the way you and your company approach marketing.* And we'll say it again: This is an approach that has proven successful in dozens of companies, large and small, with big or small budgets. The net goal is to create change so that an organization's advertising works and improves.

This is an approach that has proven successful in dozens of companies, large and small, with big or small budgets. . . . so that an organization's advertising works and improves.

The painful reality that led us to develop our approach was our disappointment in helping companies that conducted the first few studies that measured the effectiveness of their marketing. We'd come back with these amazing insights and some of these companies would get stuck in the knowing versus doing gap. The benefits to companies were so clear—remixing the media without spending a single dollar more to produce incremental increases in sales to the tune of over $1 billion in the case of a couple of the larger companies we worked with. And yet, the implementation of the findings, which in a couple cases were independently validated by actual sales figures, was far less ambitious than we would have suspected. We were stunned by this reaction, or lack of action. As we studied the issue, discovered the problems described in Part I, and worked with more great companies, we recognized the need to implement a new approach to addressing the knowing versus doing gap.

Our solution in essence *forces* marketers and their organization's key participants to think about the *possible upside* and, more important, the *downside* of their marketing plans, and to agree in advance what "Plan B" might be if their initial marketing plans fail in one area or another, and then map out an action plan in some detail. We found this simple process (paired with gold-standard research) to be extraordinarily powerful in improving the real results of every advertising campaign to which it was applied.

OUR COP ENSURES ACCOUNTABILITY

Our solution, based on our direct experience, is that marketers need a *COP*— a Communication Optimization Process paired with marketing effectiveness measurement. The COP is an authoritative process to enforce

- the *alignment* of your marketing plans to definitions of success,
- development and application of marketing *best practices*, and
- agreement to specific marketing *actions* (what Johnson & Johnson called *Action Standards*).

The process does not require a major overhaul of your (or any) organization's structure, a redesign of your entire marketing process, or a rewriting of the laws of how agencies, marketers, and media owners work together. The process is more like a metaphorical *traffic cop* who waves cars around an accident to keep the flow of traffic moving. Similarly, the marketing function needs a COP to help direct the marketing team to be accountable in four ways:

1. The team as a whole must be accountable to the marketing goal itself.
2. Each team member must be accountable to the others.
3. There must be accountability in measurement of marketing effectiveness.
4. There must be accountability in taking action to improve marketing.

Accountability in this four-step method produces superior results. Let's look at a metaphorical traffic accident. Based on the stakes in marketing, the collision of what the well-meaning team hoped would happen and the reality of a missed goal must feel like a gruesome 20-car pileup. When there is a *wreck* in marketing, the best way to move forward to success is to find a way to drive around it. Because the goal is to get to where you were heading—creating marketing that provides growth and profit to the business.

It is clear that CEOs and CFOs want better results from their investments, marketers want better results, and advertising agencies want their clients to be successful; but the process and measurement leading to better results has been elusive for most. Because business schools don't teach it (yet), top companies are developing their own approaches to marketing accountability. We've seen a few different approaches, and we found the COP, or a variation of it, to produce the most success.

Let's be clear, though: Our COP is a *helpful* traffic cop with a badge and a smile and a strong desire to "serve and protect." Our marketing COP is not an authoritative, mean SOB with a gun and an attitude. Nothing could be more destructive to marketing accountability than a heavy-handed process. The culture of marketing would reject it, and an overbearing process itself would destroy the creative process and collective approach needed to solve difficult marketing problems. Our process, our COP, takes an entirely different approach. The most important tools are not the COP's gun or handcuffs, they are his or her eyes and hands. Eyes that see what sticks and hands that wave people through, offering guidance to get marketers to where they are intending to go and maintaining the rules of the road for the good of all.

Our COP is a helpful traffic cop with a badge and a smile and a strong desire to "serve and protect."

HOW OUR COP WORKS

So now that you've met our marketing "COP," let's look at how the process really works. The foundation of what makes this hands-on approach work revolves around three meetings. The first meeting brings the entire team together to develop a shared definition of success. The second meeting is oriented around *scenario planning*, and the meeting maps the actions to be taken, depending on different outcomes of the campaign. The third meeting connects the definition of success and scenario planning with marketing effectiveness measurement to confirm which specific actions will be triggered based on campaign performance. We will illustrate these steps in Chapter 7. In our experience, the COP uses scenario planning plus measurement (what you might call *trust but verify*) and a precommitment to action. If it were a formula, it would look like this:

Scenario Planning + Measurement + Action = Same budget, better results

Same budget, better results means increased marketing profit without necessarily spending more on marketing. Scenario planning adds the following four benefits to the marketing function:

1. It *focuses attention on improving marketing* with marketing effectiveness measurement as opposed to using measurement as a report card.
2. It *cuts across company silos* and achieves the teamwork and preplanning that are critical to the continuous improvement of marketing.
3. It *cuts down dramatically on the Monday-morning quarterbacking* that occurs when the marketing and advertising team fails to define expectations and action plans up front, before the campaign is launched, which then leaves room for others to criticize and argue, "If I had my way, we wouldn't have made that mistake."
4. And, perhaps most important, it *provides a process* to ensure that the results are acted on to improve marketing return on investment. After all, ROI research that isn't applied is *worthless*.

USING OUR COP TO IMPROVE
THE 4Ms OF ADVERTISING

The COP helps the marketing team see things it might otherwise miss. Furthermore, as a result of the first meeting, which explores the definition and dynamics of success, the COP produces a clear understanding of the dynamics of the entire business situation. For example, imagine you're stuck in your car trying to navigate around an accident. The COP can see things that you might miss from your vantage point. And, with better visibility, the COP helps by applying order, breaking gridlock, and ensuring that everyone gets to where they need to go as quickly as they possibly can.

Similarly, consider the dynamics of a marketing campaign. We've found nine discrete facets to advertising effectiveness that can be grouped into four categories we call the 4Ms. The 4Ms stand for motivations, message, media, and maximization You might view these as the map upon which you make decisions (see Figure 6.1).

Surprisingly, our research revealed that most marketers don't address two-thirds of the facets outlined in Figure 6.1 and tend to think about and manage *only a couple* of these facets. As a result, of the 36 campaigns we worked with to measure and optimize their marketing ROI, all but one of them had areas where they could make adjustments and achieve significantly greater ROI from marketing. If we take the first campaigns we measured prior to applying the learning as a cross-section of current marketing success rates, *more than*

FIGURE 6.1 The 4Ms

Motivations (strategy)			Message (creative)		Media (allocation)		Maximization (ROI)	
Consumer Needs	Positioning	Segmentation	Message Communication	Touchpoint Integration	Media Mechanics	Psychologics	Intra-Media Optimization	Extra-Media Optimization

one-third of advertising spent could be considered to have been wasted because it didn't address one or more critical facets of the 4Ms. We can now respond to John Wanamaker's famous complaint, "I know half my advertising is wasted; I'm just not sure which half." We can know which half is wasted, and we can fix it.

Take the first M, motivations, as an example of where a COP can make a difference. Harvard professor Clay Christiansen and Taddy Hall, the Chief Strategy Officer of the Advertising Research Foundation (ARF), calculated that 90 percent of new product introductions fail. In their *Harvard Business Review* article, "Marketing Malpractice," they put the blame squarely on *flawed understanding of consumer motivations* that produced these doomed products and their corresponding advertising campaigns.[1]

Our own research pinpoints a similarly disturbing fact: Most companies don't have any systematic *process* in place to make important, critical marketing decisions for getting at consumer motivations, which is the first of the 4Ms. In fact, many of the decisions pertaining to all of the nine facets of marketing and advertising are seemingly made somewhat ad hoc in nearly a third of the companies we've studied. As a result of failing to understand the first of the 4Ms, motivation, $53.5 billion is wasted in advertising each year. Waste, or missed opportunity for expanded marketing profit, occurs at each of the 4Ms. And don't forget our research and analysis has been conducted among many of the top 100 global advertising companies. Because these companies are probably better than most at marketing, our estimate of the percent of companies missing the mark on motivation and the cost in terms of waste is likely conservative!

Sure, most companies do research here and there, but they don't have a *comprehensive, holistic view* of all the facets they need to measure to make good marketing decisions. They also don't have a feedback loop to apply the learning, and that's a shame because such insight can have dramatic impact on the success of marketing.

Most companies do research here and there, but they don't have a comprehensive, holistic view of all the facets they need to measure to make good marketing decisions.

Here's an example. A marketer had a Poker TV program to promote. Like many other companies, this marketer jumped straight to "creative messaging" for its poker program. They looked at their poker program with a multimillion-dollar jackpot for the winner and decided that the multimillion-dollar jackpot would motivate consumers to watch, and therefore, the jackpot should be the focus of the marketing message. Unfortunately, the decision to make the jackpot the focal point of the advertising wasn't based on any research of consumers' underlying motivations. It was based on gut. Intuition said: Because poker is about winning money, let's focus on the high stakes.

When the marketing team got the results from our research on ad effectiveness, the network found that viewers were more strongly motivated by the *quality of competition* and *specific game strategies* than by the size of the jackpot. People watched the show because they wanted to learn how the best poker players play so they could play better themselves.

When marketing focuses on the right motivations, everything that follows is more efficient and more effective (motivations can make the difference between success and failure).

Our research has shown that you can't just "skip over" any of the nine facets of the 4Ms because missing some of them can lead to invalidating any other "right" decisions, and may doom the entire campaign to failure. Think of the facets as land mines and potholes. Some of the nine facets are small potholes, and stepping in them will cause you to twist an ankle. They'll erode your marketing ROI, but they won't kill you. However, some are land mines and, well, we know what can happen if we miss seeing those.

To give the examples of land mines, where missing them means that everything else has a high chance of failure, consider the following:

- Brand positioning involves understanding your *consumers' motivations* and why your consumers buy your brand instead of the competition's. If you mess this up and you position your brand in a way that it doesn't solve a consumer problem, *everything* you do afterwards is going to be suboptimal, or possibly worthless.
- Similarly, if you translate that consumer-motivation statement into an ad that doesn't resonate with consumers or doesn't communicate the right message to consumers, nothing you do afterwards in terms of tweaking your media allocation between TV, magazines, and online, etc., is going to make that much of a difference.

If you get the first two Ms right—motivations and messaging—it will matter less if you get the absolutely best possible media schedule. The media mix is important, but if it is built on a solid foundation in terms of motivation and message, then problems with the media mix are more akin to potholes than land mines.

OUR COP HELPS FOCUS ON WHAT'S MOST IMPORTANT

If you want your marketing and advertising to have a better-than-average shot at being effective and successful (and not just an extravagant waste of money, no matter how fun your ads are!), you need to follow the process, and work with the COP, in a systematic way. Our COP doesn't simply or blindly enforce the "laws" of marketing success; instead, it provides a way of approaching marketing that helps marketing groups focus on *what matters* and on what needs to be done to ensure marketing success. That's where *scenario planning* can help because it breaks marketing inertia, changes the marketing culture, and improves advertising results.

Scenario planning makes you think about your preparedness for what needs to happen in "what-if" cases.

Scenario planning is a term most often applied to an approach that military intelligence and government policymakers take in developing options for an uncertain future. The benefits are obvious in that scenario planning makes you think about your preparedness for what needs to happen in "what-if" cases. That way, the groups who are affected are in agreement about what should be done and are able to respond quickly, rather than not at all.

When scenario planning is applied to marketing, we find that groups are encouraged to invest their attention on figuring out what are the right metrics for success before the campaign begins. They select milestones to plan when to take action and use the data to determine which plans to activate. Scenario planning dovetails with institutionalized knowledge (the knowledge storehouse) so that learning from each campaign makes the next campaign more effective.

For example, several clients have transformed marketing by using research to analyze and improve each campaign. Each year, we at Marketing Evolution pull the research from all the campaigns we've measured and perform a "benchmark" analysis to summarize for the marketing team what were the most effective strategies for media targeting, flighting (the pattern of when ads run on-air), advertising weight level, etc. We do this across different types of ad campaigns so that the marketer can achieve a deeper understanding of how marketing works in different situations.

The benchmark analysis and related marketing team meeting maps "ideal media plans" to achieve success for different types of marketing situations, and feeds the marketing teams knowledge storehouse of institutionalized learning (which survives even if the champion of the marketing program leaves). These marketers learn from both success and failure. Unfortunately, most marketing organizations don't analyze the reasons for success or failure; they move on too quickly to the next program without institutionalizing learning. For perspective, and to improve marketing's chances of success, let's take a look at some entirely different spheres of life to better consider the state of marketing in terms of applied learning to improve success and survival.

WHAT MARKETERS CAN LEARN FROM MOUNTAIN CLIMBERS

Cotton kills is an expression used by mountaineers. Why do we mention it in a book about marketing? Because mountaineers know something that marketers could learn from. Marketers could learn that embracing failure, learning from it, and applying the lessons can improve their survival.

Marketers do not embrace the f-word—*failure*. And, based on our work in more than two dozen countries, the level of denial in marketing is pandemic. Yet, much can be learned from failure. Each year, the *American Alpine Journal* delivers a thick volume chronicling failures of mountaineers. The point is to help others learn from those failures and to take specific action to avoid failure in the future.

For example, ever heard of the Marty Hoey knot? It's an extra twist added to the previous way that mountaineers tied their safety harnesses. It's named for, you guessed it, Marty Hoey. You might think, as a marketer, how flattering it is to have invented a knot and have it branded with your name. But Hoey is not the person who discovered the Marty Hoey knot. She is the one who sadly died on Mount Everest, due to a knot that, as it turned out, was not sufficient to prevent disaster. The new knot was invented as a way to save lives and as a tribute to Marty's life.

What are the marketing failures that you've learned from, that your company has learned from? Which of those lessons borne of failures are worthy of bearing your name as a tribute? (Or would it be taken in your marketing organization culture as an insult to attach your name to something that had been developed and had failed?) Remember the Japanese manufacturing concept we discussed in Chapter 3—that a defect is a treasure? The COP creates an environment where failure is neither personalized nor shameful; rather, the process makes it easy to quickly recognize points of failure and to adapt in order to get marketing on the right path to success and increased profit. We've found that knowing why something fails, and adjusting accordingly, can be worth millions of dollars in marketing ROI.

Let's go back to the expression, *Cotton kills.* What do mountaineers know about cotton that causes them to not use it in back-country conditions and to use such a harsh expression as "cotton kills"? Cotton kills because it fails to wick moisture away from the body and instead traps it—and in cold weather conditions that can induce hypothermia. Mountaineering is as much about preparing for the downside as it is about climbing a mountain. Mountain climbers *assume* that things will go wrong and that conditions could change. To not plan accordingly for the downside can be the difference between life and death. Therefore, mountaineers pack the right synthetic clothing. Look inside a mountaineer's backpack. Any mountaineer worth his carabineers can be found carrying a waterproof jacket shell, even in sunny weather, just in case. They will also carry waterproof matches, iodine to make safe water, ropes, and extra food. They do this because they want to be able to climb another day should things not go as planned. *Cotton kills* is a simple expression used among mountaineers as a reminder to pack for the downside. Marketers could learn from this.

Mountain climbers assume that things will go wrong and that conditions could change. To not plan for the downside can be the difference between life and death. . . . Marketers could learn from this.

What's in your marketing plan backpack? The COP's scenario planning generates the list of "things to take with you" just in case your sunny forecast turns to drizzle and snow. If things don't go as hoped, these action plans may guarantee you get to climb another day.

Marketers Are Overly Optimistic: We Need to *Consider* Failure In Order to *Avoid* Failure

Scenario planning is about planning for both the upside and the downside. Yet many marketers just don't do this. For example, at our own companies, we use an assessment test during job interviews, to give us bell-shaped-curve benchmarks on core personality attributes of job candidates in an effort to ensure that we have the right people for the right jobs. One of the elements this assessment determines is if candidates question the information they are given, or if they accept things at face value. We interview lots of marketing people, and we've been surprised to see that marketing people consistently score very, very high (e.g., in the top 15 percent to 20 percent of the U.S. population) in the trait of *trusting* what they hear and expecting things to work out for the best.

Our conclusion is that marketing people are not suspicious of what they hear and read in marketing plans and agency briefs. They don't naturally think of the downsides. They accept that all will work out. And although we appreciate positive attitudes, this trait is often the difference between success and failure. It is particularly problematic in that many marketers assume that others in the business share the same definition of success for a marketing program. To trust everything or everyone is deadly. Our COP adds a trust-but-verify balance to marketing planning.

> *Marketing people are not suspicious of what they hear and read in marketing plans and agency briefs. They don't naturally think of the downsides.*

To illuminate, confront, and manage the downside risk, the COP helps marketers get consensus about the following three things:

1. Explicit, agreed on definition of success ("Are we all aiming for the same goal?")

2. Agreement on how success will be achieved by advertising/marketing (because not all company goals can be achieved by marketing)
3. Group exploration of what could go wrong and what will be done to address it if it does go wrong

To address the third point, marketers must have a very clear understanding of the dynamics that determine success. And the 4Ms—motivation, message, media, and maximization—are those broad dynamics.

Few marketers voluntarily explore what could go wrong in a marketing program. And yet, the exploration of what could go wrong is vital to developing plans to minimize failure and maximize the chances of success. Scenario planning starts with how marketing is *intended* to work and then moves through a process of mapping action plans based on possible outcomes from marketing. Scenario planning along with gold-standard measurement are the keys to the COP system that helps overcome the dysfunctional dynamics outlined in Part I.

Scenario Planning Builds Consensus

The point of scenario planning is to *build consensus* across all key decision makers in advertising, in terms of how the marketing is intended to work, and to agree on the definitions of what constitutes a successful marketing campaign. Equally important, scenario planning builds consensus on what *actions* are to be taken depending on different outcomes of the results prior to receiving those results.

Here is an illustration of the importance of scenario planning. Imagine a group of friends decides to get together to have some fun on a Friday night. Think about how widely the possible options of "getting together to have fun" could span. For some, it might be a quiet dinner; others might want to have a wild night out on the town. So it's probably a good idea for this group of friends to discuss briefly—*before* Friday night—what *everyone* would *agree* would be "fun."

The same applies to your marketing and advertising team: You need to agree in advance what your goals are and how you're going to achieve them. Because we *choose* our friends, such a group is generally somewhat unified on what they want to do. However, in companies, people come to work with many different life experiences, educational backgrounds, levels of work experience, job functions, and, therefore, goals—all of which play a major role in increasing the odds that they all don't see the world in the same way. Also, friends can opt out and just do their own thing if they don't agree with the group. Companies can't have employees selectively opting out of working toward the same goal.

With success defined, the team can begin playing the what-if game, as seen in the following examples:

- "What if we missed the mark of our advertising campaign because of a suboptimal media mix?"
- "What if the messaging isn't changing consumers' attitudes?"
- "What if sales are not impacted?"
- "What if we are under-spent in TV?"

And we need to address the following:

- "What would we do?"
- "Who would do it?"
- "When would it be done?"

Of course, this thinking process begs this question: "How can we know such things?" But set that question aside for a moment. As Harvard professor Gerald Zaltman argues, marketers would benefit by occasionally considering: "If this idea were true, would it change how I think or behave?"[3] Note that scenario planning is *not* a creative brainstorming session to come up with the campaign or the creative message, nor is it about "advertising by committee." It is making sure that the brand managers, marketers, agency creatives, finance managers, researchers, media planners, and others are aligned to the *same goal*, are aware of the *same potential downsides*, and are in *agreement* on the same action standards based on different outcomes. Therefore, each person brings his or her unique perspective to the process. The value of scenario planning is that it helps the team agree in advance on what drives business success and, therefore, what should be the advertising goals. It also helps the team think more deeply about success dynamics and to plan how to adapt if the actual results differ from expectations.

Marketers would benefit by occasionally considering: "If this idea were true, would it change how I think or behave?"

So in the end, the formula for our solution is simple:

Scenario Planning + Measurement + Action = Increased Marketing Profit

We've seen this work again and again to create real change. Applying these three items in light of the 4Ms of motivation, message, media, and maximization is a surefire approach to making sure that nothing gets missed that could sink your whole marketing campaign. Making sure that there is a Plan B and having the measurement to know if Plan A is working seems simple enough, but, as we've said, it is not being done. The next chapter describes how scenario planning works—and how it can work for you.

The COP in
Three Simple Steps

A marketing COP can help you bring together the marketing team to achieve accountability and improved results. There are three steps to the process that can be accomplished in three meetings. This chapter offers an end-to-end view. If you want more information on these three meetings, Appendix A provides additional background on scenario planning.

STEP 1: GET CONSENSUS ON WHAT YOUR SPECIFIC GOALS ARE FOR EACH AD CAMPAIGN

The first thing you need to do—and anyone should be able to do this, at any level—is to request a meeting with those involved in a particular marketing campaign. This will include brand managers, finance people, media team, and everyone who will be involved in or has valuable input to the marketing and advertising campaign. It's good to have an objective facilitator. If you're the facilitator of that meeting, you'll then have the following two objectives:

1. Get an *unambiguous, clear definition* of *what success will look like* for this campaign
2. Define specifically *how each marketing element* (i.e., advertising, direct mail, skywriting—whatever!) *will contribute to that success*

Don't be surprised if it takes 90 minutes to get five or more people to agree on what defines success and how each marketing element contributes to success. It is worth having a meeting to define success even if your campaign is *already* produced and you are doing the scenario planning simply as a double check before optimizing the media mix.

The reason you need to define success at the outset is that people often have different ideas about how a marketing program should work; therefore, they have different expectations and definitions of success. In our research with more than 30 of the top 100 marketers, we found that *87 percent of their teams started with divergent definitions of success.* You might have a definition of success in your mind that you think everyone agrees with; don't be so certain. Odds are that at least one of the key stakeholders has a very different definition of success. And even when the definition of success on the surface seems clear and mutually agreed upon, scratch the surface and you will likely find that there is a lot less agreement on what success is.

The value of the COP will become most obvious the moment you hear one of the participants answer, "The goal of this campaign is *A, B,* and *C.*" Jump on that goal definition with politeness and ask, "If you achieved A, but not B or C, is that success?" What about B, but not A or C? Check all the combinations, and you'll find that the multiple goals have a distinct possibility of crashing together in a way that makes it ambiguous to define whether the campaign should be defined as success. By interrogating the different goals and definitions of success, you can get to what that person really defines as success. Involve the entire group in the discussion so there is consensus as to whether goal A really is more important than B or C, for example.

> *Multiple goals have a distinct possibility of crashing together in a way that makes it hard to define whether the campaign should be considered a success.*

The COP can help here, too. Think of this process as everyone coming to a five-way intersection, with no traffic lights or "Stop" signs. Each person, based on his or her goals and definition of success, might have a different view of who should proceed first. And that could easily result in a five-car accident. So the COP needs to make sure that those five drivers agree on what the appropriate traffic flow should be by prioritizing goals to arrive at a definition of success that works for everyone.

And, again, this doesn't mean that this is advertising by committee. It's about making sure the group is driving toward the same goal. We've found that people come with very different sets of implicit definitions of success—for example, that someone in finance has ideas that could be in conflict with what one marketer might know to be true or not true about the brand. In addition, promotions people have expectations that may be different from the agency's goals, and so on. Let's examine this with an example.

Consider our experience working with a number of marketers launching new line extensions. The line extension could be a new formula of Colgate toothpaste, or a new soap, such as the Dove Nutrium bar, or a new menu item at McDonald's. The COP conversations have been amazingly similar across a range of line extensions. Not surprisingly, when asked what defines success, the answer is generally unanimous: The definition of success for the advertising is *sales*. Is *sales* a straightforward and unambiguous definition of success? No. *Sales* is actually pretty vague.

"Sales of what?" we ask in the first meeting. "Of this new product," answers someone. But someone else answers: "Sales on the entire brand line counts as success, too." The line extension is meant to have a halo effect across the entire brand. "In fact," another chimes in, "the ad for the line extension is really to drive interest and communicate relevancy." So, what is success? Does success consist of sales of the new line extension or sales of the overall brand, or is it interest and relevancy?

This isn't a hypothetical discussion. This dialogue unequivocally illustrates that marketers need *to squeeze every bit of ambiguity out of their definition of success*. Question the wording. Push the point. What if sales of the overall brand went down, but sales for the line extension went up: Is that success? Some may answer no, cannibalization isn't success. For others, cannibalizing yourself is better than your competitors eating your lunch. When we facilitate these meetings, we politely challenge the definition of success with "what ifs" until *everyone agrees* to exactly what constitutes success.

In most cases, sales for the line extension were prioritized as the highest goal of the campaign, with a caveat that if advertising for the line extension increases overall brand sales, "We'll take that as success too." In our experience, it is perfectly acceptable to have a prioritized definition of success. So, sales of the line extension first and secondarily increased sales for the overall brand sounds like a pretty clear definition of success, doesn't it? But is it? In some cases, *where* the sales come from is part of the definition of success. "Does it matter to the team where the sales come from?" we asked. For example, if you were McDonald's and discussing the Grilled Chicken Flatbread Sandwich, the sales could come from the following three sources:

1. New consumers, who are attracted by the novelty of the new sandwich
2. Existing customers, who may come more often (i.e., increasing visits to McDonald's)
3. Existing customers, who are visiting at the same frequency but are now spending a little more than they otherwise would have to buy one more item (the new Grilled Chicken Flatbread Sandwich)

Where sales come from may or may not be relevant. In working with the Olay brand of Procter & Gamble, it mattered whether they were attracting new customers or selling to existing customers. For McDonald's, they defined their target as "people who eat." In other words, everyone; and they were happy to get sales from any source, though they suspected that the flatbread sandwich would likely bring in consumers who would ultimately buy a burger. For Philips and their high-end electric shaver, the sales focus was divided among two targets, gift givers (mostly women) and males buying for themselves. Does your advertising campaign aim to generate sales by specifically targeting one group over another? If you had success with one segment, but not another, would that still be success? This question will help the group define and focus on whether there are different priorities (and definitions of success) by consumer segment.

The final issue for the group to consider and discuss (after clearly articulating goals, priorities, and consumer-segment priorities) is a deceptively simple question: "Why would these consumers take the action we have defined as success?" In other words, what motivates consumers, and how is our marketing tapping into that motivation? Checking that the marketing plan is matched to consumer motivations is critical. Recall that our poker client started with the assumption that the motivation to watch their poker program was the huge jackpot. Even if the assumptions prove to be wrong, having explicitly listed and discussed them will make it easier to develop scenario plans if the motivation is off-base, and to "trust but verify" when the campaign is in market. When the client learned that a more powerful motivation for watching the Poker program was the quality of the competition, the client was in a great position to leverage that learning and make the appropriate adjustments.

Consensus is the name of the success definition game. Everyone needs to contribute and agree with what exactly defines success for that campaign. If we want our marketing to stick, we need to know and all agree to what success looks like. The first meeting creates a one-page memo, distributed to the team, that summarizes a shared definition of success. It doesn't guarantee that the marketing plan will achieve success, but we've found that the discussion alone generated a deeper degree of alignment and, after the results are in, at least one person recognized that a few changes to his or her part of the marketing program would be in the overall interest to help the company achieve the agreed-upon definition of success.

> *If we want our marketing to stick, we need to know and all agree to what success looks like.*

STEP 2: CREATE DECISION TREES TO AGREE ON ACTION PLANS

The second meeting is scenario planning where we map out possible outcomes and agreement on the next step. We call these maps *decision trees*. Each tree branch ends with an *action plan*. Your decision trees should map possible outcomes from the research to related action plans. In other words, you should decide in advance that if x happens, you'll do a, and if y happens, you'll do b. *This decision tree includes not only what needs to be done, but who will do it, and when it will be done.* Plan on spending 90 minutes for this meeting, and use the first 10 minutes to recap the agreed-upon definition of success and prioritization of goals (reconfirm that everyone agrees with the definition of success before moving on to the decision trees).

Let's return to our metaphor, introduced in Chapter 6, of a group of friends who decide to get together to have some fun. If this group applied scenario planning (albeit in an informal way), the group, as mentioned, would have to come to consensus on what would be "fun" for *everyone*. Let's say that going to see a certain movie is what the group agrees on. Everyone jumps into their cars and heads for the theater, but, oops, the movie they want to see isn't playing. Now what? Does the group have a backup plan, or will everyone just stand in front of the theater debating whether to see a *different* movie, or will they do something entirely different?

If the group of friends had conducted a scenario-planning meeting, they would ask: "What could go wrong with our plan to see a movie? And, what would we do in such an event?" Let's say one scenario is that the movie isn't playing at the time they want to see it. You can create a simple form of a decision tree, a simple illustration to help you map possible outcomes and subsequent action plans. In this example, your decision tree should branch out from your ideal plan for the evening's fun to include seeing a different movie, or going out for dinner, or hitting a club, or even playing miniature golf instead. Of course, you'd want to prioritize which one of these activities you would do next because you can't do all of them at once. Figure 7.1 shows what this might look like.

We realize you're not *actually* going to draw up such a plan just to make plans with friends on a Friday night and have all your friends sign it! But we're showing you this simple decision tree to illustrate how to think about potential failure when you're creating plans—especially expensive marketing and advertising plans. It has benefited our clients greatly to decide *in advance* what they might do if they don't achieve their desired goal, and we believe it can help your marketing too.

FIGURE 7.1 A Simple Decision Tree for Friday Night Fun with Friends

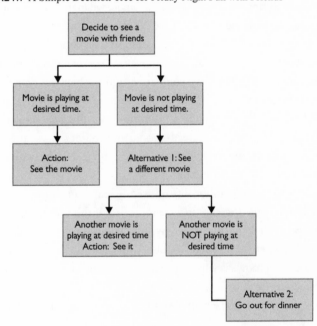

Here's the important point: The mere identification of potential problems often leads to a realization that someone should do some leg work to make sure the problem is avoided in the first place. In this case, that might mean checking for movie times on the Internet before they leave the office or house. Such a step can save wasted time of everyone jumping in cars, driving to the theater only to find out the movie isn't playing anymore.

> *The mere identification of potential problems often leads to a realization that someone should do some leg work to make sure the problem is avoided in the first place.*

In marketing, the Association of National Advertisers (ANA) estimates that 70 percent of marketing staff time is spent on *rework.*[1] To extend the metaphor, our COP helps direct traffic so that you and your friends aren't driving all over town wasting valuable time trying to find a theater showing the movie you want to see when you want to see it, or trying to find a restaurant on a Friday night that you can get into, or trying to find something else that's fun to do. The COP helps you *plan ahead.* The COP helps cut down on re-work. Similarly, marketers have lots of steps they can take that are the equivalent of checking the movie times. These steps can save loads of money and lots of time. And we'll share these steps throughout the book. Again, you don't need formal scenario planning for a group of friends who are just looking to have some fun, but those marketers who fail to define success and develop decisions trees often fail completely. Worst of all is that they fail and may not even know it or have a clue as to why.

Let's return to the example of McDonald's. McDonald's first defined success as awareness of the *Grilled Chicken Flatbread Sandwich.* They justified the focus on awareness instead of sales because the purpose of the advertising was to get consumers to think of McDonald's as offering more than burgers. They wanted to communicate that McDonald's has "new tastes." Secondarily, success for McDonald's was *sales across the entire menu.* If a consumer came in because the flatbread sandwich whetted their appetite, but they bought a Big Mac instead, that was just fine. McDonald's marketers defined their target segment broadly, and they assumed that most *awareness* would come from consumers who are not currently major buyers of McDonald's, and *sales* would likely come from existing customers; however, whether sales came from new or existing consumers wouldn't define whether the campaign was a success or not.

Why would consumers buy the product? What are the reasons a consumer would "hire" the flatbread sandwich? The McDonald's team defined the following two motivations for this new menu item:

1. Combination of great flavors
2. New, different, exciting—a novelty

These two motivations are *bridges* that connect the marketer's goal of selling with the consumer's goal of fulfilling needs and wants. McDonald's belief is that to the extent that consumers see the product as new or a tasty combination of great flavors, then all things being equal, McDonald's cash register should ring.

Once you have gone through a recap of the definition of success from the first meeting (the definition of success is circulated in writing prior to the second scenario planning meeting) and confirmed that you have agreement on that definition of success, then it's time to delve into the 4Ms. Our experience has proven the 4Ms (motivation, message, media mix, and maximization) to be an excellent way to map appropriate action plans based on the potential outcomes of the advertising measurement (and don't worry, we'll get to gold-standard measurement of advertising effectiveness later).

For the campaign to be successful at building awareness, the advertising must simply connect the McDonald's brand with the new flatbread sandwich. For the campaign to achieve the secondary objective of sales for the product, the advertising must first tap into the right consumer *motivation* (the first M) for hiring the brand. In other words, the assumption is that consumers will buy the flatbread sandwich because it is a combination of great flavors and it is new. But what if this assumption is wrong?

What if, overnight, consumers' preferences changed, and most consumers cared only about "low-calorie, recognizable" food such as carrot sticks? Would the advertising that the agency is developing be successful? No. The consumer motivation to buy that the team assumes is "a combination of great flavors" and the "new." The team is developing ads to speak to that motivation—not to the recognizable, low-cal diet food. Fortunately, the odds that consumers' tastes would change overnight is not so high, so this example is a bit of an exaggeration. Scenario planning simply asks: "What if we're wrong and consumers are motivated by something else?" And scenario planning allows action standards to be set, ensuring quick course adjustments if necessary.

The next M is message. The assumption is that the message will be effective if it shows an appetizing view of the food, which will speak to the "great combination of flavors" with the word "new." And the assumption is that people will connect the ad to McDonald's. The ad uses McDonald's red and yellow color palette and the golden arches. That's a very good assumption and probably right, based on our measurement experience with other brands, but what if that doesn't work? Are there alternative approaches that McDonald's should be considering to try different communication styles, such as showing someone eating and enjoying the food? To get across the message of combination of great flavors, should McDonald's show the sandwich being assembled, or should they just show the finished product in all its glory?

> *The assumption is that showing an appetizing view of the food, with the McDonald's red and yellow color palette and the golden arches would be effective. But what if that doesn't work?*

Many marketers are finding that trying different communication approaches and measuring which work best provides a clear path to success. Develop and measure four or five ads and then quickly adjust in order to run only the most successful ads. But what if none of them work? What is the action plan then? With scenario planning, the marketing team has a back-up plan.

The next M is media mix. Media mix refers to which communication channels you will use to carry the message. What are the best media to use and what combination of media and spending level is optimal? What if we find out that a certain media is achieving impact at a much lower cost than another? What if there is the opportunity to get better results without spending a single dollar more? How much flexibility is built into your planning to take advantage of such an insight? What is the plan of action and who will be responsible for making the changes? Here too, scenario planning plots the course.

The fourth and final M is maximization. What if the marketer got the motivations right, nailed the messaging, and had an optimal mix among the media they were employing, what else should the marketer do to further extend their effectiveness? What other marketing programs would help maximize results? Maximization is where advertising becomes an intense competitive weapon for building your business and your career.

The 4Ms is such a powerful organizing principle for marketing, we will return to it in detail in Part III. In scenario planning, we use the 4Ms to identify what could happen and what action would be taken to give the marketer the best chance of success. The results from this second meeting are a memo summarizing what defines success followed by the decision trees for each of the 4Ms. This memo specifically details who will take what action and when, in response to possibly missing the mark on any one of the 4Ms.

STEP 3: LINK MARKETING EFFECTIVENESS MEASUREMENT WITH ACTION PLANS

How do you know whether you've achieved success and whether there is room for optimization? This requires data and analysis. With an unambiguous definition of success and clearly laid-out plans of what action to take under different scenarios, analysis of marketing effectiveness data tells marketers where the campaign is working as planned and where it is not working. Having the data in real time, when the marketer can do something about it, is the equivalent of a traffic cop using his or her eyes to see what is happening around an accident and then directing traffic accordingly. "Measurement" is essential. Remember, the formula for COP is as follows:

Scenario Planning + Measurement + Action = Same Budget, Better Results

With the COP, the marketing team has already contemplated what to do if the marketing plan was suboptimal in one area or another; therefore, scenario planning combined with the data leads to continuous improvement and marketing optimization.

Sometimes a little extra push is necessary. That extra push is a reminder for key members of the team to take action as planned and as agreed to by the entire group. So when we do scenario planning with our clients, we circulate a short document stating the definition of success of the campaign (as the group agreed on it) and the decision trees, with clearly spelled-out action plans, (including *who* will take the action and *when* it will be taken). We circulate the document and give everyone a week to review it and recommend any edits to the document. We then have everyone in the group sign it. This creates a personal and group commitment to the action plans and allows group members to hold each other accountable for following through.

When the campaign starts and data begins to come in, we present the marketing effectiveness data we collect in the context of decision trees. By having all the key parties who are involved in the execution of the marketing plans on the same page with decision trees, it's easy to link your data analysis back to your scenario planning/action plans—in other words, review what you've done (i.e., analyze the data of how your ads worked), and what could go wrong, and see how those results compare to your original plans and goals.

We've noted that our philosophy is that accountability isn't marketing effectiveness measurement only; it's helping marketers do something *about* the measurement. And the scenario-planning process is our approach to delivering according to this philosophy. For example, what if you found that the $25 million spent on TV was beyond the point of saturation and had a lower ROI than if you had spent that same money in other channels of communication? What would you do differently? What would you do for the next budget cycle? Or, if you could, what would you do in *this* budget cycle? Scenario planning is all about sticking to your goals and sticking to your commitment to success. Let's move on to Part III and the 4Ms, beginning with motivation, to ensure understanding of customers' needs so you can position your message accordingly.

> *Accountability isn't measurement only; it's helping marketers do something about the measurement.*

How to Use a "COP" to Direct Your Marketing Campaigns

1. Apply the COP—Communication Optimization Process—to help the marketing team see things it might otherwise miss. Marketing people tend not to think of the downsides. They often accept that everything will work out. And although we like a positive attitude, the ability to also see the downside is often the difference between success and failure at their jobs.

2. The first part of the COP solution is making sure that there is *alignment* of your marketing goals and plans. Remember that only in rare instances have we seen alignment to how success is defined among all members of a marketing team. So you need to bring together people who may normally not sit down together and come to a detailed definition of success.

3. The next part of our COP is the decision tree. Go through each of the 4Ms—motivations, message, media mix, and maximization—and confirm or get agreement to clearly spelled-out action plans, including *who* will take the action and *when* it will be taken in the event that the marketing plan is missing the mark. This plan should then be circulated for review and editing. Everyone in the group should sign the action plan because signing it creates a personal and group commitment to the action plan.

4. Finally, be sure to link the gold-standard marketing effectiveness measurement of each M to the action plan. Accountability isn't measurement only; it's doing something about the measurement. And the scenario-planning process is our approach to delivering according to this philosophy.

PART THREE

Guaranteeing Your Advertising Works

Actions You Can Take Today

to Fix Your Own Advertising—

Insights from Research

on $1 Billion in Ad Spending

Motivations and Your Customers' Needs

Now that you know the basics of how to do scenario planning, let's get into the nitty-gritty of improving each one of the 4Ms. The 4Ms are our framework for guaranteeing your advertising succeeds. The 4Ms are motivations, message, media mix, and maximization. The first M—motivations—is the most important because, based on the research we've conducted, an estimated *$53.5 billion is wasted* in marketing as a result of missing the mark on consumers' motivations. To avoid this problem, marketers need to make sure they know what their customers think—and want—before they do *any* marketing or advertising in any medium. This chapter shows how marketers can use the first of our 4Ms to map and manage consumer insights.

There are three key facets of motivation to ensure marketing success:

1. *Motivation & needs*—understand why consumers buy a product: Why do they "hire" your brand? What are the attitudes and beliefs that lead a consumer to buy one brand over another in your category?
2. *Positioning*—know how to differentiate your product from your key competitors: What really makes your product, in the mind of the consumer, different and special?

3. *Segmentation*—recognize how different groups of consumers might choose to buy your products differently: You might need to be something slightly different for one segment of consumers (in terms of motivation and positioning) as compared to another segment of consumers.

These three facets of *motivation* are the three fundamental things a marketer has to get right for the rest of the marketing campaign to work. Motivations is a great place to start, too, because a marketer who misses on motivation has a disturbingly high rate of campaign failure. Of the 36 marketers we studied, one-third did not get consumer motivation right—and they are some of the best marketers in the business. It should be obvious that getting motivation right is critical to success.

This chapter focuses on the first two of these three facets: (1) understanding your customers' needs and (2) positioning the marketing message accordingly.

CUSTOMER MOTIVATION IS OFTEN DRIVEN BY THE EMOTIONAL AND SOCIAL DIMENSIONS OF A BRAND

Motivation is probably best illustrated by looking at a few products. What motivations compel some consumers to prefer, for example, a Rolex over a Tag Heuer watch? Target over Wal-Mart stores? Or a Ford F-150 over a Dodge Ram full-size truck? Or even preferring Colgate Total toothpaste over Colgate Gum Protection Formula, when the latter is the exact same product as the former yet did not succeed in the marketplace? In each of those pairs (and there are many, many others), the functional attributes are very similar. Yet if you talk to the people who bought one of those products or shop at one of those stores, they will tell you that the products or stores they chose are different.

What the consumer means is that the *brands* are different. The brands are different because the brands tap into different consumer motivations for buying. It comes down not so much to the *physical* attributes of the product or the store, but more to the difference in how consumers are satisfying certain sets of needs for their underlying motivations for buying those brands—the emotional and social dimensions of the brand.

A careful study of why these companies missed the mark reveals that the most common cause is *lack of process*—which brings us back to our COP.

Motivations is a great place to start, too, because a marketer who misses on motivation has a disturbingly high rate of campaign failure. Of the 36 marketers we studied, one-third did not get consumer motivation right—and they are some of the best marketers in the business.

The COP could blow the whistle on the missed motivations and force a healthy group discussion by asking the following:

- Are the assumptions of what *motivates* a consumer to hire the brand written down somewhere for everyone to see and everyone to approve?
- Does your *positioning* versus your competition's make sense given the reasons why consumers "hire" one brand (or even one category) over another?
- Are different consumer *segments* motivated by different things? And, how does the marketing strategy align with the segmentation? Do you know the value of each segment (often called market-sizing)?

Here's an example: Compare Rolex, Tag Heuer, and Timex

Functionally, all these watches tell time. So why does someone hire a Tag instead of a Timex? Is it to tell time? Not exactly. After all, a $10 Timex can do that job. Luxury watches like Rolex and Tag are hired to tell time *and* to communicate something about the individual, both to the self and to others.

A framework we use to understand consumer motivation is to break it down into functional, social, and emotional benefits, as follows:

- The *primary functional benefit* of the watch is telling time. But the added functional benefits of a luxury watch are similar to jewelry—something you might wear when you dress up. There is also another segment of consumers who wear the luxury watch every day.
- The *social motivation* is what the brand communicates within society. Both Rolex and Tag are *badge* brands that tell something about the individual wearing them. At the risk of oversimplification, just as a badge on a police officer says, "I'm an officer of the law," a Rolex on the wrist says, "I'm successful in an establishment sort of way." A Tag Heuer on the wrist says, "I'm successful, and I'm defined by more than my career—I'm

adventurous and sporty, too." When a Tag is given as a gift, the meaning of the brand is similar to when the person buys for himself, but it says something important about how the gift giver views the recipient.

In terms of *emotional benefits,* Rolex and Tag each say something to the individual who buys it. For some people, for example, it says, "I've earned this." Understanding the meaning of your brand in the hearts and minds of consumers is central to motivation analysis.

Here's another example: Target versus Wal-Mart

The prices are not that different at Target and Wal-Mart,[1] and the products they carry are not that different either. But in our research, we've learned that the *positioning* of Target is vastly different from Wal-Mart. Some upscale consumers in suburbia refer to Target by a pseudo-aristocratically French-sounding "Tarjhay," and perceive Target as a more socially acceptable place to shop compared to Wal-Mart. Target has positioned itself around style while Wal-Mart has positioned itself around the tag line "Always low prices. *Always.*" For those consumers who are upscale (or if they fancy themselves as upscale), they perceive Target as having higher quality products, whereas "Wal-Mart suffers from a perception that its merchandise is lower quality, and that turns off consumers who can afford better.[2] If you're going to buy the exact same thing, and if you're going to pay very close to the same price, then the motivation for somebody to shop at a Target instead of a Wal-Mart has a lot to do with this brand *perception* of Target as being more upscale. For those motivated to spend no more than they need to, Wal-Mart is thought of as being the lowest-price store—absolutely the place to go. It's about saving every penny. For some Wal-Mart shoppers it is a badge of pride that they got the best deal or the lowest price (even if they are affluent consumers).

Some readers might think of this motivation analysis as "Advertising 101," but given that one-third of marketing failures can be traced to a miss on motivation, it's important that these critical foundational principles are put into practice. To recap, remember that you should

- *understand your consumers' motivations'* as the starting point for developing any effective marketing and advertising campaign;
- comprehend why a consumer hires *your* brand instead of your competitor's; and

■ know what your consumers' *perceptions* are related to functional, emotional, and social aspects of the brand because the decision to buy is not just about product or price or placement or packaging, but about *perception.*

Effectiveness in messaging depends on understanding common motivation and applying this understanding to messaging. A COP can help. While most marketers know that this is important, it doesn't always translate into meaningful messages; therefore, 36 percent of the best marketers missed the mark. The COP process enforces "the law of the land" for every marketing and advertising campaign you do. The COP systematically gets the assumptions on the table for everyone to see and collectively consider. As discussed in Part I, there are a lot of possible roadblocks to interfere with a marketing campaign's success, but our COP process really helps drive around all of them and arrive where you wanted to go.

> *Effectiveness in messaging depends on understanding common motivation and applying this understanding to messaging.*

Here's an example from ING Financial Services of how a COP could help a marketer to change

When the company first launched in the United States, ING's TV ads asked, "What is ING?" and answered, "ING is new and innovative." The focus on fresh thinking and innovation as the motivation hot buttons is very different for the financial world. However, people who want financial advice generally don't care as much about how *fresh* their advisor's thinking is, or even whether it's innovative, for that matter. Instead, consumers tend to put the greatest emphasis on a company that *understands* their particular investing situations and challenges. So this begs the question, why would a consumer hire the ING brand in terms of functional, emotional, and social benefits?

The *emotional connection* in selecting a bank is often a desire for *security* and the consumer's self-centered belief that "this bank understands me and my needs." Or, "I've developed a history with this institution, and even if it is not a great relationship, there is more fear in the unknown and an unproven bank, especially considering the complexity and fine print in the financial world."

The *social aspects* of motivation also matter to some consumers. For those who want to use their bank for name-dropping *badge value,* Morgan Stanley and Merrill Lynch benefit from this social motivation. Yet how different are these banks really on the functional aspects of what they deliver?

Perhaps ING initially said, "Hire us because we are innovative," because they were afraid that no one would even notice them if they simply catered to the same core motivations that many other financial institutions address. ING Financial Services figured out that its positioning for ING could be better regarding its consumers' motivations, and the company adapted accordingly. ING adjusted its approach to motivations. ING's new campaign says, "Hire us because we make a complex [financial] world simple." ING is the kind of company that listens to consumers and makes adjustments as required to get to the motivations that really resonate.

CLOSE THE GAPS IN KNOWLEDGE ABOUT YOUR CUSTOMERS' MOTIVATIONS

In our experience, understanding why consumers hire your brand and stating that in writing during scenario planning dramatically improve your marketing campaign's chances of success. We've found that writing it down and getting consensus reveals most weaknesses in logic. Recall that, in scenario planning, you start by developing an unambiguous definition of success; as part of that definition process the marketing team will build consensus and agree on the issues related to customer segmentation and motivation. And you need to do at least some research to make sure you're going down the right path in your positioning versus your competition.

Here's an example from McDonald's

When we worked with McDonald's, the marketing team defined the primary goal as awareness for the new flatbread sandwich. The secondary goal was sales. The group came to consensus that the consumer motivation for buying this new sandwich was the perception that "it was new and different and had a combination of great flavors." The ad agency nodded in agreement; briefs were written that were intended to make the food the hero of the ad campaign.

When the agency delivered the online ads, it showed a gorgeous image of the sandwich with pepper jack cheese, chunks of grilled chicken, fresh lettuce, and luscious tomatoes and a yellow thought bubble with the word "new." The ad was so good it should have included a warning: "Not responsible for consumers eating their computer screens." But *what if* instead of that excellent food as hero advertisement the agency delivered, they handed McDonald's a crazed-looking chicken wearing a red and yellow wrestling leotard with the question, "What can satisfy the savage beast?" No appetizing view of the flatbread sandwich. No mention of the combination of great flavors. No mention of "new" or the limited-time availability. Just a crazy chicken in a wrestling suit and the question: "What can satisfy the savage beast?"

As discussed in Chapter 7, scenario planning would allow the client to say, "Whoa there, wrestling chicken: Before you body slam yourself into the media plan and cost the company millions, explain what you have to do with the consumers' motivations of 'new and a combination of great flavors'?"

The answer could be that when the consumer runs a computer mouse over the wrestling chicken, the online ad magically expands and shows an appetizing view of the food that can satisfy the savage beast. Would this ad—that requires a consumer's interaction to communicate a combination of great flavors—work? Without data, it's impossible to know for certain. If you have a COP to blow the whistle on the crazy chicken and say, "Let's trust, but verify. Let's measure how well crazy chicken does versus some other alternatives." Perhaps the crazy chicken represents a meaningful breakthrough in effective advertising. Perhaps it's just a creative way to waste a lot of the company's hard-earned money.

TAKING INVENTORY OF CONSUMERS' MOTIVATIONS

If taking inventory of consumers' motivations is new to you, here are some guidelines for how you can organize your data from your research in order to help ensure you tap into your customers' motivations. There are three levels to the motivation-discovery process. The first level is the category, the second is the class, and the third is the brand. For example, Automobiles is a category. Within that category are several classes, such as sedan, sport utility vehicle (SUV), or sports car. Within each class there are several competing brands. Less expensive and lower involvement products, such as toothpaste, may require positioning only around the category level of motivations. More expensive and higher involvement products, such as automobiles, may need to carefully consider and apply all three levels of consumer motivations to be effective.

Level 1: Know Why Customers Hire the Category of Products

"What is the purpose of this category of products?" What do consumers hire this category of products to do in terms of functional, social, and emotional benefits? For example, if your product is cars, you might start with the following general answer:

Functional: To provide transportation

Keep in mind, though, that in most cases, the *generic* description of the purpose of the category of products is too functional to capture all the motivating benefits of individual brands. So you need to probe deeper and look at the emotional and social needs. What are consumers signaling to themselves by buying in this category? What are they signaling to others?

In complex and fragmented categories (with hundreds of choices) such as automobiles, positioning around the reasons consumers hire the category is generally not sufficient. Marketers need to look into the second and third levels of motivations that address why the consumer selects one class of products in the category over another or one brand over another. But in lower involvement products such as toothpaste, understanding the consumers' motivations for buying the category is often sufficient.

"What is the purpose of this category of products?" What do consumers hire this category to do in terms of functional, social, and emotional benefits?

Here's an example from Colgate

Let's take a look at a product whose success and failure was entirely determined by the marketers' understanding and articulation of consumers' motivations around why they buy the category. The product is Colgate Gum Protection; it was a dud. The sales were mediocre at best.[3] Yet it was a really great product with clinically proven results. Fortunately—and amazingly—

Colgate turned around its failure almost overnight by re-branding the product and by focusing the new brand on a different set of motivations. Here's what happened.

Colgate Gum Protection formula was launched globally in the early 1990s, and it achieved only a paltry market share. This was a marketplace failure by all accounts, even though the toothpaste functionally had so much going for it: The toothpaste used a new chemical compound, called *triclosan*, that was a break-through chemical that had real clinical results proving the product helped reverse gingivitis and helped protect teeth longer than many other toothpastes.

The problem was with the first ad campaign that showed white-coated dentists in their offices, recommending Colgate Gum Protection to their patients. We think Colgate was selling a solution that wasn't central to why consumers buy toothpaste. We think Colgate's assumption behind this campaign was that consumers trust their dentists to "treat their teeth and gums" (much the way a doctor prescribes medication to treat a disease). The ads mentioned other benefits, too, but what we suspect consumers really heard from those initial ads was: "Buy this brand because it will help you with your *gingivitis*." Colgate was scratching an itch the consumers didn't have!

This shows how Colgate may have gotten its *message wrong*—and the message may have been wrong because the consumers' *motivation* may have been wrong. The message focused on *dentists*—based on a premise that consumers would want a toothpaste to reverse the disease in their mouths, to "protect their gums against gingivitis." But the image most of us have of gingivitis is of people who have really nasty teeth and receding gum lines, whose teeth are about to fall out; and that is *not* an image that most people want to associate *themselves* with. There is an aspect of consumer-buying motivation for even a low-involvement product like toothpaste that is tied to social acceptance and personal relevance. So, the idea that the Colgate Gum Protection product was for "people like me" was likely rejected by consumers.

There is an aspect of consumer-buying motivation for even a low-involvement product such as toothpaste that is tied to social acceptance and personal relevance.

So how did Colgate turn this misstep into an absolute success? It used the exact same triclosan formula—the same toothpaste, the same chemical compounds, even the same flavor—but Colgate changed its marketing by focusing on different consumer motivations. As one Colgate executive put it: "It was a real challenge to narrow the message and sort out the most compelling advantages and turn it into a high-share mass market product when it does so much you can do a five-minute infomercial on it."[4] The Colgate marketers realized that positioning around the motivation of "long-lasting protection" was the focal point of consumers' motivation to try something new in the category. White coat dentists were replaced by hurried executives going about a busy day with the sound of brushing in the background to communicate their Colgate Total toothpaste was still working to produce that bright smile and fresh breath. Now, *that's* something a consumer can relate to!

Colgate also changed the name of the product, from "Colgate Gum Protection" to the new "Total" name, and they ditched the clinical-looking "Gum Protection Formula" lettering and changed the packaging, from a pharmaceutical look to a more kinetic logo with brighter red and white colors. Packaging, after all, is part of the *message*.

The new campaign was an instant success—in every country, in all regions of the world, and across different cultures. Even in the United States, where Colgate had trailed the Crest brand of Procter & Gamble (P&G) for 35 years, Colgate dethroned the king by achieving dollar share of more than 10 percent of the $1.5 billion category with Colgate Total in the first few months of the launch. This pushed Colgate's overall share to 25 percent, just past P&G's leading position.[5]

Moreover, as a testament to the power of getting motivations and messaging right, consumers even liked the flavor—when the flavor hadn't even changed! The renamed and repackaged toothpaste had the exact same formula as before. But in the previous market research, when Colgate had its motivation and positioning wrong, consumers indicated they didn't like the flavor: They said it tasted like medicine. Yet with the new campaign, the same flavor *tasted better.*

In retrospect, perhaps if Colgate had the benefit of scenario planning to force it to explicitly list its consumers' motivations assumptions, the company might have avoided its initial stumble in marketing this great product innovation. Perhaps if it had a COP back then, someone would have challenged the notion that consumers' most burning need in the toothpaste category is "stopping their gingivitis." Perhaps not. Gingivitis does affect the majority of consumers to some degree, and therefore maybe it was reasonable to believe consumers would be motivated to protect their gums and deal proactively with their gingivitis. In either case, scenario planning helps marketers react quickly and adjust accordingly. Colgate now implements scenario planning as part of its marketing process.

Clearly, even large successful companies with brilliant marketers still occasionally get consumers' motivations for hiring the category of products wrong. So it's great to see that for the exact same product, a company can go from getting it wrong to reevaluating its marketing, changing it, and then getting it right and becoming a success.

Colgate is a good illustration of level 1, knowing why consumers hire a category of products. Consumers hire toothpaste for protection against cavities and bad breath, and Colgate found success tapping into the idea of longer-lasting protection producing bright smiles and peace of mind knowing that the toothpaste is still working in between brushing. Positioning a lower involvement product like toothpaste around a category benefit works. But what if the product is higher involvement, with lots more choice among competing brands? Here is where marketers need to consider level 2 and level 3 motivations.

> *It's great to see that for the exact same product, a company can go from getting it wrong to reevaluating its marketing, changing it, and then getting it right and becoming a success.*

Level 2: Know Why Customers Choose a Particular *Class* of Brands

Knowing why some people select one class of brands over another class of brands in the same category is key to success. For example, ask the following questions:

- Why would a consumer choose a luxury car over an economy car?
- Why would a consumer choose a sport utility vehicle (SUV) over a minivan?
- Why would a consumer choose a microbrew over a mainstream brand of beer?

■ Why would a consumer choose a generic medication over a branded medication?

These questions will provide insight about the deeper functional benefits. The answers to these questions will tap into the attitudinal beliefs that motivate purchases. Brainstorm and research the list of functional and attitudinal benefits that describe why a consumer might choose one class of brands over another within the same category. But you need to dig still deeper.

Take the SUV and minivan question, for example. A very good predictor of buying a minivan is the arrival of a second child. In fact, the best predictor for buying an SUV is also the arrival of a second child. Both the SUV and minivan provide the same *functional* benefit of transportation for a growing family. So why do some moms go for the minivan, whereas others wouldn't be caught dead in a minivan and instead opt for an SUV?

The answer is found more often in the *social* and *emotional motivations* of the brand rather than the functional differences. Research has found that the women who define themselves first and foremost as "moms" opt for the minivan; the women who define themselves by who they were *before* they were moms often opt for the SUV.

For men, the social and emotional aspects of selecting an SUV over a minivan are even more starkly defined. For some men, driving a minivan just doesn't seem manly.[6] Dodge attempted to address this motivation barrier with the introduction of a powerful "Hemi" branded engine into its minivan. The Hemi engine is derived from Dodge's muscle cars and trucks—masculine-targeted vehicles to be sure. The TV advertisement shows a father with his baby son at the open hood of the Dodge minivan pointing out the one thing he needs to know: It has a Hemi.

> *Why do some moms go for the minivan, whereas others wouldn't be caught dead in one? The answer is found in the social and emotional motivations of the brand rather than the functional differences.*

Level 3: Know Why Customers Choose a *Specific* Brand

Next, let's turn to the motivation and positioning of one brand over another within the same category. For example, ask the following questions:

- Why would a consumer who has decided to buy an SUV pick a Toyota Sequoia over a Tahoe? Or a Tahoe over a Denali?
- Why would a beer drinker buy Sam Adams over Heineken?

In our research process, we develop a list of attributes that captures all three levels: (1) the reasons why consumers might hire one brand over another within the same class of brands, (2) why consumers select one class of brands over another, and (3) why consumers buy in the category in the first place. Remember, your motivation list should cover not only why the consumer selects *your* brand, but also why the consumer selects *competitive* brands. This list will prove important. It is a central part of marketing effectiveness measurement. It is also useful for brainstorming how creative messages connect with core motivations.

In the example shown in Figure 8.1, if you were working for the Denali brand, you would certainly want to probe the perception of excellent handling, even though this is likely an attribute that attracts consumers to select a competitive vehicle, such as Porsche's Cayenne. Also, consider whether there are certain occasions that lead a consumer to select one brand over another, then on other occasions change his or her choice. Perhaps the advantage of Denali over the Cayenne is the extra back seats in the Denali. And, even if it is rarely used, the idea that "it's there when you need it" might connect with the social aspect of providing room for visiting family or being able to accommodate visiting friends (or the kids' friends). You'd also want to probe issues of fuel efficiency. It may be as important to understand reasons against buying as it is to understand reasons to buy. Translate these situations into attribute statements and add them to your list.

Figure 8.1 is a visual representation of the steps in this brainstorming process.

Compare your brainstormed list to what is already known about consumer perceptions of your brand. You may want to create a "brand elements table" that illustrates the different types of appeals advertising might make to ensure your brainstormed list covers all the bases. Figure 8.2 shows an example.

The list we've used is not perfect for every brand or every category, but it's a good framework to start with. It's a list that we've found useful across most categories. This list is translated into marketing measurement. The measurement of motivations not only allows the ability to ensure marketing messages are connecting with the motivations that matter to consumers, it also allows for an amazingly rich insight on what competitive brands are tapping into. For example, when we worked with Target, we examined how significant a threat

FIGURE 8.1 Sample Brainstorm Framework for Understanding Why Customers Buy a Particular Automobile Brand

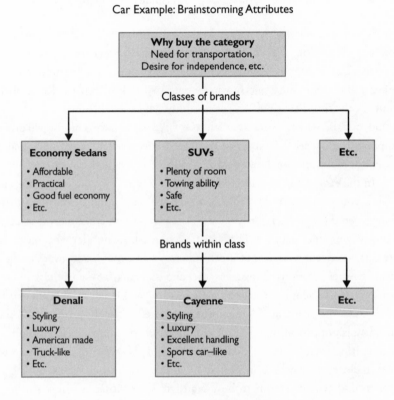

Car Example: Brainstorming Attributes

Wal-Mart's announcement that they intended to move up-market was to Target. The strengths, weaknesses, opportunities, and threats (SWOT) analysis allows brands to examine consumers' motivations for selecting different brands and to understand how linking a brand with key motivations creates barriers for competitors.

All marketers would agree that getting consumer motivations right is critical to the success of the campaign. Still, we found that several of the major marketers we've worked with had suboptimal results because they were not aligned with the most important consumer motivations. And although it might be understandable that getting motivations right is very difficult given the unique, interdependent mix of consumer motivation, needs, positioning, and segmentation, the motivation phase of the marketing plan is the bedrock

FIGURE 8.2 Sample Consumer Motivations for Different Brands

Overall Brand Elements	How the Consumer Internalizes the Element	Examples of Attribute Statements	Tangible versus Intangible
Rational (mind)	What do I know about the brand?	"Mercedes makes luxury automobiles." "Dove makes skin products for women."	⬇ Tangible
Physical (senses)	How does this brand feel to the touch?	"The Jaguar looks sleek and feels plush." Victoria's Secret makes silky lingerie."	
Emotional (feelings)	How do I feel about the brand?	"In a Jeep, I'll have exciting adventures." "Allstate will make me secure."	⬇ Intangible
Status (identity)	What do other people think of me if I own this brand?	"The Cadillac parked in my driveway will impress my neighbors." "The Nike swoosh is for winners."	
Time genre (cultural age)	Where does this brand live in time, i.e., is it old fashioned, classic, contemporary, etc.?	"The Acura is futuristic." "Target is hipper than other discount stores."	
Fictional (beliefs)	Things I believe about the brand based on lore and fantasy.	"Driving a Hummer means I'm a rugged individualist ready to conquer what life puts in front of me." "Crystal Light Lemonade is a healthy beverage."	

of everything else that follows. Weakness in determining motivation can make everything else fall apart.

In our experience, the reason most marketers got motivation wrong is that they did not have a COP to make sure they got to the optimal answers. The marketer needs to be really clear why the consumers buy (or hire) the category;

why they choose classes of brands within that category; and, of course, why they buy the specific brand over another in that category. Moreover, we've found it beneficial to understand this within the functional, emotional, and social aspects of the category and brand. The COP approach has been found to keep everything on the straight and narrow path by ensuring that marketers are asking the right questions.

The motivation phase of the marketing plan is the bedrock of everything else that follows. Weakness in determining motivation can make everything else fall apart.

Once you've worked out an understanding of customers' true motivations, you're ready to consider different segments of the target market. For that, we turn to Chapter 9.

CHAPTER NINE

Motivations, Segmentation, and Positioning

Previously we introduced the following three critical levels to understanding your customers' true motivations:

1. Level 1: Know why customers hire the category of products.
2. Level 2: Know why customers choose a particular *class* of brands.
3. Level 3: Know why customers choose a *specific* brand.

This chapter continues with our analysis of motivation and covers a closely related marketing decision: segmenting and positioning your targeted customer base.

GET YOUR SEGMENTATION AND POSITIONING RIGHT

As mentioned earlier, we've found that focusing on the functional, social, and emotional reasons why a consumer hires a brand can be applied to the vast majority of purchase categories and nearly all brands. Different consumers may have different reasons for hiring a brand. Segmentation is a critical part of getting consumer motivations right. Segmentation and positioning are closely related. Let's look at some case studies of segmentation and positioning.

The Colgate example described in Chapter 8 hints at a broader issue: segmentation. As mentioned, the sales of Colgate Gum Protection were unimpressive at best. But there were sales, and that means that Colgate's initial positioning appealed to some consumers (albeit not many). When Colgate figured out the *motivations* for the majority of its consumers, the insight allowed the company to re-launch the product with new motivation positioning, aimed at a larger, potentially more profitable segment, and the company achieved significantly better results. How can a marketer sort through the segments and focus on the most profitable opportunity? If you use focus groups you can almost always find at least one person who hires your brand for the reason you think they hire the brand (in other words, marketers are inclined to hear what they want to hear in a focus group). But does that really mean that there is a *large enough segment* that is motivated by that need? Maybe not—and that's why having a statistically valid (e.g., not a focus group) way of calculating the market size of people motivated by different factors is important to success.

> *Marketers are inclined to hear what they want to hear in a focus group.*

Here's an example from Jell-O. Kraft's Jell-O brand launched a fourth-quarter marketing campaign that focused on providing recipe ideas for special occasions and holidays—in other words, *only four times a year:* Christmas, Halloween, Thanksgiving, and New Year's.

Although it's true that some consumers hire Jell-O to make an orange Jell-O fruit ring for Thanksgiving, the research found that the *size* of the segment motivated to buy Jell-O for a recipe was much smaller than the segment that is motivated to buy Jell-O as an *everyday* delicious and *economical* snack. If their entire strategy rested on holiday recipes, we estimate that millions of sales would be left on the table (and the product would never make it to the family table) because the Jell-O recipe advertising strategy does sell, but the company could tap into a different motivation that could sell *more*—specifically, positioning the brand as an everyday economical snack.

Our experience is that many ad agencies, with the complicity of their clients, approach research with an eye on validating their ideas. If their "big idea" is to provide recipes, then that's what they test. But that approach can miss the *bigger opportunities* that come from more exhaustive analysis of what motivates consumers to buy. That approach of validating the "big idea" may in fact validate a good "small idea." The bigger idea may sit on the sidelines, unexamined by the research. A better approach examines the size and value of different consumer segments (grouped by common motivations). Is your brand casting the net wide enough? If not, the brand may be missing bigger opportunities, and it could be costing the marketer dearly.

Kraft used different media to address different consumer segments. As Kathy Olvany-Riordan, Kraft's vice president of global digital and consumer relationship marketing, points out, the Internet has allowed Kraft to focus on segments of consumers motivated by different needs. "Traditionally, we'd have to pick a singular focus. Jell-O could be positioned as a healthy snack, or (included in recipes) it could be an indulgence. With mass marketing, we'd have to pick the positioning with the most business opportunity and develop a 30-second TV ad that appealed to the middle of the road. But the Internet is much more targeted and it allows us to have very consumer-centric messages that amplify our positioning much better." In other words, Kraft can communicate "healthy snack" and "indulgence" to two different segments of consumers. But not all marketers are as savvy as Kraft. We've seen marketers latch on to a segment of consumers without ever checking to see if their focus was indeed the most profitable group.

THE *SIZE* OF THE CUSTOMER SEGMENT
MATTERS LESS THAN ITS *VALUE*

Volkswagen, Ford, and other auto manufacturers understand the importance of segmentation. Ford understands the power of being able to talk differently to people who are at different stages of the purchase process. This is called a *purchase funnel:* The big mouth of the funnel is the general population, which isn't currently looking for a new car, and the narrow end of the funnel is those people who are in the market and about to make a decision about buying a car within the next six months.

In our work with Volkswagen, Ford, and other automotive brands, we've found that even though the in-market target audience is just a *sliver* of the size of the pie compared to the overall population that will buy a new vehicle at some time further out than six months, they are *more valuable* because they represent immediate sales. In other words, *the size of the segment matters less than the value of that segment.* To neglect the *value* of a segment can be a disaster. Therefore, the marketing team must consider the value of the segments of the targeted consumer base.

In our practice, we encourage marketers to perform what is called *needs-based* segmentation, where marketers take into account the motivation and the financial value of consumers as well as media usage variables to develop segments. These segments of consumers are distinct in why they hire a brand and can be prioritized by profit potential to the company. Simpler (and often good) segmentation can also be done looking at different financial value of customer groups (as suggested in Garth Hallberg's book)[1] or by developing portfolios of customers (as suggested by Peppers & Rodgers).[2] The key point is to consider the following three questions in segmentation:

1. Do different segments have different motivations?
2. Is there different financial value for different segments?
3. Do the different segments use different media so that the marketer can actually deliver the right message to the right segment?

There can be a deeper analysis here; however, if your segmentation scheme answers these three questions, you should do just fine.

Here's an example from the Warner Brothers' Movie *Constantine*

This example illustrates the need to consider the motivations of different segments. If you didn't see the movie *Constantine,* it is best described as a cross between *The Matrix, Seven,* and *The Exorcist.* Keanu Reeves is the star, and he is attractive to women because he's Keanu Reeves. His good looks and appeal certainly motivates one segment of consumers. The other segment of consumers motivated to see *Constantine* tends to be the younger, male audience who is interested in the action/adventure, supernatural, demon-fighting element of *Constantine.*

As a marketer, you have to make a decision: Are you going to try to be all things to all people? Or are you going to focus on one of the segments because the motivations are *incompatible*—for instance, the motivations for the segment of women that think Keanu Reeves is hot would probably most appreciate a butt shot of Keanu Reeves in the ad somehow paired with his kind, winning smile. In contrast, though, the consumer segment that is interested in the action/supernatural components of the movie itself will be turned off by a kind smile and Keanu's posterior—unless it's getting kicked in an action sequence!

The more you emphasize the action and adventure aspect of the film and show that fighting part in the advertising, the more you appeal to one segment and alienate the other. You see, movies get caught in the crosshairs where their marketers have to decide: Is the focal point of this movie *romance* or is it *action/adventure?* And how do you position the film or recut the film? Movies that sometimes try to be all things to all people end up bombing.

That decision of which direction to go with segmentation is an important one that requires some research and a COP discussion. Consider consumers' motivations and the product itself, and what it can reasonably deliver, and then size up the markets and calculate the financial value of each segment. Measure up the competition focused on each segment, and choose your battle.

> *The decision of which direction to go with segmentation is an important one that requires some research and a COP discussion. Consider consumers' motivations and the product itself and what it can reasonably deliver, and then size up the markets and calculate the financial value of each segment. Measure up the competition focused on each segment, and choose your battle.*

For example, we'd suspect with Will Smith's *Hitch* in theaters at the same time as *Constantine,* and because the story line of *Constantine* lent itself more to action than romance, Warner Brothers chose the action/adventure aspect of its film in order to capture a younger male segment of the consumer market, leaving female movie fans to go see *Hitch,* a movie that was perceived as very formidable competition in the "date" movie motivation category. Part of the process is targeting the messages by media to the appropriate segments. In some cases (i.e., for some products), marketers are able to see that somebody's inherent interest and the way you segment the category does influence what type of media they use. That's the case with the *Constantine* example: If you go toward more of the sci-fi, supernatural, action/adventure side of the audience, you'll find that people interested in those categories read very different types of magazines than the women who are interested in a romantic Keanu Reeves. The woman who finds Keanu Reeves attractive is much more likely to read *People, InStyle,* and *InTouch* magazines, whereas the person who is interested in the action/adventure part is much more likely to be reading *Sports Illustrated, Stuff, Maxim,* and *Car & Driver.*

In the end, *Constantine's* marketers opted for the action/adventure, supernatural focus in their advertising, and it was a good choice: The movie wasn't a runaway blockbuster, but its opening weekend was $34.5 million,[3] which is not bad at all.

MAKE SURE YOUR MEDIA CHOICES SUPPORT YOUR TARGETED SEGMENTS

When looking at your segmentation, ask whether you can buy the media to support that segmentation. For example, for Colgate's Gum Protection Formula toothpaste, there certainly was no media that specifically targets consumers who have gingivitis—such as a magazine called *In Touch with Gingivitis.* This makes communicating to individual segments with specific messages difficult. It's a limited segmentation if you can't deliver targeted messages to each segment separately.

Most of the time, media choices and their respective return on investment (ROI) are not intuitive—analysis is required. For example, is it better to buy advertising in *Fortune* magazine or on CNET, the Computer Network Web site, to reach information technology (IT) decision makers at the level of vice president? If you guessed that CNET has a higher percent of VP IT decision makers, you're right. But having the highest concentration of a segment is not the only consideration. Cost to reach each person within the segment is also important. As we learned through our work with VeriSign, *Fortune's* cost per person reached is lower than CNET's in reaching IT professionals on an audience basis. But that too is not the end of the story. For VeriSign, CNET was more effective, which in their case was the number of leads generated for their sales force by the ads; and when cost per person impacted was calculated, CNET came out on top by far in terms of efficiency in reaching the audience.

Unfortunately, marketers won't find the measurement of impact (whether it is leads, sales, or changes in brand perceptions) by segment in their traditional media-planning tools. *The cost per impact is the most important measure and it*

Most of the time, media choices and their respective ROIs are not intuitive—analysis is required.

requires marketers to engage in their own analysis. Marketers need to know: For every dollar I spend in each media vehicle, where do I get the biggest bang for my buck? To arrive at this measure requires customized marketing ROI measurement that links consumer motivations and segmentation to observation of advertising effectiveness. The measurement provides the marketer with the data and insights to manage and optimize the marketing programs.

KEEP UP WITH EVOLVING CONSUMER MOTIVATIONS

If you think you have a lock on consumers' current motivations, remember consumer motivations change. Competitors change their positioning—sometimes to one-up your brand. As a result, segmentations may need to change really fast.

A trap that marketers occasionally step into is the belief in the unchanging segmentation. Many marketers spend a lot of time and money on a segmentation scheme and assume that the consumers' motivations and segmentation will remain stable; therefore, they don't revisit those assumptions on a regular basis. These marketers get stuck in a trap and never move, but consumers keep moving, and, pretty soon, the marketers' great segmentation is not only out of date, but it is also leading them to make the wrong decisions about consumer motivations.

Here's an example from Aqua Net hair spray

Do you remember women's hair in the '70s and '80s? The smell of Aqua Net was in the air, and, in the '70's, women appeared to be three inches taller thanks to the extra-hold hair spray plastering their hair in an everlasting "do." The '80s saw a resculpting of hair into the shape reminiscent of a wave curl that would make a surfer long for the beaches. What would you do if you were selling hair spray and competing against the king of hair sprays, Aqua Net?

You might start by figuring out the king's weaknesses—the areas where women were dissatisfied with the product—and then position your brand in that niche. For example, one thing you might have heard from women is, "I like the holding power of Aqua Net, but it sure does hurt when I try to comb it out." Aha! That's an insight on motivations. A competing brand would use the insight to position its product as providing holding power while also being easy to brush out. As styles changed, for example, Vidal Sassoon came along with a new reason for women to hire that brand: "Flexible hold" was its promise. [4]

Within a few short years, consumer motivations changed. The reasons a woman would hire one brand over another changed, but Aqua Net didn't. Aqua Net went from market dominance in the 1980s to only a 4.4 percent market share in 2001. Its prospects for growth marginalized to aging consumers who use the product out of habit. As one research company reported, hair sprays have been losing popularity for some years, overtaken by more contemporary and multifunction styling products that offer both style and hold. [5]

Consumers' motivations can and do change. The approach to advertising measurement should integrate motivations measurement so that the brand can determine whether consumers' preferences are moving. Marketers can play a role in helping to redefine motivations.

Here's another example from Ford's F-150 Truck

The Ford F-150 truck is a great example of a company that both understands its consumers' motivations and uses good marketing to develop a positioning advantage with that insight.

Ford applies the typical automotive segmentation among people who are looking for a new vehicle right now (called *in-market* consumers) and those who aren't. But keep in mind that those people who aren't in-market right now but typically buy or lease new vehicles will *eventually* want new vehicles at some point in the future. And the segments can be targeted with different media choices. In-market consumers can be found concentrated online at automotive sites and in magazines focused on automotive reviews.

Ford also tries to leverage the changing motivation for consumers to hire the F-150. The 2004 Ford F-150 was a totally new design for the vehicle. Visually, the truck looks decidedly different than other trucks—that is, it's always a truck, but the style is definitely very different, both inside and out.

Ford and its advertising agency, J. Walker Thompson (JWT) Detroit, had insight that full-size truck buyers wanted the luxury of a car in a rugged and tough truck. As contradictory as these ideas might sound at first, Ford delivered. The motivations and messages tapped into the exceptionally quiet interior and the excellent ride. Prior to the campaign, less than one in three truck *intenders* (i.e., people intending to buy a truck) would describe the F-150 as having an "exceptionally quiet interior" (30 percent) or an "excellent ride" (29 percent). Ford's ad campaign moved this perception by +13 points (from 30 percent to 43 percent agreement with "exceptionally quiet interior") and by +16 points (from 29 percent to 45 percent agreement with "excellent ride"). And Ford accomplished this without sacrificing "rugged and tough," an impression that started out at 41 percent before the campaign and moved by +12 points to 53 percent by the end of the campaign.[6] Ford successfully tapped into a motivation insight, repositioned its brand, and grabbed market share from its competitors.

Motivations for buying a full-size truck have changed in the 20-year history of the F-150. Ford is astute in changing with consumer demands, and the company's research systems are becoming increasingly tuned to not only understanding consumer motivations, but tracking how the motivations change over time in connection with marketing efforts.

As we indicated in both this chapter and the last, getting motivation right is mission critical. It is the foundation of the entire campaign. And when a strong foundation is combined with an optimized segmentation, the brand has a real shot at accelerating its growth. An optimized segmentation is one that focuses the right message on a segment that is large enough to have maximum impact on revenues and profit. For many brands, the sweet spot is a high-impact message directed at a segment of the audience that can be targeted appropriately with the right slice of media. Even better is the ability to deliver targeted messages to different segments. Kraft is pursuing this strategy and delivering distinct messages to different segments. The targeted messages tap into different motivations and take advantage of the fact that these segments use different media. Once you've researched your consumer segments and know what the motivation is for each, you should move on to the next M— *messaging*—to improve your prospects of getting your marketing to stick.

The sweet spot is a high-impact message directed at a segment of the audience that can be targeted appropriately with the right slice of media.

10

Messaging and Advertisements That Stick

Remember the childhood game of telephone? You start off with a phrase and then pass it to the first kid, who in turn whispers it in the ear of the next, and so on. The punch line comes at the end, when the last kid in the line repeats what he "heard," and it turns out that the phrase is completely muddled and has an entirely different meaning than what you said in the first place. Everyone laughs—it's funny how our brain works and fills in, writes over, and otherwise distorts what was said to create its own meaning. It's funny in the game of telephone. It's not so funny in the real-world, high-stakes game of advertising.

Of the 30+ companies we worked with, studied, and discuss in this book, an astonishing 31 percent got their messaging wrong in at least one or more of the media we measured—or at least the consumer heard it wrong (meaning the message did not contribute to sales, or it didn't create its intended change in the consumers' brand perceptions). Sometimes the message was wrong in a particular area, and the marketer had systems in place to catch it, fix it, and improve results. But more often, the marketer had no mechanism in place to guarantee effective messaging. If these marketers are indicative of patterns in the marketplace, then a total of $35.8 billion dollars each year is lost in lost marketing productivity.

Obviously, this is disturbing. The core of advertising is the advertisements themselves, which really makes one wonder: Why do many marketers get messaging wrong? This is, on one hand, very perplexing, and on the other, it demonstrates the real state of advertising today.

Although our primary focus in this book is advertising, the implication of messaging applies broadly. It applies not only to the ads themselves but also to the messages that the sales force communicates directly, to the product packaging, to the distribution channel—to every "touchpoint" that consumers come in contact with. Everything about the brand communicates meaning and should be managed as a message.

This chapter and the next two deal with the issue of why marketers' messages so often fail to stick and how a COP helps put messaging on the right track, across the entire consumer experience.

Be warned: Some of the following is a little heady because it looks at the theoretical underpinnings of how consumers create meaning. We do that because of all the areas in which we work with marketers, messaging is the one that almost everyone—including the CFO and CEO—believes they know well, yet the research confirms the way messaging works is more complex and varied than most of us were taught. Neuroscience and observation-based experiments of advertising suggest that some theories of how messaging works need to be re-examined. Some of the communication theories that may have made sense, or seemed to help marketers at one time, now appear to be wrong and appear to undermine success.

Advertising messaging isn't the first place to experience a total overhaul in underlying theories. What conventional wisdom or common practice says is right at the time and seems to make a lot of sense can be overturned by a scientific breakthrough that sheds new light. Looking back, it might seem silly that we ever thought that the old way was right—and sometimes in retrospect, it might just seem . . . well . . . crazy. For example, consider the area of medicine: At one time, bloodletting was thought to be the cure for what ails you. Bloodletting was based on people's theory that the human body had four humors (i.e., critical fluids) that needed to be kept in balance. The fluids were blood, phlegm, black bile, and yellow bile. The theory arose from those in medicine who believed the body was naturally expelling these humors in an effort to seek balance; for example, coughing up phlegm or having spontaneous nose bleeds and vomiting were thought to be examples of the body "seeking balance" by expelling out-of-balance humors. To a lot of medical professionals of a certain era, bloodletting seemed a reasonable and intuitive medical practice—for everything from fever to anemia. Bloodletting had a long history, and it was held up by generations of medical professionals as "the way to do it."

Have you ever wondered what are the marketing practices that we take for granted as "the way you do it" that will be proven someday to be the marketing equivalents of bloodletting? We have—and one marketing practice we take for granted that is turning out to be off-base is the model for how consumers process advertising messages. Bloodletting didn't always kill, but it never helped— and the same can be said for marketers' views on how messaging works. Many marketers either explicitly or implicitly assume that consumers *actively* process what the marketer has to say in "high-attention" mode—almost like a good student in a classroom actively and attentively takes notes to learn what the teacher has to say. Maybe that was the way it worked in marketing at one time (which is debatable), but that's not at all the way most advertisements are processed by consumers today.

> *Bloodletting doesn't always kill, but it never helped—and the same could be said for marketers' views on how messaging works.*

Instead, the evidence suggests "low-attention" processing is a more accurate model of how consumers process advertising. The erroneous view held by many marketers of high-attention processing of marketing messages is a consequence of the distorted lens. Marketers do pay a lot more attention to advertising than consumers do. Like bloodletting, the erroneous view doesn't always kill a marketing message, but applying this flawed model rarely helps a campaign succeed. And, in some cases we've measured, the assumption of high-attention processing has killed a campaign's success.

To be more specific, what is a marketer's equivalent of the flawed four humors model that led to bloodletting? Following are the three issues we have to contend with:

1. Consumers don't always hear the advertising message in the same way the marketer intended it to be heard.
2. Marketers see their own marketing messages differently than consumers. (This goes back to the distorted lens discussed in Part I.)
3. Marketers require a foundation built on a new generation of measurement and a focus on results over deadlines.

CONSUMERS DON'T ALWAYS HEAR
THE ADVERTISING IN THE SAME WAY THE
MARKETER INTENDED IT TO BE HEARD

The way meaning is created in advertising is not unlike the game of telephone. Brain scientists like Marketing Evolution's Dr. Krag Ferenz (who holds a PhD in brain sciences and psychology from Dartmouth) will tell you that we interpret meaning starting with our own *frames of reference*. These frames exert an incredibly powerful influence on messages and will distort meaning to fit our world view. Our brain fills in gaps with its best guess. For example, remember Colgate Gum Protection toothpaste described in Chapter 8? We don't think Colgate's message was intended to be solely about gingivitis, but the gums with gingivitis seems to be the message consumers "heard"—and the brand's impact was affected.

You need our friendly marketing COP—the Communication Optimization Process—for messaging. How else can you ensure that your message is truly effective? How do you safeguard against marketing's distorted lens? How do you ensure that you are catering to consumer motivations and developing an advertisement that connects to those motivations and are not just being sold a bill of goods from a creative voice in love with its "big idea"? Without a COP, marketers are prone to believe their own marketing spin and create messages that work for them. With a COP, marketers have a process to ensure the message connects with consumers' motivations. The COP maps out the action to be taken if the ads do not achieve the intended results. And, the COP enforces consideration of the action to take in the event that the ad doesn't work as planned generally encourages marketers to do more testing up front. The COP helps the marketer to focus on what the consumer is hearing from the marketing messages. Which brings us to the second issue.

Without a COP, marketers are prone to believe their own marketing spin and create messages that work for them. With a COP, marketers have a process to ensure the message connects with consumer motivations.

MARKETERS SEE THEIR OWN MARKETING FROM THEIR OWN LENS, COLORED BY THEIR EXPERIENCE WORKING FOR THE BRAND

This goes back to the distorted lens we previously discussed in detail in Chapter 3. Probably the greatest distortion that we see by marketers is that they assume that because they did some focus groups and they created messages based on that research, the consumers therefore will hear the message in the same way the marketer intended. If only it were that easy. But nothing could be further from the truth. Really, nothing. Because consumers hear based on their collective experience.

If it's not problematic enough that consumers don't always hear what the marketer intended to say, consider how marketer's natural inclination to become wrapped up in their brands creates an invisible challenge to see messaging the same way a consumer will. To build on the discussion of the distorted lens, marketers' experiences with and exposure to their messaging is vastly different from the way that consumers are exposed to and experience it. We need to recognize that coming into work for a brand causes us to lose the perspective that a consumer approaches the brand with.

For example, we were at a meeting with executives from a major conglomerate that made all kinds of food and other products. Everyone went around the room and introduced themselves and what they did. We came to a 50-ish balding man in a nice suit. He said, "I'm so-and-so and I'm in women's underwear." Hmm . . . a bald man in women's underwear. Anywhere else, that'd be funny. He wasn't laughing; he was serious. He worked in the apparel division, responsible for women's undergarments, and he had been in the company for 17 years. He had lost perspective to the point that saying "Hi there, I'm in women's underwear" to a stranger did not sound peculiar.

As marketers, we become so absorbed in our companies and our brands that they are our life: We spend more time with our brands than we do with our loved ones. But our consumers usually think about our brands for only a few seconds at a time. It is impossible for us to capture the innocence of seeing a message for the brand for the first time the way a consumer does.

The conditions under which marketers first see the message for the brand is in a conference room, studying story boards and working with the agency to craft a message that is perfect for their strategy. Visualize for a moment the consumer's experience. Picture your typical consumer. Place that image of the

> *As marketers, we spend more time with our brands than we do with our loved ones, but our consumers usually think about our brands for only a few seconds at a time.*

consumer into the environment where he or she sees and hears the ad message. Maybe that is in an office, at a desk with the clutter, the pictures of their families, the people in the next cubicle. See the distractions and the long to-do lists. Or maybe the consumer is at home, with the TV on, but they're not on the couch; instead, the TV is merely on to keep them company while they attend to ten other things. Again, really try to visualize how the marketing message comes into their world.

Or maybe the message is an online ad consumers may only glance at, spending only 12 percent of their time on the page looking at the ad and the other 88 percent focused on the non-advertising content.[1] The marketer's ad is definitely there, in their peripheral vision, and it probably gets an occasional glance for a few seconds, but it's not the focal point of their media experience. Or maybe the marketer's sales pitch is delivered by a rep for a pharmaceutical company in the hallway of a doctor's office. The doctor gives the pitch only three minutes—and she may *want* to listen, may *try* to listen, but can't help but think about 50 other things that are higher on her list than the details of the marketer's new medication.

The first realization is that *the marketers' brand* is most likely *not* at the top of the consumers' lists of things to think about. What do consumers hear? How does it change their perception of the marketer's brand? What influence does it have on the consumer buying the marketer's product? How can you optimize the marketing message to increase its effectiveness? When one considers the daunting challenge of getting inside a consumer's head to answer these questions and understand how messaging is working, it is shocking to hear marketers suggest that one can be successful by relying on gut instinct. How could we ever expect to answer such complex questions without a solid scientific measurement?

Understanding what marketers are up against in terms of ensuring that consumers hear the message right in that game of "telephone" we call advertising would lead one to assume that plenty of research should be in practice to ensure success. But, too often, marketers and their advertising agencies are more focused on getting the ads up and live than on ensuring that the results of those ads will meet their objectives. This leads us to the third issue marketers require: A foundation built on a new generation of measurement and a focus on results over deadlines.

HOW TO AVOID MARKETING QUICKSAND

So why do so many messages miss their mark? After all, smart marketers work hard every day to create effective messages, but there are a number of factors that nullify this hard work. It's the same issue that nearly nullified the hard work of thousands of workers as they built the 59-story Citicorp building in New York. After investing millions and millions of dollars constructing the Citicorp building in Manhattan, the company discovered the whole thing was in danger of toppling over. The reason: a faulty foundation. The soil beneath the building was faulty. It was like building on quicksand.[2]

Similarly, many marketers have invested millions and millions of dollars only to discover their message strategy is about to topple over because it was built on a quicksand foundation. Fortunately for Citicorp, science came to the rescue, and engineers found that by injecting a chemical into the soil it would start a process that turned the faulty foundation into a solid block of concrete.

> *Many marketers have invested millions and millions of dollars only to discover their message strategy is about to topple over because it was built on a faulty foundation.*

Marketers have that same opportunity to turn their quicksand foundation into a rock-solid base on which to build successful messaging. The fix requires marketers to realize that some of the underlying premises of message development need to be considered and reengineered. Better measurement can start a process that ultimately produces a much better foundation. Let's look at the following two problems with our foundation that could be improved:

1. Marketers' processes often focus on *deadlines,* but they skip the critical issue of effectiveness.

2. When measurement of message effectiveness does occur, marketers are prone to measure the wrong metric—often measuring a consumer's self-stated reasons for buying or *recall* of the ad, but consumers are notoriously inaccurate in reporting why they did what they did or believe what they believe based on introspection within a survey. Instead, marketers need a new generation of their measurements based on scientific observation with well-constructed experiments in the real world in order to learn how advertising is influencing change in the consumers' attitudes or buying behaviors.

Nearly one-third (31 percent) of the campaigns we studied had some or all of their messages fail to produce the intended effect. Lack of modern measurement or inappropriate measurement is the quicksand foundation of most messaging. It is a contributing factor to the marketers' messages we studied that topple over into failure. So, how can marketers convert the quicksand to a rock-solid foundation to improve their success rate in messaging? To answer that, let's look at the two problems listed above in more detail.

THE PRESSURE OF *DEADLINES* DISTRACT FROM A NEEDED FOCUS ON ENSURING *RESULTS*

Marketers' processes often focus on the very tangible action of completing the message by a *deadline,* and often they don't give adequate time to focus on the important but intangible task of making sure the messaging is really *effective.* To understand the magnitude of this second problem, consider the situation Procter & Gamble (P&G) faced.

Prior to an important measurement of advertising effectiveness in relation to sales, P&G's marketers measured five different online ads so that they could pick the best performing ones. But, in this market test, none of the ads was strong enough for the P&G team. We believe the ads underperformed because they were too linear, meaning that they slowly unfolded a story that reserved revealing P&G's Olay brand until the last second or two of the ad. That approach may (or may not) work for TV, but it for sure doesn't work in online, where the ads are not intrusive, often sharing the page with the content the consumer came to read.

The ad started with an image of beauty, built to a message, "Love the skin you're in," then concluded a second or two later with the appearance of the

Olay logo. But, by the time the story tied the image of beauty with the Olay brand mark, few consumers were paying attention. Therefore, P&G saw no lift in purchase intent, the metric that they defined in scenario planning as the criteria for success in creative measurement. This learning was valuable to P&G because it helped them go back to the drawing board and create new ads for this important campaign (which was particularly important because it was being heavily researched to determine the linkage between advertising and sales among different media). But P&G didn't have time to redo the ads. What should they do?

The ads underperformed because they were too linear, meaning that they slowly unfolded a story that reserved revealing P&G's Olay brand until the last second or two of the ad. That approach may (or may not) work for TV, but it for sure doesn't work in online.

P&G was on a deadline. It needed to run the ads *now* to have them in-market to measure actual impact on sales and have the data in time for budget planning. If P&G stopped and went back to the drawing board to redo the ads, they could lose a couple weeks. This measurement was a critical input for P&G to determine optimal budget allocation in the marketing mix as part of its annual planning agenda. If it missed this window, it might be another year before this learning could influence budgets. What would you do?

Most marketers, we've found, favor meeting the deadline and rationalize why the ad is good enough. To P&G's credit, it cancelled the first couple weeks of its media and worked furiously to redo the ads, (and we worked furiously to repeat the measurement with the new ads). Within a few weeks, P&G had another set of ads developed based on the insights of the first creative test.

The new ads worked very well, where the others had performed well below P&G's expectations. Figures 10.1 and 10.2 compare the old ad to the new ad. To learn more, P&G kept one set of the new ads nearly identical to the old ads and only changed the timing of when the Olay brand mark appears.

The new "Ad B," (Figure 10.2) used the exact same woman, the same message, the same logo, the same color, but this time, the attractive woman appeared at one end of the advertisement, and the Olay logo appeared

FIGURE 10.1 Ad A—Not Effective

FIGURE 10.2 Ad B—Effective

simultaneously at the other end of the advertisement, like book ends. The goal with this layout was to *connect* the image of beauty with the Olay brand instantly, rather than wait for the inner story to unfold (as with the old ad). A second or two later, the phrase "love the skin you're in" appeared in the center between the image of beauty (i.e., the woman) and the Olay brand, reinforcing the connection between the two. This ad worked well in boosting purchase intent, and follow-up research showed that it produced a 14 percent lift in sales volume, based on tracking actual purchasers. P&G's focus on results over deadline paid off, big time.

It paid off because P&G recognized its old ads weren't working, and even though creating a new ad meant pushing back the launch deadline by a few weeks and potentially paying media cancellation fees, P&G's marketers recognized that meeting the deadline with messaging that didn't work would not produce success. Success wasn't defined as *meeting the deadline* to have an advertisement ready; instead, the campaign would be successful if it *produced sales results.*

Yet, more often than not, the current marketing process focuses on deadlines rather than results. In fact, in many cases, marketers don't have the immediate feedback that P&G had to say, "Wait a minute, none of these ads are working to our standards; we need to extract learning on why they are failing and apply it to new ads to fix the problem." P&G gets it. P&G used a new generation of research based on design of experiments to measure which messages work best. P&G also created other versions of the ad that had the logo and image of the woman appear at the same time, but positioned closer to one another in the ad. They created versions that used a different color palette, some that included the image of the product packaging, and experimented with other ad layouts. All of the new ads built on the insight of having the image of beauty appear with the logo from at the start of the advertisement, and these new set of ads performed very well.

> *More often than not, the marketing process focuses on deadlines rather than results.*

P&G has a COP that remains true to the goals of the campaign and P&G experiments to learn what works best. This might sound simple, but in many organizations, without a COP, there is the advertisement and the deadline and no intermediary measure of likelihood of success to help the marketer recognize early on if the campaign will achieve the intended results.

> *In many cases, marketers don't have the immediate feedback that P&G had to say, "Wait a minute, none of these ads are working to our standards; we need to extract learning on why they are failing and apply it to new ads to fix the problem."*

So how does your process work? Is it deadline driven or results driven? How do you ensure that your message will produce the results you want? Do you experiment with different message execution to learn what works best? Are you measuring the right things? Too often, when measurement of message effectiveness does occur, marketers are prone to measure the wrong metric, specifically measuring consumers' *recall* of the ad or self-stated perception of how advertising influences them and not the underlying change in consumers' *understanding* of the brand, or change in purchase behavior of an exposed group as opposed to a control group.

MARKETERS WHO MEASURE THE WRONG THING GET FAULTY ANSWERS

We know that some marketers are skeptical of research. They mistrust it. In part, that's because there are some rather antiquated research approaches to advertising that were developed more than 30 years ago, based on a theory of how consumers process advertising developed over 100 years ago when horses and buggies ran in the streets and no one had ever seen a motion picture.[3] Although the obsolete theories have been discredited in the past 15 years by advances in neuroscience, some research companies and the marketers that use them have legacy problems, where they have invested a lot of money in infrastructure to measure marketing in a certain way, based on outdated theories of how consumers process advertising.

Two common mistakes in measurement based on obsolete theory are

1. a focus on ad recall, and
2. asking consumers to introspect and offer their own opinions of how advertising influenced them.

Whether consumers remember an ad or not has little relationship to the actual impact that the ad has in influencing their attitudes about the brand or sales. And asking consumers directly if they bought something or felt differently because of advertising has proven faulty and problematic. Advertising works whether consumers consciously know it or not (and, in fact, consumers are particularly bad at remembering what influenced them). Let's first examine why ad recall is a poor basis for summarizing the effectiveness of advertising and messaging.

Advertising works whether consumers consciously know it or not (and, in fact, consumers are particularly bad at remembering what influenced them).

THE PERILS OF AD RECALL

The most common ad-testing techniques that are used now grew out of very dated and incorrect assumptions about how advertising works. As veteran advertising researcher Jon Howard-Spink rightly complained:

> Look at most advertising research today (and the advertising it is researching), and it still starts from the same premise: your advertising has to have been consciously attended to [by consumers] if it is to be effective, and the [ad] awareness score has always been deemed as good a guide as any to whether you have achieved this. [4]

Spink argues that this "hegemony of ad awareness" may be coming to a close thanks to advances in neuroscience proving that consumers are influenced by ads even when they don't consciously recall having seen an ad.

Spink quoted the work of Dr. Daniel Schacter, professor of psychology at Harvard:

> You may think that because you pay little attention to commercials . . . your judgments about products are unaffected. . . . But a recent experiment showed that people tend to prefer products featured in ads they barely glanced at several minutes earlier . . . even when they have no explicit memory of having seen the ad. [5]

Spink also cited Robert Heath, a Professor at the University of Bath in the United Kingdom, who developed important empirical evidence that showed that the consumer's processing of advertising is "Low-Attention Processing" (LAP). [6] In other words, we *don't* pay a lot of attention to the ads, but we *do* process the ads at some level, and the messages *do* influence our attitudes and behavior.

In summary, ad recall measures don't equate to whether the ad worked or didn't work—period. Spink provided direct evidence of the point based on his own company's measurement of their Amoy's Straight to Wok noodles, a consumer packaged-goods brand. At 20 seconds long, the straight-to-wok noodle ad shows (in close-up) a stir fry dish being cooked in a wok, to which (in slow motion) Straight to Wok noodles are added: The thought was that because a stir fry is so quick to cook with Straight to Wok noodles, things had to be slowed down.

According to Spink, what was striking about this ad was "its virtual invisibility" in terms of ad recall. The pretest, rooted in old-world ad thinking, suggested the ad should be tossed in the rubbish bin because it would not create sufficient "ad recall." And the pretest was right about one thing: When the ad ran, the ad did *not* create much ad recall among consumers. But the conclusion that the ad should be thrown out was *wrong*. Despite the fact that plenty of money was spent (enough to put the ad in front of each consumer seven times on average) in the first few weeks that the campaign was launched, the ad achieved only 15 percent ad awareness recall based on this survey question: "Have you seen advertising for Amoy Straight to Wok Noodles recently?" Spink's query is that if consumers are processing the ad in low-attention mode, why should they remember something as insignificant in their lives as *if they saw the ad recently?* So why do many marketers focus on ad recall? Perhaps it's because that's the metric certain research companies found easiest to ask about when they developed their research services 30 years ago. And, since then, these research companies have norms, and now they are locked into doing things a certain way, whether it makes any sense or not.

Spink points out that advertising can very well influence the consumer's belief about the brand, and it's the change in consumer beliefs that we should measure. As Spink put it: "Although the [advertisement] is not memorable, maybe even eminently forgettable (it is just a stir fry in a wok), it was well branded . . . with clear, compelling message." By *observing changes in consumers' attitudes and behaviors,* Amoy could get a much more reliable measure of advertising effectiveness. The research showed that the predictor of sales success is *not ad awareness recall;* it is the *meaning* consumers attach to the brand. Observing if consumer perceptions such as "authentic" and other key attributes increased with the ad and the meaning consumers attached to the brand is a better predictor of sales success. Spink concluded, "People were aware of exciting news from Amoy—just not where they had heard it."

While ad recall wouldn't have predicted this, the Amoy ad did in fact significantly increase sales by 15 share points, and the sales results have been broadly replicated with each subsequent burst of advertising activity. The metric ad re-

The research showed that the predictor of sales success is not ad awareness recall; it is the meaning consumers attach to the brand.

call provided misdirection and almost led to killing sales by suggesting pulling a good advertisement.

So if ad recall isn't a model to help marketers measure and understand success, what is? The answer is to recognize that observing changes in opinions and behaviors using the scientific practice of *design of experiments* is the path to enlightenment. Here's another way to think about it. In the best-selling book, *Freakonomics,* the award-winning economist Stephen Levitt shares the example of a small business owner who sells bagels in company lunchrooms using the honor system. You want a bagel, you put your money in the payment box and help yourself. Only, some people help themselves without paying. The business owner might be interested to find out which signs (advertisements, really) affixed to the bagel and payment box reduce white-collar theft and produce the highest profit. How can one know which signs work best? Should we ask if the consumer "recalls the sign?" No, that doesn't yield insight as to whether the message worked or not. Should we ask a consumer, "So, which sign makes you less likely to steal?" No, we're not likely to get an accurate answer from that self-reported direct question approach. Instead, the bagel owner has a broad enough customer base that he can (and did) deliver *different* messages to a randomized list of customers and observed which messages worked best. This scientific practice of creating an experiment by randomizing the assignment of the population to exposed and control groups has been a cornerstone of scientific inquiry and it can and should be applied to advertising (in fact, this gold-standard approach is the basis of our research).

DON'T ASK, BECAUSE CONSUMERS CAN'T TELL: THE PITFALLS OF ASKING CONSUMERS TO INTROSPECT ON ADVERTISING'S INFLUENCE ON THEM

The point that observing changes in consumer attitudes and behaviors is the way to measure message effectiveness leads us to confront a second common mistake in advertising measurement, and that's the practice of asking consumers to directly state if advertising influenced their attitudes or behavior. The truth is, consumers can't introspect on how advertising and marketing influences them. Our brains aren't wired that way.

> *"In actuality, consumers have far less access to their own mental activities than marketers give them credit for."*

Dr. Gerald Zaltman of Harvard, in his book, *How Customers Think,* noted: "In actuality, consumers have far less access to their own mental activities than marketers give them credit for."[7] Zaltman backed up his point with several examples, including Dr. Lowenstein's quote: "Self-reporting methodologies . . . that rely on conscious reflection might not provide any substantial insight into what really motivated a particular action or decision."[8]

Dr. Ferenz supports this idea, as expressed in the following:

> If you really want to get an accurate and powerful read on how consumers are influenced by advertising, you need to adhere to the scientific method. You need to establish exposed and control groups beforehand and carefully measure differences in consumers' attitudes and behaviors between groups, rather than relying on consumers' memories of what they saw and how it made them feel.[9]

Dr. Ferenz's point makes clear the insight of neuroscience to marketing and underscores Dr. Zaltman's and Dr. Lowenstein's point nicely.

Research from P&G on the implications of misattribution is eye-opening. In a carefully controlled field experiment, we measured online advertising for a couple of P&G shampoo brands. The only difference between the exposed and control group of respondents was the exposure to online ads. And yet, when consumers were asked, "Where did you see ads for brand X?" it wasn't Internet ads that were attributed to the increase. Instead, it was television advertising and magazine advertising. See Figure 10.3. To reiterate, there was no difference in exposure to TV or magazine advertising between exposed and control groups. Therefore, if consumers could accurately self-report ad recall, there should have been no difference between exposed and control groups. In

FIGURE 10.3 P&G Shampoo Brands: Question to Consumers: "Where Was the Ad?"

Brand Y Advertising Recall	Control (n = 271)	Exposed (n = 1,162)	Δ
TV	77%	82%	5%
Radio	9	7	−2
Internet	9	9	Not Sig.
Bilboards	5	5	Not Sig.
Newspaper	9	7	2
Magazine	27	29	2

Brand X Advertising Recall	Control (n = 228)	Exposed (n = 1,609)	Δ
TV	39%	51%	12%
Radio	8	5	−3
Internet	10	10	Not Sig.
Bilboards	3	3	Not Sig.
Newspaper	3	4	Not Sig.
Magazine	26	27	Not Sig.

fact, for one of the brands, TV wasn't even on air. The only difference between exposed and control groups was that the exposed group was delivered *online* advertisements while the control group was given a placebo ad. And yet, consumers' self-reported data doesn't accurately reflect the source of ad exposure.

The explanation for these results is that advertising isn't important enough to consumers for them to make a careful mental note of "I just saw shampoo brand X advertised, and it was being advertised on the Internet." If you work for the brand, maybe you would make that mental note, but your consumers won't. So, when a survey asks consumers, "Where did you see the ad?" the consumer might be aware that they have indeed seen an ad, and they will likely *guess* where they might have seen it. But, it is a *guess,* and not a very good one. In this case, most consumers *guessed* television is where they saw the ad—wrong, it was the Internet.

Perhaps because the ad was visual, guessing the visual media of TV and magazine increased while guessing radio decreased. The type of brand may also play a role in misattribution. We can imagine that if the brand was eBay and eBay were doing a magazine ad or a TV ad, it might get misattributed to the Internet because that is where consumers might *guess* (incorrectly, in this case) that eBay would be advertising.

The implications of the P&G research are a warning call. If a marketer were to use consumers' self-stated ad recall by media, then the Internet ad (which drove effect) would not get credit. Using this erroneous data, the marketer would eliminate the Internet and increase magazine and TV spending. But that change in budget allocation would actually undercut marketing effectiveness because it was the Internet ads that were producing the effect (television and magazine were simply gaining credit because of consumers' inability to accurately report where ad exposure comes from).

We've seen this misattribution work the other way, too. In another study, this time for a high-tech consumer electronics product, out-of-home and local market television (SpotTV, as its called) were misattributed to Internet ads. In other words, in the cities where these offline ads were running on billboards and on television, consumers reported seeing more Internet ads even though the number of Internet ads was constant.

Marketers who rely on self-stated recall of ads by media, or who rely on consumers' self-stated answers to which media made them buy the product, are likely to draw *incorrect* conclusions about what is truly influencing consumers' attitudes and behaviors. Worse, the evidence suggests that relying on such data to make budget allocation decisions across media will actually hurt marketing ROI rather than help it. P&G did not make this mistake. Instead, they used the *design of experiments observation* of difference between exposed and control groups to understand how advertising influences a range of brand attitudes and beliefs (including the perception of where the consumer saw the advertising). As a result of their research, we have an important insight about advertising misattribution, and the dangers involved in using it for advertising effectiveness analysis.

> *Marketers who rely on self-stated recall of ads by media, or who rely on consumers' self-stated answers to which media made them buy the product, are likely to draw incorrect conclusions about what is truly influencing consumer attitudes and behaviors.*

What do we learn when we apply the proper design of experiments observational approach to marketing effectiveness measurement? The research used for the 30 marketers for this book to measure messaging works through setting up scientific measurement of control groups and exposed groups. These randomized experiments are the gold standard in research in a range of fields. These scientific experiments capture changes in consumer attitudes and behaviors by observing changes over time and between exposed and control groups. Our research across more than 30 in-market campaigns arrives at the same conclusions that Spink did: The right insight won't come from *advertising awareness recall,* nor will it come from asking consumers to tell you directly if they bought your product because of advertising. Instead, the right insight comes from measuring the *meaning* and the *action* that the marketing stimulates (with or without the consumers' explicit knowledge) by using scientific observation in a randomized experiment.

> *Are you certain your ads are effective and not part of the annual $35.8 billion in waste due to ineffective messages?*

In Chapter 11, we'll look at how we can use observation-based field experiments to enhance our effectiveness in marketing and our knowledge of why some ads stick and others don't. In the end, because our research with 30 of the world's best marketers suggests that nearly a third of the ads fail, every reader should take note. If some of the marketers we studied didn't get it right, are you certain your ads are effective and not part of the annual $35.8 billion in waste due to ineffective messages?

Marketers face a host of challenges. Consumers don't interpret the messaging in the way the marketer intended, and that problem begs for research to confirm whether the message is achieving the results the marketer is counting on. Marketers can often be bad judges of their own messaging because they are too close to their own brands, and the deadline tends to override the need to ensure that the ads are effective, which creates the ultimate scenario for throwing good money after bad. And finally, if the marketers use old-world approaches such as self-stated probability of exposure or ad recall, or consumer-stated reasons for buying, to determine advertising effectiveness and to reallocate budget, they may do more harm than good. The challenges are many but there are solutions.

11

Messaging and the Transformation from Intuition to Science

If there is a name to know besides Enzo Ferrari in Ferrari racing history, it is Luigi Chinetti. Luigi put Ferrari on the map by winning the first post–World War II Le Mans endurance race; before then, Ferrari was an obscure Italian name. In the 1940s, when vehicle reliability was still a problem, winning the grueling 24-hour race at Le Mans proved that cars had both the speed and the stamina to race hard and win. To win a 24-hour endurance race took some planning. All racers had to have a feel for how far they could push their race cars to win the race, but they could not push their cars so far that they overstrained them and caused a breakdown. "To finish first, you first must finish," the saying went.

Luigi's intuition came from his training at technical school and his practical experience. The mythology and lore around him states that because his father was an engineer and Luigi had mechanical understanding in his blood. Luigi was reported to have great intuition and was very successful. Luigi once explained, "I can hold a connecting rod in my hand. I can tell you how many RPM I can get out of it and where it is going to break."[1] His mechanical background was a definite plus in endurance racing. The mythology that developed around Luigi and his natural talent often brushes under the carpet the mechanical breakdowns he experienced at Sebring and the other endurance racing miscalculations he made and, instead, focuses on his magical touch.

Racing in the '40s and '50s was not unlike marketing today. There was an art—an intuitive sense that made the difference between winning and losing. Such an intuitive feel was thought to be essential to Luigi's success. As Matt Stone, executive editor of *Motor Trend Magazine* put it, "Luigi was simpatico with the machinery, and that allowed him to be a successful endurance racer." [2] Discussion of successful marketers often adopts similar rhetoric, celebrating their intuitive feel and brushing their miscalculations under the carpet.

WHAT MARKETERS CAN LEARN FROM RACE-CAR DRIVERS

Marketing in many ways parallels race-car driving. Many marketers believe that their success is determined by an intuitive sense for the consumer—to know by touching a campaign how many sales it's good for and when the campaign will break down and need to be replaced by a new creative campaign. Thus, "I know a good ad when I see it," has won fame and laurels for some, but the approach is rather antiquated. It may have worked for the legends of advertising, such as Leo Burnett, Jerry Della Femina, and Bill Bernbach, who developed their marketing craft in the same era that Luigi was racing his Ferraris, but times have changed. Marketing can take the lead from racing and move from intuition to science by integrating talent and science together. Advertising legend David Ogilvy was an early proponent of blending the science-based research with marketing and the power of this blend is remarkable.

In motor racing today, F1 is the premier international racing venue where Ferrari now puts its time and investment and Ferrari uses science. In a single weekend, Ferrari gathers more than 4,000 data points and applies the analysis to get the performance edge. Teams of statisticians are employed to analyze the data and recommend adjustments in real time. Sure, skill and talent play a major role in success. Talent and science are *complements,* not competitors. Watch a practice session the day before the big race, and you'll see the drivers pull into the pit and a computer screen is popped in front of the driver while the pit crew refuels and swaps tires. The talented driver is studying data output and will adjust driving accordingly. Headphones fitted into the racer's helmet allow the team to feed insights from statistical analysis and computer models to the driver. The fact that F1-Racing teams gather more data in a single weekend than most marketers gather in an entire year should give marketers reason to pause and consider: "Can we improve our success rate with more intensive analysis?"

The fact that F1-Racing teams gather more data in a single weekend than most marketers gather in an entire year should give marketers reason to pause and consider: "Can we improve our success rate with more intensive analysis?"

Even amateur race drivers today may apply more science to do well in a race worth only a trophy than many marketers do in a race for market share worth hundreds of millions of dollars. A friend and ex-Microsoft marketer, Will Diefenbach, drove in the 24-hour race at Daytona. He is a very good amateur race-car driver. He races for Team Seattle, on behalf of the Seattle Children's Hospital (drivers raise donations for every lap they complete), and the degree of science and data that supports an amateur racer would cause those marketers that rely on intuition alone to blush in embarrassment.

Team Seattle pretests a few times before the car enters the race. They gather hundreds of data points, and they benchmark against the best. For example, benchmarking involves hooking sensors up to the car and having a champion driver take the car around the track, synchronized with a timing device. The sensors provide a map of exactly how much the gas or brake pedals were applied, which gear the car was in, and a host of other vehicle-cornering and assorted dynamics for every moment on the track. Diefenbach uses this data to compare his driving with that of the best. He sees exactly where he was losing time to the pro, and he can diagnose where he should adjust his approach and where he can stick to his approach because he is doing as well as the best drivers. Out of the 12 turns, he was as fast as the pro on 9. Knowing this allows Will to focus on the 3 turns where he was performing suboptimally.

The best marketers do the exact same thing with advertising. They give the campaign a spin before entering the race. The best marketers benchmark performance and constantly challenge their advertising to see if they can achieve better results. They diagnose where changes to their approach can boost performance, and where they are doing as well as possible. The best marketers complement a talented team with scientific data and analysis.

So how can marketers supercharge their advertising performance? Once you've visualized your consumer's world; once you've realized that getting the right results from your marketing campaign is more important than just having an ad ready by the deadline; and once you start measuring by using the

> *The best marketers . . . give the ad campaign a spin before entering the race. The best marketers benchmark performance and constantly challenge their advertising to see if they can achieve better results.*

right tools and are asking the right questions about your marketing (which should focus on advertising *effectiveness* rather than how well consumers *recall* or think it affects them), you can really start honing your marketing message so it wins the race.

EFFECTIVE MESSAGING REVEALED THROUGH A/B SPLIT TESTS

Marketers and researchers are only really beginning to understand how messages work in consumers' minds. The role of emotional response in advertising and the linkage between brand beliefs and behaviors is an area that begs for much more research. We are humbled by how much more we have to learn about effective messaging. And one of the most powerful and easily accessible tools at a marketer's fingertips is the A/B split test.

Whether one focuses on emotion or behavior, the A/B split test is a measurement approach that allows marketers to learn whether one message produces a better response compared to another ad message with all other variables controlled for. The ability to hold constant all other factors that can influence a marketer's success is made possible by one of the most important scientific tools—design of experiments—which uses randomized exposed and control groups. An experiment using exposed and control groups lets the marketer observe the *true* effect of messaging alone. Let's take a look at how these powerful exposed/control and A/B split tools work, and what we are learning from their application to marketing.

Gaining insight about marketing is a tricky challenge. A senior marketing executive once shared an interesting experience he had in its ice cream novelty business in Europe (*novelties* are the single-serve products such as ice cream sandwiches and drumsticks that are bought at convenience stores and corner news stores). The marketing department would pat itself on the back when sales went up, and it would blame the weather when sales went down.

But when corporate management conducted a careful study of what was driving the sales, it found most of the sales occurred during the summer, and the hotter it was on a weekend, the better for sales. And, the better the company's distribution was (that is, if the consumer only had to walk a few steps to a corner store or newsstand to buy the product), the better its market share. The marketers were right: Bad marketing wasn't to blame when sales went down. It was indeed cool weather or rain that killed sales. However, marketing was also wrong. When sales went up, the advertising could claim little credit. It was the heat of the sun and the company's distribution that explained almost all its sales lift.

So how can a marketer isolate the impact of different messages with so many other variables influencing ultimate success? The foundation of our research is observation of actual effect through randomized control and exposed groups. Other parts of the business, such as manufacturing, use this tool and call it "design of experiments." For the measurement of messages, we use design of experiments to conduct A/B split tests in the field (not in an artificial laboratory). [3]

Imagine two groups of 500 consumers going about their day and, in the natural course of things, using media. Without even being aware of it, we control which ad is delivered to them as they use media. Based on randomization, one group sees ad A for the brand, the other sees ad B for the same brand as part of consumers' normal media use. The delivery of message A and message B is randomized to ensure that the two groups see different ads. Thanks to the power of randomization, the groups of consumers are equivalent in every respect, except for the fact that one saw message A and the other saw message B. An important variation on the A/B split introduces a third group, called a *control*. The control group is given a *placebo* ad for a completely unrelated brand to measure the baseline consumer relationship with the brand without exposure to advertising. This group is called a control group because it is used to effectively "control" for *all* the outside influences aside from the advertising. To explain further, in the *controlled experiments*, a randomly selected holdout group sees a control advertisement, such as a public service ad for the Red Cross. This produces additional power to the experiment in that we can measure and isolate the underlying base sales and brand equity from the incremental impact of advertising that the A/B groups see. We can also track changes between exposed and control groups over time and integrate competitive analysis.

A/B split testing comes from direct mail marketing, where savvy direct marketers found that they could randomly divide the list of names that would receive a mailing, deliver different messages, and then measure, in the real world, which messages performed better.[4] The scientific precision of this approach captured our imagination, and we adapted it to measuring two or more advertisements. We learned to measure more than response rates as direct marketers would do, because for most marketers, success is defined by less-visible "branding" measures, such as product awareness, brand perceptions, and purchase intention. The measurement is captured through identical surveys given to a random sample of consumers at some point after in-market exposure to the advertisements. We also use this A/B approach to measure sales, which allows the calculation of profit and return on investment (ROI) in relation to advertising expenditures.

A/B split testing comes from direct mail marketing, where savvy direct marketers found that they could randomly divide the list of names that would receive a mailing, deliver different messages, and then measure, in the real world, which messages performed better.

Measuring the A/B Split for *Wired* Magazine's Web Site

In 1995, one of the authors performed the first A/B split tests of an online creative ad campaign. We were measuring HotWired (*Wired* magazine's Web site) advertising on Netscape.com. The goal was to encourage people on Netscape's home page to click over to HotWired.com and give the Web site a try. In other words, HotWired wanted to induce trial of their Web site, hopefully acquiring new consumers for that Web site. We measured the percentage of consumers who clicked on the ad on Netscape to visit HotWired. Because each page viewed has a direct financial value to an online publisher (it's the same as a sale because the Web site generates revenue by charging marketers for each consumer who sees their ad on one of HotWired's pages), we could calculate the impact of a dollar spent on advertising and the dollar returned in sales. We found that certain rich-media ads (i.e., ads with motion) worked better than those that were static. Tracking clicks and counting subsequent page views was a fine way of qualifying ROI for an online publication like

HotWired because each click and subsequent page viewed literally represents revenue value as HotWired sells ads on their pages.

But what about companies such as IBM? Should they analyze and adjust their ad tactics based on "click-through"? Maybe, but a click is not always the real value the marketer is after. In fact, next to ad recall, click measurement is the most overrated and error-prone success metric that marketers might use. Sure, IBM would like to have information technology (IT) buyers and decision makers click on its ads and visit its Web site. But that's looking at things through the marketer's lens. Let's look at this from the consumer's perspective.

Measuring A/B Splits for IBM Online Ads

Picture this: Fifteen minutes before an IT decision maker's next meeting, he or she is on the Internet pulling down tech news to catch up on the latest trends. Because he or she is searching the Net in a hurry, he or she glances at an online advertisement but doesn't click on it. Does that mean that the ad wasn't effective? The answer to that question depends on what constitutes success. If success is a sale, then "clickthrough" is not useful in calculating the ROI of the advertisement. If success is an IT decision maker believing that IBM technology or services are worth a premium, then clickthrough is not useful in calculating the ROI of the advertisement. If success is IBM is increasing the number of people aware that IBM offers a certain product or service, then, similarly, clickthrough is worthless. As we said, in most cases, the clickthrough is not integral to success. So, if click-through isn't the ROI metric, how can we measure marketing ROI?

If IBM's focus is increasing the belief that IBM is the world leader in technology (because consumers who hold that opinion are more likely to pay a premium to have IBM products or services, or are more likely to be receptive to a salesperson from IBM), then IBM must measure the *consumer's mind,* not the computer mouse action. We can measure the consumer's mind through surveys where we quantify branding metrics. The three most common branding metrics are

1. *brand awareness,* including unaided awareness of the brand (which measures how top-of-mind the brand is compared to competitors) and aided awareness (which measures recognition of the brand within the product category);

2. *brand imagery* (e.g., agreement with statements such as "the brand is growing more popular," or "the brand is for people like me," or "the brand is good value for the money," or "the brand is a world leader in technology," or "I love the brand," etc.); and

3. *intent to purchase* (which many marketers have found is a good predictor of sales).

If IBM's focus is increasing the belief that IBM is the world leader in technology . . . then IBM must measure the consumer's mind, not the computer mouse action.

If a consumer answers that he or she "strongly agrees" with a brand image statement such as "IBM is the world leader in technology," what does that mean? Can we credit advertising with forming the consumer's opinion? The answer to that question is "No!" The simple fact that a survey finds that a certain percentage of consumers strongly agree that IBM is a world leader in technology cannot just be attributed to advertising effect because so many different things might have influenced that opinion. This is where a control group and observation through A/B splits plays a critical role in answering the ROI question.

So here's the scenario: Two groups of consumers are *randomly* divided into exposed and control groups, and because of randomization, the two groups are identical in all respects except for the one variable we aim to isolate. In IBM's case, the exposed group is delivered the IBM ad, and the control group is delivered a placebo ad for a public service such as a Red Cross advertisement, or something unrelated to technology. We can then ask the two groups of consumers if they strongly agree that IBM is a world leader in technology and compare the relative difference in responses between the two groups. If the two groups have the same percentage that strongly agree—in other words, if the two groups show no difference—that means that advertising had no impact.

The level of agreement among the control group, the ones who saw only the Red Cross ad, is caused by all other marketing factors. If, on the other hand, the exposed group has a higher percentage of consumers who strongly agree that IBM is a world leader in technology, we know it was that advertising that caused the difference and no other factor caused that effect.

This is the same rigorous level of proof that exacting sciences such as physics and biology hold up as the gold standard. It allows marketers to isolate the effect of advertising in the complex environment of the real world and to calculate the true cost to influence consumers' attitudes and beliefs about a brand. When we know that the marketer spent X amount on advertising and the researchers were able to see that Y consumers changed their view, we can then calculate cost per impact and ROI.

Why should it matter to the CFO that consumers strongly agree that IBM is a world leader in technology? The reason it should matter to a CFO is because causing a change in perception of a brand (in this case, a positive change in perception of IBM as a world leader in technology) is part of the chain of events that leads to sales. We can document this linkage between branding and sales and assign a dollar value to increasing the perception. By using design of experiments, we can pinpoint if it was the advertisement that caused this positive improvement in the number of people that state that "IBM is a world leader in technology." We further can extend our measurement to directly measuring the impact on sales too, assuming we set up the A/B split test and collect the measurement of those who bought. This is much more powerful than measuring the click of a computer mouse.

> *By using design of experiments, we can pinpoint if it was the advertisement that caused a positive improvement.*

In the vast majority of circumstances, marketers can move to measuring whether a campaign achieved intended results. The benefits of measuring actual advertising messaging can be the difference between success and failure.

For example, for IBM, we measured the side-by-side performance of two ads for IBM's Deep Blue versus Kasparov Chess Match.[5] In addition to the A/B split, we also used a control group. This allowed us to specifically isolate the effect of the online ad from all the other marketing and public relations activity for the world-chess champion Garry Kasparov's match with IBM's Deep Blue computer. Based on the results, if IBM reached 25 million users with the ad, 12 million of them would have already heard about the Kasparov versus Deep Blue match.[6]

Ad A used the IBM logo combined with the text "intuition vs. analysis, man vs. machine" as the hook and it made 2 million more people aware of the IBM event. Ad B used the same IBM logo, but this time used a close-up shot of Kasparov's eyes (made to look sinister), and then converted the image of the eyes into the text "man vs. machine." This ad made a little over 3 million more people aware of the IBM event. In other words, Ad B was 50 percent more effective— that's a big difference between the two ads. In fact, the 50 percent difference is a larger boost than is typical when an advertiser increases its ad size from banners to skyscrapers or large rectangles.[7] The key to success is the promotion of man versus machine, using the eyes of Kasparov paired with a persistent IBM logo.

Because Web sites charge the same amount for ads that work and ads that don't, the IBM case study makes a clear argument for experimenting to ensure you are using your best creative effort and thus getting the most bang for your buck.

INSIGHTS ON MESSAGE EFFECTIVENESS REVEALED THROUGH EXPERIMENTS

As we've measured literally hundreds and hundreds of advertisements across different media, in the real world, most with A/B split designs, we've gained insights on how consumers process advertisements. The advertisements that work best, almost without exception, are the ones with clear branding and relatively straightforward messaging. We've seen the pattern beyond the borders of the United States also. We've seen it in the United Kingdom, in Australia, in Austria, in the Netherlands, and in Hong Kong too. In fact, wherever we have conducted research, we have found, without exception, the same mental process at work.[8] Advertisements that link the brand with the meaning that is being created by the *visual imagery* perform better. Let's look at several companies that used A/B splits to get messaging right.

How Naming the Brand Clarifies the Message

Consider the two ads from Volvo measured in Australia, shown in Figure 11.1. Can you tell the difference between these two ads for Volvo? Could these two ads really perform that differently for Volvo? If you think the difference between including the brand name in the ad on each frame (especially the first frame of the ad) is more than a subtle difference, you're right. In fact, ad B (on the right) produced 86 percent more value across the key

FIGURE 11.1 Volvo Ads (3 Frames of an Animated Online Ad)

Ad A   Ad B

branding metrics for Volvo. With the Volvo name in the first frame, it was far more successful.

As we observed with Procter & Gamble's Olay advertising, the difference between success and failure was the result of whether or not the advertisement connected the *visual image* of beauty (personified by the woman in the ad) with the *Olay name and logo*. When another version of the ad showed the image of the woman first, and then a few seconds later showed the Olay logo, our research revealed that the ad did not work nearly as well. There are two reasons for the ad working better: The first is that consumers can recognize the brand and that communicates relevance to the consumer; and the second is framing the meaning and story of the ad with a specific brand.

Channel 9, the leading TV network in Australia, has done some fascinating neuroscientific work on using brand names within an ad. Consumers wore a specialized hat with neurosensors and goggles that tracked where the consumer's eyes were looking while simultaneously measuring blood flow to various parts of the brain where memory is encoded. While these are not field experiments, the research helps understand consumer engagement with an advertisement. There is an unmistakable increase in consumer engagement and memory encoding when a familiar brand appears in the ad—so it's wise to introduce the brand *earlier* in the message. Marketers are encouraged to challenge the dominant practice of waiting to reveal the brand logo and name until the end of television and online advertisements.

The principles learned through online A/B split testing apply to TV, magazine, out of home, and indeed all media. Here's an example from magazines: A magazine advertisement shows a close-up side profile picture of a man's face. The copy below reads:

You're playing poker. They're playing you.

In the right corner is the word "Tilt" as if on a Las Vegas billboard filled with lights and under it is "Thursday's 9PM, ESPN." What is Tilt? Might it refer to a new poker competition on ESPN? Or maybe it's a poker reality show?

Actually, it's a reference to a dramatic series set in the seedy underworld of Las Vegas that revolves around fictional high-stakes poker players. An examination of the magazine ad suggests that the ad requires the consumer to be familiar with the character featured in the advertisement (in this case, the character is named Everest). The magazine copy is sparse, it may appeal to those who like to play or watch poker, but on its own, is it enough information to resonate with people who are interested in a dramatic series?

Try this exercise—it's not meant to replace proper research, but it might help frame the challenge of conveying meaning and influencing consumers: Take one of your ads. Think about the advertisement from the perspective of a consumer who knows nothing about your product. Glance at it for no more than three seconds because that's the amount of time, on average, a consumer will look at it. Look away and think about the meaning the consumer would take from the ad. Are there enough cues to communicate the meaning of the brand, what the product promise is, and why a consumer would want to hire the brand? Advertising an entirely new idea is challenging.

Now consider the case of ESPN's *Dream Job*. Based on findings presented at the 2004 Marketing Accountability Forum hosted by the ANA(EN), ESPN nailed it. The magazine ad shows an empty chair behind the sports center news desk with the *headline text* "Sports Center anchor wanted, no experience necessary." The body copy adds, "Watch one fan's dreams become a reality." This ad really seems to work to get the idea across. The best ads work both as stand alones and in concert with ads in other media. *Dream Job* advertising in TV used a similar look and feel, which helped reinforce the message for consumers who saw both the TV and the magazine ads.[9]

People say, "a picture is worth a thousand words," but for iconic imagery, the marketer should aim for the picture to capture the essence of *a singular concept*. If the ad is intended to reinforce or shape perceptions, a visual message should communicate the essence of the brand promise. Together, the logo and the image should be easily understood at a glance.

Here's another example: Consider the image of the woman used as an icon in Figure 11.2. This ad conveys Olay's promise of beauty and science.

FIGURE 11.2 Olay Magazine Ad

LEVERAGING IMAGERY TRANSFER

If a picture is worth a thousand words, what should marketers do with radio? The radio ad should work as a stand-alone message to tap consumers' motivations and connect it with the brand. And in a cross-media campaign, radio should also leverage the content of television advertising. The theoretical underpinnings of this approach is called "imagery transfer,"[10] and the evidence suggests that when a radio ad is similar to the TV ad, the audio in a radio spot can trigger a mental replay of the TV images in the minds of consumers. Radio can be effective in cross-media campaigns, but the marketer has to figure out how to convey meaning using sound.

Evidence suggests that when a radio ad is similar to the TV ad, the audio in a radio spot can trigger a mental replay of the TV images in the minds of consumers.

For example, we have several clients that have been challenged to communicate the core idea of a brand without the visual aid. Some have cued into the voice-over used in the TV ad in an attempt to connect a TV ad to a radio ad. But, if the voice message is merely the same voice as the TV ad and isn't communicating the key motivating factors that matter to the consumer, this approach fails to produce an impact in the radio ad. Success in radio ads comes from tapping into the core motivations for why consumers would care about the claim the marketer is making and buy the product.

The difference between success and failure is knowing that the messaging works; therefore, we strongly urge marketers to consider pretesting TV ads, extracting insight from the ads in terms of the elements that tap into the motivations of the consumer and applying those elements to radio ads. It may not be what the voice- over says, it may be the imagery that matters. In such cases, figuring out how to convey the imagery with sound in radio is key to success.

MAKE SURE YOUR MESSAGE CONNECTS CLEARLY TO YOUR BRAND

Consider the case of Colgate Oxygen toothpaste and its competition, Aquafresh Extreme Clean. Aquafresh Extreme Clean was the first product on the market in the United Kingdom to develop bubbles in your mouth that work to clean between your teeth to give an "extreme clean." Colgate had its own product called Colgate Oxygen that had a "sensorial benefit" (as they put it). Tiny oxygen bubbles clean between the teeth, and the popping bubbles give the mouth a fresh, clean feeling.

From the consumers' standpoint, the Colgate and Aquafresh products were similar innovations in toothpaste. Unfortunately for Colgate, Aquafresh launched first. When the Colgate ads first began to run, they actually helped increase awareness for Aquafresh—its *competition*—which obviously was not the result Colgate wanted!

The technical term for this phenomenon, in marketing research speak, is the *halo effect*. It occurs to some extent because consumers are not paying full attention to marketing messages and will occasionally connect the benefit you are marketing to one of your other products, or to your competition's product instead. We raise this issue here to encourage marketers to ensure that your message is connected to your brand. In cases where your product is very similar to the competition, or your advertisement plays on similar visual imagery, there is often a spillover, or halo affect, on other brands, and your brand gets less benefit than it should from your media dollars.

You can minimize advertising for your competition by making sure your message is well branded and is backed by an adequate media plan. That's what Colgate did. As the Colgate Oxygen campaign expanded across media, our research showed that consumers were less likely to connect Colgate's message with the Aquafresh product. Over time, thanks to the well-branded messages running across multiple media, Colgate got the benefit of its advertising. In a way, the use of multiple touchpoints helped Colgate overcome a potentially "me too" visual and product and take ownership of the sensorial benefit of oxygen bubbles in toothpaste from the competition.

In the end, messaging is critical to any success. In many campaigns, it is the difference between any success and failure. In today's world, it is not good enough to use intuition and talent alone. As in car racing, a marketer should use science and data to complement talent. Knowing what's working and making it work harder based on testing is essential. Isolating the effect of advertising should be done through scientific observation using tools like the A/B splits that isolate the effect of the message.

This scientific approach will increase the likelihood of overall success and start to make CFOs happy when marketers are able to show they know what the cost of meeting the goal is, whether that be in building awareness, driving particular brand imagery, purchase intent, or even sales.

Chapter 12 looks at how consistency in messaging across every point of contact with a consumer can lead to the marketing nirvana of synergy, where multiple-message touchpoints work to do more than one touchpoint can. We will expand on the value of managing the message across touchpoints and address how a COP can improve message effectiveness and overall marketing ROI.

Messaging Across Consumer Touchpoints

The last point that's important for marketers to understand with respect to messaging is the concept of messaging *integration and reinforcement* across the many ways a brand comes in contact with consumers. This is often called touchpoint *integration*. This consistency in tone, messaging, visual representation, and more is the hallmark of great brands such as Starbucks, McDonald's, JetBlue, and many others.

Touchpoints are all the places the consumer encounters your brand, whether it is an ad in a magazine, or on television, the Web, an in-store display, or the truck carrying your product. Do the touchpoints right, and you can produce synergy. Do the touchpoints wrong, and you can undermine success and even counteract the good work already done. This chapter explores the importance of touchpoint integration and ties together the concepts of messaging by showing how a communication optimization process—or COP—can help marketers get messaging right and improve overall return on investment (ROI). If touchpoint integration is the pinnacle of a well-functioning marketing message, then touchpoint interference is the nadir.

WHY TOUCHPOINTS ARE SO IMPORTANT

Let's consider the flip side, touchpoint interference, by considering the problems that occur when messages are not well coordinated and interfere with one another. What message are you communicating about your brand through the ancillary services you offer? Have you asked: "How do I make sure that the message I'm trying to convey with my product and my service experience is what my consumers are hearing and that it's the message I want them to hear?" To answer that question, you may find a COP helpful.

Colgate Oxygen Toothpaste Example

Consider the results of Colgate Oxygen toothpaste ads in the United Kingdom, shown in Figure 12.1. Notice how purchase intent increases with the 30-second TV ad and drops during the 20-second TV ad but it appears to pick back up by 28/05/05—why?

What did consumers hear in the 30-second TV ad that made the awareness, purchase intent, and sales increase so well? What did the 20-second TV ad do to cause consumers' purchase intent to decline?

It turned out that, in a move to save money, Colgate had cut down the 30-second ad to 20 seconds and had combined that 20 seconds with a 10-second ad for another Colgate Palmolive product—which it turns out was a deodorant. The combination of 10 seconds of a sweaty tennis player and deodorant with the 20-second toothpaste ad that focuses on oxygen bubbles bursting in your mouth and producing a new level of clean just didn't jibe. Colgate was sending consumers mixed messages, literally, and it was creating confused meaning. Consumers didn't separate the two messages enough, and the combination led consumers to take away the wrong message. No one had thought to check to see whether the messages for Oxygen toothpaste and a deodorant would work *with* one another. The focus had simply been on saving money, and there wasn't a process to check for message compatibility. Fortunately, Colgate is a smart company. And the moment its marketers saw the data for the 20-second commercial, they knew what went wrong.

But companies need more than an *autopsy* reporting why the campaign failed. They need systems in place to reduce the likelihood of the problem occurring in the first place (or again). They need a COP, not a coroner. Colgate's mixed message, which undermined effectiveness to consumers, is a phenomenon we have observed in more than 10 percent of the brands we've studied; therefore, we explicitly discuss touchpoint review as part of the COP discussion.

FIGURE 12.1 Overall Campaign Results

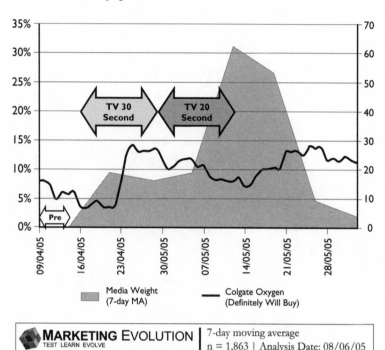

Companies need more than an autopsy reporting why the campaign failed. They need systems in place to reduce the likelihood of the problem occurring in the first place (or again).

Target Example

Another manifestation of mixed messages occurs when marketers shift from one focus to another, as Target did in its "Fashion for All" campaign that we measured. The campaign had two different points of focus: apparel and housewares. The fashion campaign is a brilliant television, magazine, newspaper, and online campaign. The ROI against sales and profit is impressive.

The apparel advertisement runs around the same time as a Target housewares campaign. Take a look at the data shown in Figure 12.2. It shows that consumers' association of Target as a place to buy apparel increases during the

FIGURE 12.2 Target Graph

When you think of purchasing apparel for yourself or your family, which stores come to mind first? (Trended: Those answering "Target")

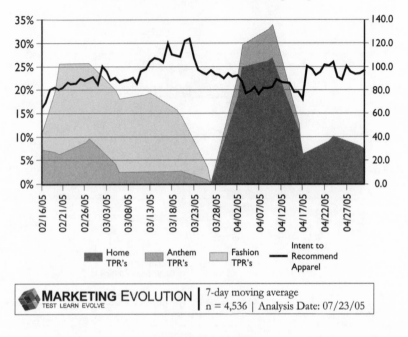

MARKETING EVOLUTION
TEST LEARN EVOLVE | 7-day moving average
n = 4,536 | Analysis Date: 07/23/05

apparel campaign but decreases quickly during the housewares advertising. Every time the housewares message runs, it undercuts perceptions of Target's apparel—why does this occur?

The perception "undercut" occurs because consumers aren't spending their time focused on trying to sort out what Target does and does not offer. Remember, the ads are in the consumers' *peripheral vision.* They hear whispers in the game of telephone, and when housewares are advertised they play back the message that "Target = housewares"—and that meaning undercuts "Target = apparel."

Meaning is susceptible to distortion by consumers, who are processing messages in "low-attention" mode. Marketers need to make it *easy* for consumers to connect meaning to the brand. Consumers pick up patterns from the environment so marketers need to help consumers see the pattern of a consistent benefit that caters to their motivations for hiring the brand. Marketers can do this by ensuring the consistency of visual look and feel of the message across media. Target's very well-branded design and emotional energy levels add power to the Target messages, but they don't overcome the conflict in what Target means.

Consumers pick up patterns from the environment, so marketers need to help consumers see the pattern of a consistent benefit that caters to their motivations.

MAKE SURE EVERY CONSUMER TOUCHPOINT SUPPORTS THE BRAND YOU ARE CREATING

Messaging is more than advertising. Therefore, marketers should think broadly about touchpoint integration. Think about the coordination of sales-force messages with direct mail, advertising, etc. Think about the salesperson who has to push too broad of a portfolio of products—and therefore muddles the meaning and benefits. Think about the look and feel of the stores. Think about the design and colors. Think about the scent and other sensory inputs generated by the product.

Everything the consumer experiences should communicate the benefit in connection with the brand. Think beyond the traditional definition of marketing materials (i.e., ads and brochures) and think about package design, facilities, and sales force.

Starbucks' Example

The lid on the Starbucks cup is totally different from the lids that donned coffee cups before Starbucks reinvented the coffee category. If you think about it, the Starbucks cup lid *communicates* something. It is part of the Starbucks message. We take it for granted that the lid just feels right when you hold it to your mouth and sip a $4.50 latte.

Now go back to how coffee lids looked before Starbucks worked directly with its supplier to change the lids that were little plastic flimsy things, where you had to pull back the tab and tear it off to make a little coffee hole. Starbucks said, "The feel of the lid must communicate quality." The *experience with the product* is a message, and Starbucks managed it as such. The company worked with the lid supplier, SOLO, and they jointly designed the current lid. The current lid helps to justify the coffee for which consumers pay a premium. Sure, the lid costs Starbucks about three times more, but Starbucks made the call that it was worth it and is consistent with the premium price it's charging.

So Starbucks developed the premium lid and used thicker paper for its cups, instead of Styrofoam. The company wanted the product to communicate "premium quality." And they get the message across brilliantly.[1]

This all begs the question, have you considered the silent communicators of your brand? Have you tested or measured the effect of different packaging? How about the impact of store layout? The dress of your sales force? The services that go along with the product? Do all your touchpoints contribute to the meaning you are aiming to convey? Think about the following examples, and see if you can apply what these companies did to *your* marketing.

> Have you considered the silent communicators of your brand?

Target adopted a new packaging for the pills dispensed through Target pharmacies. The new packaging was meant to convey the "design" leadership of Target as well as be easier for consumers to use by improving the ability to tell whose medicine was in the bottle (no more having to read the tiny lettering, which is a real problem for older people, many of whom require reading glasses).[2]

Crayola builds the smell into its crayons. That smell is part of the company's message. Similarly, Rolls Royce found that sales were better for its new cars once the company discovered the appeal of the "old" smell of leather. It is actually a more complex odor than just the smell of leather. It reportedly contains more than 800 components and is designed to replicate the smell of the 1965 Rolls Royce. The smell is sprayed in at the factory.[3]

Consider the full sensory brand experience. Singapore Airlines does so: Its flight attendants not only have a uniform that is coordinated with the color palette of the airline, Singapore Airline manages the fragrances they wear as well. In fact, Singapore Airlines is so detailed about the touchpoints that it manages its color palette down to the *eye shadow* flight attendants can wear.[4]

Sound may also be part of your message. United Airlines has a sound signature that plays as part of its preflight announcements and in all its advertising. One of the Japanese car brands (the Acura RSX) found that the sound of the car door closing was used as an indication for consumers in determining car quality. Therefore, the company designed a system that produced the sound most associated with a heavy car door closing. Every touchpoint communicates a message. Elevators in the Disney Building in Burbank California play the sound of the Disneyland theme park train whistle when the doors close. Intel pays part of the advertising bill of computer manufacturers that use Intel chips (such as Dell) if the computer manufacturer includes a trade-marked Intel sound to signify that Intel is inside.

The *service* marketers wrap around the product also communicates a message. When FedEx began to provide tracking codes to allow consumers to see where their packages were in the delivery process, the company communicated "reliability." Brands that provide call services, Web site support, or other services should work to optimize the message that comes across in each of the interactions with consumers.[5]

Moreover, brands should consider whether there is more that can be done to extend the brand message through services, as Coca-Cola® is doing with iCoke at *www.coke.com*. Because Coke sees connecting people as one of its brand benefits, its iCoke brings together people with common interests. For example, the common interest could be around football (Coke is a big sponsor of the Federation Internationale de Football Association [FIFA]) or around music (there is a mixing room where you can make your own tunes). Coca-Cola's iCoke is a Web site experience that creates community. Coke uses the Web site to extend the meaning of the brand.

HOW A COP HELPS WITH TOUCHPOINT INTEGRATION

A COP can help ensure marketers leverage the power of *surround-sound marketing*. Surround-sound marketing is a way of thinking about touchpoint integration. The ideal situation is for the elements of the marketing program to work the way a surround-sound stereo system works—where each message plays the role of one of the speakers in the surround-sound stereo system. By working together, each one doing something slightly different, but all working together in concert, the totality of the system creates a more powerful experience for consumers, and the marketer achieves better results.

The elements of the marketing program should work the way a surround-sound stereo system works.

Let's take two examples from our research—one where the marketer got touchpoint integration wrong within its advertising and one where the marketer got it right.

Kimberly-Clark Example

There were two TV ads. The first TV ad was flirtatious: It showed an attractive young woman driving a convertible sports car down a dusty road, splashing a young guy with water, and offering him a Kleenex Soft Pack. The second TV ad showed a cute kid in the backseat of a car; in the car's front seat is a dog with his head out the window, jowls to the wind. As drool forms on the dog's mouth, the kid grabs for the Kleenex Soft Pack as his best defense. A cute ad—but not integrated with the first TV ad.

The campaign's magazine ad appeared to us to use a completely different approach: It looked like a family picture from a trip across the country, with the family standing under a giant statue of Paul Bunyan in a kitsch tourist trap that you'd find in the middle of nowhere. The visual look and images were entirely different from the TV ads.

And the Kleenex online ad looked completely different to us from the TV and magazine ads. It used a pure white background with a picture showing a briefcase and the Kleenex packed inside.

Unfortunately, Kimberly-Clark didn't have a COP to catch this lack of integration during its approval process. The company did realize surround-sound marketing might have been important when it got back poor results from the campaign measurement.

Unilever Dove Nutrium Soap Bar Example

Unilever recognized that its whole product promise was about a bar of soap that nurtures your skin and provides nutrition to your skin, so *Nutrium* was a good name for it. The reason to believe that this product does what it promises is based on the idea that the soap's pink stripes do moisturize and nourish the skin (the soap contains vitamin E), and the white stripe contains cleansers that clean your skin. Together, the soap produces a perfect product for your skin.

Unilever used surround-sound marketing to carry those pink-and-white stripes very effectively across the TV ad, which showed the pink-and-white stripes coming together, mixing together, blending together, and then resolving into the pink-and-white bar.

FIGURE 12.3 TV, Magazine, and Online Nutrium Ads

Photographs by Robin Broadbent used with permission

Unilever carried this idea across in the magazine part of its ad campaign: The print ads were a big picture of a pink-and-white striped bar and an explanation in the body copy about how it was nutrition for your skin, containing Vitamin E. As can be seen in Figure 12.3, the online advertisement also played on the same visual theme and had, as the main feature, the pink-and-white stripe Nutrium bar.

Touchpoint integration occurs when the meaning across touchpoints is so well integrated that marketers achieve synergy (i.e., the total effect is greater than the sum of the parts). When it's not well integrated, marketers can actually undermine their success.

How do you create an effective surround-sound message? Every marketing campaign has to start with a strategy. Though this is a simple concept that all marketers understand, the strategy most often gets focused around how the advertising communicates the message. But that may miss the value of all the nonadvertising communicators such as the sales force, direct mail, public relations, events, and so forth. As more companies move toward an integrated communication plan, the strategy requires a consistency of *voice* to the consumer through all of the touchpoints controlled by the marketing department. However, the concept used for the traditional advertising vehicles does not always translate easily to other activities such as events, salesforce communications, etc. We suggest that marketers focus on the consistency of the *voice* (e.g., tone, style, messaging, etc.). The *voice* doesn't have to start with the advertising creative activity itself. It may start with a sales strategy, or event, and the *voice* can carry over to advertising. Because the *voice* may emerge from many different places within marketing, it requires a more conceptual COP and channel-planning approach that begins earlier in the marketing process to ensure that all marketing vehicles (and agencies) are singing with the same *voice*.

Based on our research, we found that it was more effective for the consumer to see the ads in different media than it was to see the ad three times on television. Why is surround-sound marketing better than blasting the message out in a single media? The reason surround-sound marketing works better is that consumers naturally scan for patterns. When a consistent look and feel to the message is carried across media, it reinforces the core message. When the same meaning is reinforced across all our physical senses (sight, taste, touch, smell, and sound), then we have even better touchpoint integration.

> *We found that it was more effective for the consumer to see the ads in different media than it was to see the ad three times on television.*

Getting motivations right followed by messaging that really works and is known to work and then reinforcing the message across touchpoints is a formula for success. We have found that the COP should have an inventory of all the touchpoints with consumers and that it should work to align those communication objectives into each touchpoint. Use the COP approach to make sure the salespeople are saying the right things, the collateral and other visuals (including the ads) support a consistent brand image, and even the scent or sounds tie the brand together. Not doing so is either a missed opportunity or, as some of the examples demonstrate, can even set the brand back.

If you want to learn more about messaging research, turn to Appendix D. The next three chapters address the third of the 4Ms—media.

CHAPTER THIRTEEN

Media Mechanics

Media Allocation's "Laws of Physics"

For big clients and agencies, media planners are the people who make recommendations to clients about *where* they should allocate their advertising money. For those in the world of media planning at the top ad agencies, one of the more prestigious accounts to work on is Procter & Gamble (P&G). P&G's brand managers and media managers are considered the smartest and most disciplined in the industry. Most media people who take their careers seriously make it a point to work on a P&G account for at least a couple of years to get trained in the company's superior approach.

P&G's renowned annual budget process had brand managers working hand in hand for a grueling four to five months of nights and weekends with their ad agency partners, including senior agency management, the account team, and the media team, to develop the brand's overall marketing plans and the advertising media plans for the following year. There was not a detail left open to question—everything had a supporting rationale. Many agency media people appreciated this level of rigor as a foundation for their careers.

In fact, years ago, a media person at one of New York's better midsize agencies was particularly energized by the P&G approach and the process P&G utilized to get the best marketing plans possible. However, there was always this gnawing feeling in the pit of his stomach that maybe the advice he and his agency were giving P&G about how to spend its media funds wasn't right. Sure, his bosses, who were media veterans of 15 years to 25 years, had a series of clear guiding principles that they applied to their media plans for P&G (and many of their other blue-chip clients), such as:

- *"Seek to maximize the media plan at the three-plus frequency level"* (because, they suggested, "everyone knows that any ads running fewer than three exposures to a consumer don't work").
- *"Your minimum reach of your target audience should be 75 percent."*
- *"Don't allocate to a second medium until you've done a 'sufficient' job on your first medium."*
- *"You need to run at least six insertions in each magazine annually."*

And so on. These were positioned as *proven* guidelines that were to be applied to each media plan.

Anyway, this media person listened to the veteran managers proclaim these guiding principles to P&G and other clients, who would generally nod their heads in agreement. And he would occasionally ask his management where these principles came from. The answers were always something to the effect of "based on my long-standing experience . . . ," and so on. After a while, this media guy was promoted, and he found himself repeating these same things in meetings, and the clients would nod. Yet his uneasy feeling wouldn't go away. Occasionally, a smart up-and-comer would ask: "Where did these principles come from?" And he'd find himself automatically responding, "Based on my long-standing experience . . . "

Occasionally, a smart up-and-comer would ask, "Where did these principles come from?"

Well, that media person is one of the authors, and it wasn't until we did the research that underlies this book that we learned that this nagging sense that something was wrong was actually *right*, and that much of what we had been handed down and taught was patently false at worst, and dubious at best. It was *mythology* that was being passed along by the elders. It was a conspiracy of unexamined and unproven "conventional wisdom," much of which turned out to be false once it was examined under the careful scrutiny of quality research. And for more than a decade, the author had worked with some of the biggest brands in the world determining the allocation for hundreds of millions of media dollars. And yet much of that counsel was wrong—*horribly, money-wastingly, dead wrong.*[1]

Most marketers are not actively involved in their media decisions; they delegate completely that responsibility to their ad agencies. Some companies realize that they should be involved, working side-by-side with their agency rather than abdicating that responsibility. For example, at a 2006 AdMap marketing accountability conference, an insider's advertising research conference, in London, Sony's Controller for Europe gave a riveting address about how CFOs look at advertising, and she ended with an off-the-cuff question: *"If marketers really care about ROI, where are the other marketers?"*[2] The room was packed with advertising agency and marketing research professionals, but with painfully few marketers.

The organizer of the AdMap Conference felt this was an important enough question that he took the podium after lunch and explained that quite a bit of effort had been taken to reach out and invite marketers, but most marketers said: "Our advertising agency handles that sort of thing for us, and so we chose not to attend." There are good, bright people at advertising agencies working diligently on behalf of clients, but the agency people in attendance were in wide agreement that it is a mistake for marketers to abdicate responsibility to the agencies alone. The marketer must get engaged and take responsibility for understanding media and marketing ROI and work side-by-side with their agency and independent ROI measurement firms.

The challenge for marketers and media people is that there are a number of "media myths," and, until recently, little research to sort through fact and fiction. This chapter sets forth some platinum principles of good media planning. Applying the learning from this chapter alone has proven to increase sales and profit from marketing substantially. As noted in earlier chapters, for Dove, we saw an increase of consumers intent to purchase by 14 percent; for Ford, we estimated that sales of the F-150 would increase by more than $500 million; and for the *E. T. the Extraterrestrial* DVD, fixing the media mix was the difference between some success and none at all. Just like motivations and messaging, media has a major impact on success.

MEDIA PLANNING SHOULD NOT BE BASED ON
"EXPERIENCE" ALONE; IT SHOULD BE *MEASURED*

If there ever was a place for a different or new orientation to the world of advertising, it is here in the planning and buying of media. In fact, this is what we originally set out to address with our research. We simply wanted to understand the relative effectiveness and cost efficiency of different media—to do real cross-media analysis. It was when we realized that ineffective ads made it very difficult (OK, impossible) to find an optimal media mix solution that we realized the need for a new approach to all of advertising. As in the first two of the 4Ms, we found the same issues with waste in the third M, media. In fact, our research has shown that $19.8 billion in media is wasted each year, as if the cash was run through a paper shredder and thrown into the garbage dumpster. In addition, we find that most marketers could get better results from the same budget. We've quantified an additional $16.9 billion in value from easily identifiable, underleveraged media in the mix.

Our sense is that many agency people and marketers are increasingly boggled by the seeming complexity of media and don't have the right tools to really treat media as an investment and, therefore, have no orientation to buy and manage it as such. Hence, the mantra of this chapter and the underlying theme of the book is this: *"Same budget, better results."* Whether you are a big media spender, or you're trying to stretch a tiny budget as far as you can, the concepts and results we'll share in this chapter will help improve your marketing ROI.

> *Many agency people and marketers are increasingly boggled by the seeming complexity of media and don't have the right tools to treat media as an investment.*

Let's start with the central question: Do you know the value of each marketing dollar? Oscar Wilde once said: "These days man knows the price of everything, but the value of nothing." This quote rings true in media where most marketers can report the cost of advertisement placement in terms of a cost per page in *People* magazine, or the cost of a TV rating point, or the cost of a Super Bowl 30-second unit (about $2,400,000 nowadays)[3], but they are generally stumped when asked to define that value of any advertising spend as it relates to a marketing goal, be it sales, brand perception, or even awareness. And yet, it is the branding and sales objectives the marketer spends the money to achieve not the ad insertion. Let's break out this central question about cost into the following series of crucial, must know, subquestions:

- If you, the brand manager, or the media planning agency, were to spend a dollar in TV, what would be the return on that dollar? What would be the return on the dollar at half the TV budget or double the TV budget?
- If you added a dollar to your magazine plan, what would be the gain in brand impact on a key perception, such as, "a brand I would recommend to friends," or on sales?
- What would a dollar be worth in a direct mail campaign, or the sponsorship of a Web site, or a conference, or the purchase of Internet search keywords?
- Or say that you had an extra dollar: Do you know where to add it to have the most value or the least (again as it relates to the business or marketing goals of the brand)?
- If you had to cut a dollar, do you know where you would cut it and what impact it would have?

If your answers to the above questions are tentative, or simply uncertain, you are not alone. The marketers who engaged in our research did so because they wanted to know the answers to these questions. They recognized that the only way to get the answers was to measure their campaigns, and then to adjust as quickly as possible to take advantage of the insights gained. This led to better marketing-mix allocation and deeper understanding about the dynamics of their consumers, their brands, their advertisements, and how to optimize sales and profits.

It could easily be said that it cost more than $1 billion to write this chapter because that's the total advertising spending we measured by the marketers who commissioned our research. This chapter culls through the spending and analyzes the effect of the dollars spent and distills the learning to help you ensure that you get better results from your budget, whether that budget is big or small.

At the heart of the problem is marketers who need to allocate their media mix and have to do so based on *guesses* rather than *empirical results based on real impact against goals.* Some marketers take the path of least thought and simply

Some marketers simply update their media budget by taking last year's budgets and making minor adjustments, but what was the basis of last year's budget? Was it a well-researched optimized mix? Or, was it a minor tweak to the previous year's budget?

update their media budget by taking last year's budgets and making minor adjustments. But what was the basis of last year's budget? Was it a well-researched optimized mix? Or, was it a minor tweak to the previous year's budget? And given the pace of change in the media landscape in the last decade—thanks to TiVo, the Internet, downloadable TV, Search advertising, digitization of out-of-home ads, mobile devices, a 150+ channel television environment in most homes, satellite radio, and accelerated guerrilla marketing, to name just a few—it is all the more important to measure the media mix.

Let's look at what marketers can do to get the *message* in front of the *right consumer* at the *right time* to achieve the most cost-effective change in attitudes and consumer-buying behavior. We do this by examining *media mechanics*— a process that encompasses coverage, frequency, pacing, and diminishing returns. Optimizing the media mix is not just about media mechanics. In the following chapter we'll focus on the *psychologics* of the media mix. *Psychologics* is a new field of study examining how the consumer psychology of meaning is created by each media type and the interaction of the entire media mix. Applying the lessons from both chapters together can vastly improve marketers' ROI. We will then examine a few case studies that get into the nitty-gritty of media mix optimization, tying together the motivation, message, and media mix. But first, let's look at wine tasting.

MEDIA MECHANICS, WINE TASTING, DIMINSHING RETURNS, AND QUINTILES

Imagine for a moment that you are at a wine tasting with an economist. The economist is trying to reduce the experience to a set of *utilities,* which is an economist's term for *units of value.* She hands you a glass. But the glass is empty. She asks you to taste and to tell her how much you like it. The glass is empty. You look at her with a puzzled stare. "There's nothing in the glass," you protest. She laughs and says, "Exactly!" Because there is nothing to taste, the *utility* you derive from tasting nothing is zero. The two of you work your way over to the bar, and the wine attendant pours you a taste. You smile; you like it. "Ah, the taste of utility," you say. The wine attendant pours another.

At a certain point in pouring another glass, the wine will become intoxicating—maybe intoxicatingly good. And at a certain point after that, the wine will become intoxicatingly bad. Your liver could revolt; you could wake up the next day with a pounding headache, cursing the ringing telephone. When you answer the ringing phone, it is your economist friend. She rubs in the fact that you had one taste too many and that illustrates her last lesson—that there was a point of *diminishing returns* where the *value* derived from each additional sip produced less and less *utility*. Pushing past the point of diminishing returns will make you sick. She laughs. You groan. Lesson learned.

Marketing is in a collective hangover. Many marketers have had "one too many" in some parts of their media mix and, as a result, have areas in their marketing mix that could be adjusted to increase the overall ROI. Media mechanics can help. The following five mechanics have to be taken into consideration:

1. No see, no hear = no impact
2. Beware of the dual diminishing returns
3. some consumers get more than their fair share
4. Reach isn't really reach
5. Outcome matters more than in-process measures

If you use these five media-mechanic principles together, you will improve your marketing ROI substantially.

MECHANICS PRINCIPLE #1:
"NO SEE, NO HEAR = NO IMPACT"

The Dove Nutrium Bar campaign had an estimated TV reach of 85 percent (*reach* is the unduplicated audience that a brand's message is exposed to). But what was the impact of TV advertising among the 15 percent that were not reached by the TV advertisement? Nothing!

The impact of TV advertising among those who were never reached by the TV ad is 0. Just like the economist who handed an empty glass of wine and asked: "Take a taste and tell me how much you like it?" If there's nothing there, it can't have value.

This is the first key point in media mechanics: *Coverage is critical.* If you don't get your well-crafted message to consumers for them to see it, hear it, and experience it, it isn't going to make a lick of difference. This is true of advertising, events, direct marketing, public relations, blogs, etc. No see, no hear = no impact. Where this becomes a challenge is that most media can only reach a percentage of the total population. For example, there's a meaningful group of people who watch little or no TV, and, therefore, you can't generally reach them in that medium; you must turn to other media.

> *There's a huge group of people who watch little or no TV, and, therefore, you can't generally reach them in that medium.*

This might not seem like such a big deal except that we see so many marketers who don't seem to think about organizing their media to reach as many people as possible in their target audience. This is particularly true for online media where many marketers just don't seem to focus on getting their advertising communications to as many as possible. So it bears repeating: If your plan doesn't reach someone, they will not get your message (and, thus, will not act).

MECHANICS PRINCIPLE #2:
BEWARE OF THE DUAL DIMINISHING RETURNS

Diminishing returns is a powerful concept in economics. The first taste of wine may be wonderful. But each additional taste tends to produce a little less value. There are two diminishing-returns forces that play an important, highly predictable, mechanical role in determining how marketers can get better results for the same budget. We call these the dual diminishing returns.

FIGURE 13.1 Diminishing Returns Chart Showing TV Only

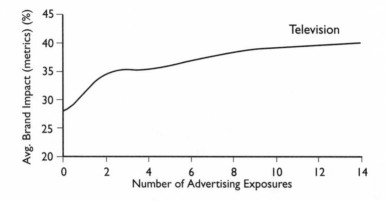

The First Diminishing Return:
Advertising Effect versus Frequency

The first type of diminishing returns is "effect versus frequency." Figure 13.1 is an important chart in marketing. It is a chart of TV frequency by purchase intent for Dove Nutrium bar's TV advertising. You can see that purchase intent increases with the first exposure to TV advertising, and then purchase intent increases at a slower rate with each subsequent impression. This is the predictable pattern observed in the vast majority of advertising campaigns (although we will discuss some exceptions in Chapter 14 where we'll discuss psychologics).

For Dove, as is true across brands, there is a diminishing return with each additional TV frequency. For Dove, the media agency reported a TV reach of 85 percent and a frequency of 6.0. Think of buying additional frequency as similar to buying additional glasses of wine. The first glass was great, so you ordered a second one, and on up to six glasses. The bartender charged you the same on glass 1, 2, and 3 as he or she does on 4, 5, and 6, but you derived a little less utility from 2, 3, 4, 5, and 6 (because of diminishing returns). If we recognize that each additional TV impression costs the marketer the same, we can quickly see that for a marketer spending money at the impression frequency of 6.0 over four weeks delivers less ROI compared to a plan with a 5.0 frequency. To know exactly how much less, we'd have to measure the effectiveness of TV. To determine if we should reallocate budget, we'd need to know the cost and effect relative to the other media Dove was running (which we did—more to the story later).

Here's an example of the first diminishing return from Procter & Gamble's Olay. P&G sought to learn more about the diminishing-return curves pattern when it was advertising its Olay product line. Initially, with online advertising, we had no idea what the optimal frequency would be. So, when the brand began to plan its online advertising, and based on our guidance, they decided to "start frequency high to see if the advertising can generate an effect." In addition, by having a range of frequency P&G hoped to plot the diminishing-returns curve to help optimize future campaigns. So they started with 5 ads per week. By comparison, in television P&G had a little less than 1.5 per week. Admittedly, 5 ads per week is a lot of advertising. Over an 8-week period of time, they delivered an average of 40 impressions to each consumer who was reached. Based on the research and looking at diminishing returns (or impact at each frequency level), we discovered that the optimal level was about 8 (in 8 weeks), which would have been 1 exposure a week. The additional 32 ads after the original 8 that they delivered had limited incremental benefit.

Because any spending after the first ad starts to produce diminishing returns, we don't want the reader to think that diminishing returns are a negative. They are what they are. The diminishing returns can be found in most facets of business. The issue is whether or not the marketer knows the diminishing-returns curves for each medium so that the marketer can optimize marketing ROI. P&G knows, and they are clear about the alternatives for reallocation that would make their marketing spending more efficient. Don't assume a magic number. There is no magic number. You need to measure the diminishing-returns curve, monitor it, and adjust accordingly, just the way P&G does.

Do you know the diminishing-returns curves for each medium so that you can optimize marketing ROI?

While there is no universal magic number, such as 1.5 impressions per week, there is a consistent pattern for a brand within a medium. This "effect to frequency" diminishing-returns concept follows the same pattern for McDonald's, Lexus, Colgate, Dove, ING, Ford, and just about every marketer we studied—although each has a different point where the core success metric (be it brand image, purchase intent, or sales) flattens out. The exceptions to this rule are few and far between. And although our research approach is more pre-

FIGURE 13.2 Diminishing-Returns Chart Showing TV and Online

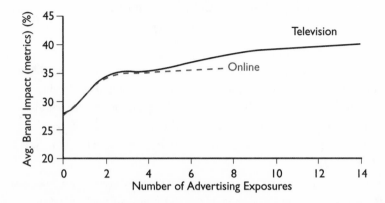

cise in picking up this pattern, we certainly aren't the first researchers to discover this pattern. Recognizing this pattern and adjusting to it is worth an increase of between 5 percent and 10 percent in marketing ROI for most brands we've worked with. But there is more to this story.

The Second Diminishing Return: Advertising Reach versus Frequency

The second of the dual diminishing returns in media is the diminishing-returns curve for "reach and frequency." Erwin Ephron observed that many marketers want to get the highest reach possible.[4] Considering principle #1 (no hear, no see = no impact), this reach goal is entirely understandable. Unfortunately, it is expensive to get a really high level of reach because there is a natural pattern where reach grows at a much slower rate, and as a consequence marketers find themselves adding unwanted frequency as they try to push their reach up higher.

Erwin suggested a better strategy. His antidote was to use more diversified media plans, which added a secondary media, as shown in Figure 13.2.

We investigated Erwin's theory for movie theatricals and found that it held true. TV and online, for example, are natural complements for theatrical movie advertising in terms of building reach just prior to opening weekend. On its surface, diversified media plans work better at expanding coverage and reducing the financial waste that accrues because of diminishing returns to frequency. As we will see after taking a look at the next principle, diversified media plans are an even more important strategy to getting your message in front of the right people.

MECHANICS PRINCIPLE #3:
SOME CONSUMERS GET MORE THAN
THEIR FAIR SHARE

Visualize yourself back at the wine bar with the economist. There is a crowd of people mingling at the bar, and others are mingling further away. It is open-bar time, meaning the drinks are being paid for by someone else. Who do you think gets their glass refilled more: the person mingling at the bar or the person mingling far away from the bar who has to work his or her way back to the bar for a refill?

You can think of media and advertising consumption in the same way. In this analogy, the media is the bar. Those consumers sitting in front of the media the whole time will get more ads than those who just periodically put themselves in front of the media, but are usually mingling away from the media (or the bar).

> *Those consumers sitting in front of the media the whole time will get more ads than those who just periodically put themselves in front of the media, but are usually mingling away from the media.*

Here's another way to visualize it. Media experts will often analyze advertising frequency by dividing all those reached into five even groups ranked by the volume of ads they see—*quintile analysis,* as it is technically called. Visualize five houses sitting next to one another on a neighborhood street out in the suburbs in any town, USA. Let's look inside each of the five houses, starting at the far right, and work our way to the left. Look through the living room window of the first house for one week, and you will see that the TV is almost always on: You've got your classic couch potatoes who perhaps don't work (at all or that much) and have few outside interests besides consuming lots of television shows. TV keeps them company. TV is their friend. Each of the other houses watches less television than this first house. The house on the other end of the block watches the least. They tend to be busy, higher-income people, who read a lot of magazines, browse the Internet, and have activities to fill their free time: If you peer into their window for a week, they do watch TV, but only a

FIGURE 13.3 Ad Campaign Results for Kleenex Soft Pack

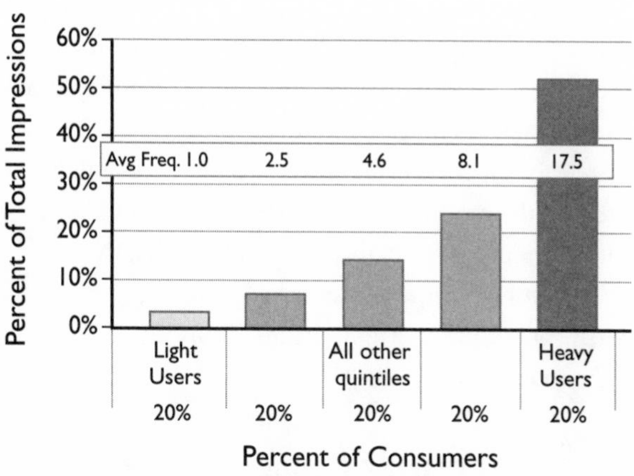

fraction of the time compared to the first TV-keeps-me-company house. Even when the fifth house's residents do watch, they may be multitasking, surfing the Internet and answering e-mails at the same time. In fact, because they don't watch that much television, an ad campaign may only reach them once over an entire month.

So what happens when you buy a chunk of TV ad space to deliver your message? Consider the results of the Kleenex Soft Pack study, shown in Figure 13.3. About half of all ads delivered were consumed by the heaviest quintile (but remember, this is only 20 percent of the total target population).

If these houses represent all households that were "reached" by the campaign, then more than half of all the money the advertiser spent on advertising would have been focused on the house with the coach potatoes. Not on purpose, mind you, but simply because those who watch more TV will see more of your ads than the house on the other end of the street, where they watched TV but not nearly as much. In fact, beyond the five houses reached, there is at least one more house that watched even *less* TV and did not see *any* of the marketer's ads. And we know the effect of those marketer's ads on them: It was *zero* because they never even saw the ads. This pattern doesn't just happen with television; it happens with magazine, radio, newspapers, Internet (although frequency at the individual user level can be controlled with the Internet), and pretty much any media that isn't individually delivered and isn't systematically controlled for delivery at the consumer level.

In the game of ad delivery, does it matter that one house hogged all the ads while the other house got none? Yes, it matters a lot because the house that hogged most of the ads is sucking down the advertiser's television budget (remember the notion that each ad costs the same). Therefore, half the budget goes to 20 percent of the population, and when you see the frequency of ads absorbed by that heavy quintile and factor in diminishing returns to ad effect, it should raise alarm bells. Unless you are specifically targeting those who consume lots of television, the people in the heaviest viewing group aren't any more likely to buy the product than the house in the middle.

But again, without individually addressable media, there is no solution to this problem. It can be mitigated somewhat by focusing on media buying to maximize reach, but *reach* does not automatically equal *effectiveness*. Which brings us to the fourth principle.

MECHANICS PRINCIPLE #4:
REACH ISN'T EFFECTIVENESS
(AND SOMETIMES REACH ISN'T REALLY "REACH")

Reaching a consumer does not automatically mean that the ad will have the influence on the consumer that the marketer is aiming for. Reach is like showing up at a factory for work. Just because someone shows up doesn't necessarily mean he or she will accomplish any meaningful work that day. Of course, showing up is the first important step. Reach is an *in-process* measurement—meaning that it isn't sufficient in and of itself to cause sales to go up. Then again, you're not even in the game if you don't have reach. If someone doesn't show up at the factory for work, it is a 100 percent guarantee that the person won't get any work done (that's a twist on principle #1—no see, no hear = no impact).

One not-so-small point about media planning is that not all impressions are created equal. For example, suppose your ad is for McDonald's Grilled Chicken Flatbread Sandwich. You can place your ad on TV at 4 AM, and you might achieve some reach, but are the people who see the McDonald's ad at 4 AM likely to be as responsive as the people who are reached around lunch time? We have the data, and the answer is absolutely *No!* The ad at 4 AM is of much lower value for the flatbread sandwich, as much as 50 percent less. The McDonald's ad works significantly better at certain times and on certain Web sites, so *reach* isn't the same as *effectiveness*. That's why good ROI advertising research, like what McDonald's executed, is so important. Because reach isn't equal to effectiveness, marketers must base their media budgets around a robust measurement of effectiveness rather than simply spending against reach alone.

One not-so-small point about media planning is that not all impressions are created equal.

The fact that reach isn't effectiveness should not be a shocker. But the fact that reach isn't really "reach" should raise eyebrows among anyone who has ever spent a single dollar on media. *Reach* is a slippery media term; in fact, most marketers aren't aware of how slippery it is. So let's take a closer look.

Just because the media research data says an ad reached a consumer, that doesn't mean the ad really did. Although a lot of money and great thinking has been put into media measurement by some large and very sophisticated companies with the help of their advertising agency clients, we've found that many in advertising who use this data are not 100 percent clear on what is being measured.

This is not to say that the industry or the companies collecting the data are doing anything wrong. A lot of very smart people have worked for a lot of years to develop audience measurement for TV and other media. The issue is this: "How does the data relate to improving marketing ROI?"

The media industry has come to call these measurements *opportunity to see* (OTS). The following reviews in broad strokes how some of the media data is captured:

- *How TV advertising is measured.* Basically, the average quarter-hour of TV programming is measured with a *People Meter* that electronically monitors what the TV is tuned to when it's on. The household that has agreed to have a People Meter capturing its TV viewing is also supposed to push a button on the People Meter device that indicates who is or who is not in the room. Research has shown that individuals are only so good at obeying. Also, the People Meter cannot determine that people are *actually* paying attention and not doing something else with their attention. This procedure might sound a little loose for an industry that captures $60 billion dollars in TV advertising in the United States each year, but this is much better than the method that was previously and is still in use in some local markets. That method is the diary, where consumers write down during an average 15-minute period what they are watching.

- *How radio advertising is measured.* Radio ratings operate as TV used to because radio relies on consumers *remembering* what they were listening to in 15-minute increments. Think about how you change radio stations in the car, usually just as an ad comes on, and then wonder how accurate radio advertising measurement is.

- *How magazine advertising is measured.* Magazines use a completely different approach. Magazine pollsters walk through a set of flash cards with magazine logos and then ask consumers if they read that magazine. If they say "yes," then bingo, that person is counted as a reader! Notice that magazine measurement doesn't measure advertising, just that the person remembers reading the magazine.

- *How Internet advertising is measured.* The Internet is different. Unlike the other media, the Internet actually does measure the ad delivered to a consumer. The Internet industry got together to create a consistently better measure that identifies when an ad is actually received by the consumer's Internet browser. The only leap of faith that needs to occur is that the consumer was looking at the screen (which is fairly likely). Unfortunately, the Internet provides a phenomenal count of ads delivered, but not a perfect percentage of audience reached because the technology of ad serving doesn't capture a "universe" measure of all the people who could have seen the ad at a given time. Therefore, the Internet measure is not perfect either, but there are efforts underway to resolve this. Still, the Internet measure is a vast improvement and an approach we hope to see other digital media emulate.

What These Measurements Mean

When marketers talk about the reach of different media, it is worth noting that reach is a rubber yardstick. Reach can stretch to include people who weren't even tuned to the station when the ad aired. It is not a consistent metric across media.[5] When Dove Nutrium's media agency Mindshare (one of the largest media buying agencies in the world) reports an 85 percent TV reach, what it really means is that 85 percent of Nielsen households were tuned to the program that included the ad in the 15-minute block of time around when the ad was aired. Odds are that some of the people weren't in the room or weren't paying attention when the Dove ad aired. In fact, some could have flipped to an entirely different channel during the commercial break, missed the entire Dove ad, then switched back for the program, and they would still be counted in the TV-reach number of 85 percent.

Reach is a rubber yardstick. Reach can stretch to include people who weren't even tuned to the station when the ad aired.

Reach is not a 100 percent accurate representation that consumers actually saw an ad. *Directionally,* the reach number is useful; for example, a campaign that has only a 50 percent television reach certainly misses more consumers than a campaign with a 75 percent television reach. But reach in one media is difficult to compare to another media because of the different methods of counting reach. Moreover, if all that marketers had was reach, they would be extremely challenged to optimize the ROI of their marketing campaigns. Reach is just not a very good measure of advertising impact. Perhaps they could make sure that their budget was buying as much reach as possible, but with the rubber-yardstick nature of reach across media, and the differential value of impressions (not all impressions produce equal impact), some marketers would be at a distinct disadvantage to other marketers who focused on how effective the spending is in buying impact on the key success metric.

The research we applied used the dollars the marketer spent on advertising in a medium relative to its impact on the actual outcome, that is, the profit, sales, or brand attitude shift (whatever the marketers defined as their goal). In this way, we bypass the inconsistencies in reach definitions across media and the ambiguity in what reach really means in favor of a concrete measure of what the marketer spent and what the marketer achieved in terms of impact on their business success.

MECHANICS PRINCIPLE #5: OUTCOME MATTERS MORE THAN IN-PROCESS MEASURES

At a conference in 2005, P&G's John Stichweh gave a wonderful presentation in which he described a little old lady with a cane, a pensioner who had invested in P&G stock, who showed up one day at P&G headquarters in Cincinnati. Because P&G is a marketing-driven company, she wanted to know what marketing was doing to make sure her stock value was being looked after. As John acted out the hypothetical conversation, he pointed the cane to other marketers in the room and said, in an old lady's voice: "Tell me, sonny, what did marketing do for the stock price today?" Did she care what the *reach* and *frequency* and *quintile analysis* showed? No! John said: "She doesn't care about these 'in-process metrics.'" She wanted to know what *sales* and *profit* were generated from marketing. "The *outcome* metric is what she cares about." John pointed out that because P&G's compensation package includes stock, he too will be a pensioner someday, and he hopes that future P&G marketers will keep focused on the *outcome,* not the in-process metrics.

In-process metrics are things like reach and frequency. No marketer buys reach and frequency for the sake of reach and frequency. Instead, marketers buy reach and frequency to get a message in front of a consumer with an understanding that the message should *convey meaning* and *connect* with the consumer in such a way that the consumer is more likely to *buy the product—* and, in doing so, generate profit from marketing.

What John's hypothetical exercise focused attention on is the fact that what really matters in the analysis is how much money the marketer put in, and how much profit, sales, purchase intent, awareness (or whatever objective the marketer set out to achieve) is produced from that investment.

Understanding the in-process mechanical dynamics of reach, diminishing returns, and layering of media can help improve the outcome, but we mustn't take our eye off the ball and get caught up in focusing only on in-process metrics. Measuring reach and frequency is akin to measuring the amount of raw materials bought or the number of production employees who showed up instead of some measure of output and, more important, profit. We'll illustrate this point through case studies in Chapter 15.

To better understand media-mix principles, let us turn our attention to the new field of media studies, psychologics, to see how we can squeeze even more out of each marketing dollar. Then we'll review some specific and detailed case studies on how we are optimizing the media mix by applying media mechanics and psychologics together. We will show how marketers can achieve better results without spending a single dollar more.

CHAPTER FOURTEEN

Media Psychologics

How Meaning is Created
Through Media Strategies

On a chilly November afternoon, I walked passed a Christmas tree farmworker in a red satin jacket. He was sitting near the building that sold artificial spray-on snow. He smiled. I smiled back politely as I tried to squeeze by. Several minutes later he called my name. I looked again and this time I recognized the Christmas tree farmworker from the advertising business. He was moonlighting (his father-in-law owned the tree farm). His day job was in advertising in a city more than a hundred miles away. Out of context, I had stared him straight in the face, and he had a good look at me, and neither recognized the other, initially. The problem we both had in recognizing one another was *context*. The phenomenon of *context recognition* is the same in marketing. The placement of marketing messages in the best context to create the intended meaning is thought of by some as the "art" of media planning. As we will see, there is a growing body of science to aid marketing decision making in this area.

Psychologics is a new field of study examining the consumer psychology of how meaning is created by each medium and by the interaction of the entire media mix. If you liked economics at school, you'll gravitate to media mechanics. If you liked psychology, you'll gravitate toward psychologics. If you liked both, then you were made for a life in media. We will break psychologics down into the following three usable pieces:

1. *Media is (part of) the message.* Selection of media to reenforce beliefs about the brand is one strategy to getting more out of your media budget.

2. *Optimize the brand impact within a media type.* Each media type is fairly diverse. So determining the optimal mix within a media type is important to getting the most out of every dollar.

3. *Surround-sound marketing.* Interaction of the message within the media can be influenced by using *surround-sound marketing,* where placing your message in multiple media can have a more powerful influence than placing it in a single media type.

This chapter shows how our research helped uncover the financial underpinnings of psychologics and how marketers can apply this concept to produce better results from the same budget. *Media mechanics* is a set of fixed relationships that resemble physical laws marketers can apply consistently across brands and campaigns. It is fairly straightforward to put media mechanics to work immediately and improve ROI. Psychologics is different. It is a collection of relationships that can be applied in very different ways to different situations. Psychologics are, in fact, more powerful than media mechanics in determining the ultimate ROI from media planning. However, it will take careful consideration about how to apply these principles to your specific marketing situation.

PSYCHOLOGICS PRINCIPLE #1: MEDIA IS (PART OF) THE MESSAGE

Marshal McLuhan was right, to a certain extent: The medium is the message. That's to say, the same message in different environments (or media) will create different meaning for the consumer.

> *The medium is the message. That is to say, the same message in different environments (or media) will create different meaning for the consumer.*

To make the point, running into a work colleague out of context on a Christmas tree farm failed to initially prompt a neural connection. Consider what meaning is created when you bring a girl to the restaurant at the Four Seasons in New York City to tell her you love her for the first time (especially if you need to stretch your budget to afford it), then consider that it has different meaning to her if you tell her you love her for the first time at a Friendly's fast-food restaurant on Interstate 80. Message in context has its own meaning. One of the authors proposed to his wife at one of the two restaurants—can you guess which restaurant? (Hint, she said, "Yes.") Let's look at some empirical evidence from the research we conducted.

Media Is the Message

When Target runs a fashion ad in *Vogue,* that says a heck of a lot more than when Target runs a fashion ad on a billboard outside of an industrial park—because *Vogue* communicates and exudes high fashion. So when people pick up *Vogue,* read it, and see the advertising, that association of Target and *Vogue* adds extra meaning to the experience.

When Volkswagen (VW) launched the redesigned Jetta, it wanted to give the impression that the Jetta was a youthful and fun to drive car. When we measured the same online ad placed in two different environments, the ad produced measurably different results on the statement "Agree/disagree: Jetta is youthful." The ad placed within an online portal's auto Web site didn't increase consumers' belief that Jetta is youthful. But when the *same ad* was placed on the same portal's music and concert Web site, consumers' perception that Jetta is youthful increased by 5 points. The ad didn't change. Both placements had a control group (so we can eliminate the audience differences). What changed was the media. The media is the message (or at least part of it). The fact that the context can influence effectiveness is what makes thoughtful media planning so important.

RANGE AND LIMITS TO THE
MEDIUM-IS-THE-MESSAGE PSYCHOLOGIC

Great media planning alone cannot carry the show. There is a limit to the media-is-the-message psychologic. We've observed a range of results depending on the nature of the brand. In research with *Wired* magazine and General Motors (GM) a few years back, we measured the influence of Oldsmobile's year-long sponsorship of Packet, a technology-oriented news Web site created by *Wired.* By placing Oldsmobile within *Wired's* Packet Web site, they hoped to shift consumers' meaning of Oldsmobile from old-fashioned to technologically sophisticated.

GM had good reason to believe that exclusive sponsorship of the technology news site *Packet* over a long period of time (such as a year) could influence consumers' attitudes. This application of psychologics rule #1, the media is the message, had been carefully researched and had worked for Levi's Dockers. Levi's Dockers brand had sponsored DreamJobs, a *Wired*-created Web site that profiled "dream jobs," where you could use your talents and still be yourself. As with most *Wired* content, research confirmed that the Web site was seen as technologically sophisticated, hip, youthful, and cutting edge. Consumers might infer that a dream job is often a casual work environment where you could be yourself and wear Dockers.

> GM had good reason to believe that sole sponsorship . . . over a long period of time (such as a year) could influence consumers' attitudes.

The research showed that just prior to the sponsorship, most people saw the Dockers brand as a bit staid, frumpy, and old. Within three months, however, thanks to the context, the tide had turned, and youthful and spirited were the Dockers attributes that were on the rise. By the end of a year, a fairly meaningful shift in perceptions had occurred among the regular visitors to the Web site. Oldsmobile hoped to replicate the media-is-the-message transference of consumers' perceptions of the media to the brand for themselves.

But, there is a limit to psychologics #1 transference. When GM tried to refresh its Oldsmobile brand, there was no shift to youthful or technologically sophisticated. As one open-ended response read:

> You can't turn my attitudes of Oldsmobile on a dime. It's great that GM is sponsoring Packet, and that's a step in the right direction, but they're going to have to do a lot more than just sponsor this one site to change my view of Oldsmobile.

As Ralph Waldo Emerson said, "What you *are* speaks so loudly I can't hear what you are saying." The product and, more importantly, the consumer's perception of the product, can make the job of repositioning a brand difficult. Still, although there are some limits to message and media interplay, it is worth specifically considering what meaning your brand is aiming to convey, and how media planning can enhance that objective. Confirm via research that what you expect is happening in terms of transference is indeed happening.

Psychologics versus Media Mechanics

There is one other caveat to include: At times, the psychologics principle will be at odds with a media-mechanics principle. VW wanted Jetta to be perceived as youthful, and advertising it on the Web portal's music site accomplished that, whereas the same portal's auto online area did not. Does that mean that VW should pull ads from the auto section of the Web site and focus on the music section? Not necessarily—because the *media-mechanics analysis* showed that there were a lot more people very close to their buying decision on the auto section than on the music section. So pulling out of the auto environment would have meant missing the reach of this important audience. And we know the impact among those not reached: It's zero. The goal of different media should be different. While the auto Web site plays less of a role in positioning Jetta as youthful, the auto section of the Web site speaks to consumers who already have a strong opinion of the position of Jetta and are narrowing their consideration to a set of cars as those consumers enter their final stretch of the information-gathering process prior to purchase.

How to Leverage the Power of "The Media Is the Message"

Generally, a certain core attribute for the individual media property, such as *Vogue, rubs off* to the advertiser. For example, if you put your advertisements online, you tend to be perceived as a bit more technologically sophisticated. Our analysis found (Oldsmobile notwithstanding) that if your brand is IBM or your brand is Verisign, just the placement of ads online (rather than just in magazines alone) increased consumer perception among business decision makers that IBM and Verisign are technological leaders. While there are limits to "the media is the message," application of psychologics has produced quantifiable benefits to brands such as AstraZeneca, Lexus, Target, VW, and more.

PSYCHOLOGICS PRINCIPLE #2:
OPTIMIZE BRAND IMPACT WITHIN EACH MEDIA

Think of each media vehicle as part of a Swiss Army Knife: As with any good knife, the Swiss Army Knife is designed first and foremost to cut. The principle way it does this is with its long blade, but it has more than one blade. Some of the more popular Swiss Army Knives have four or five different cutting instruments. In addition to the long blade, the knife might have a long serrated blade, a short blade, a hole punch, and scissors—each designed to cut in a unique way. Besides cutting, the knife might also have a toothpick, tweezers, magnifying glass, bottle opener, and a screwdriver. The Swiss Army Knife has a diverse range of applications and features.

Similarly, each media type is fairly diverse. For example, TV has ad units designed to build fast nationwide reach and awareness (i.e., prime time), but it also can be targeted to local markets and, more and more today, to a handful of postal zip codes. TV has available a short reminder ad unit, such as the 15-second spot, and longer ad units, such as the 30-minute infomercial. TV can be used for direct-response (DRTV) ads: Think of those ads with "operators standing by." And, increasingly, TV allows for ads that may invite interaction; it also can zero in on different parts of the day to target different types of consumers. TV has mixes of programs and channels, from network prime time, to niche-targeted cable channels. And, of course, a marketer can buy TV in many different ways: You can blow the entire budget in one Super Bowl spot or you can spread that budget out in all kinds of different combinations of flighting (scheduling) patterns across the year.

You can blow the entire budget in one Super Bowl spot or you can spread that budget out in all kinds of flighting patterns across the year.

Magazines are also diverse. From editorially-driven publications such as *Readers' Digest* to pretty-picture magazines such as *The Robb Report,* there are well over 10,000 different magazines to choose from in which to place advertising. There are magazines that target architects and those that target surfers (both Web and ocean surfers—but none yet targets architects who like to surf). With a couple hundred new magazines added to the market each year (and some falling by the wayside), the options always seem to be mounting (so maybe next year, surfing architects will be targetable in print).

The Internet is even more diverse—from utility sites, such as Yellow Pages online, to the critical search engines, to local newspaper sites, to content sites addressing just about every conceivable interest. There are video ads that are placed at the start of video-on-demand streams, audio ads that are placed on podcasts, classified ads that are part of online newspapers, text ads, sponsorships, rich media ads, demographic targeting, and now behavioral targeting in addition to banner ads, full-page ads, and everything in between.

Each media type is a Swiss Army Knife. Choosing the right blade within each media type depends on the marketers objective and has huge impact on the overall marketing ROI. So let's review the research and see how different marketers learned how to increase the effectiveness of a medium by optimizing each media type and thus squeeze the most out of every dollar.

A number of ways exist to increase the effectiveness of a medium. We are going to again assume—and this is a very big assumption—that the motivations and the messaging are right. Your COP process should give you a good shot at getting motivation and messaging right. To start, marketers can get more performance by scheduling the media during the right time of day (which is important for food), for day of the week (which is important for autos and entertainment), and for the right time of the year (which is what marketers of travel and cold medicine do already).

What McDonald's Learned about Choosing the Right Time of Day

For McDonald's we found that its advertising created much more impact during the four-hour period around lunchtime, 10 AM to 2 PM. In fact, they found that they could increase performance by more than 50 percent just by buying the lunch-time period. Psychologics explains this: When consumers are hungry (around lunch time) they are much more receptive to the meaning McDonald's is trying to convey as shown in Figure 14.1.

Here's another finding from McDonald's: Bigger online ads performed better. McDonald's used a combination of different online ad sizes to distribute its message, but of the six used, two stood head and shoulders above the rest. The power of the analysis isn't necessarily stating the rather intuitive finding that the bigger ads performed better at conveying the meaning of new, dif-

FIGURE 14.1 McDonald's Time-of-Day Ad Results

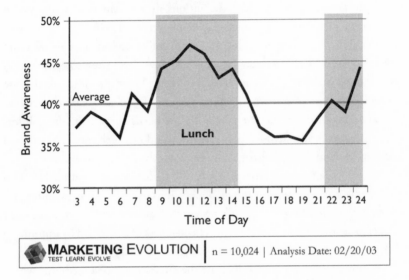

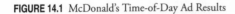

MARKETING EVOLUTION | n = 10,024 | Analysis Date: 02/20/03
TEST LEARN EVOLVE

ferent, exciting, great flavor combinations. Instead, the meaning is best conveyed by consumers seeing an appetizing picture of the food, and the larger ads simply have more space to do this. The power of the analysis is in the understanding of the financial trade-off because these larger ads do, of course, cost more than the smaller ones. However, as the analysis found, McDonald's got substantially more value by using the larger ads even after factoring in the corresponding premium.

What Target Learned about the Importance of Flighting

We've looked at data on time-of-day, let's now consider how combining unrelated products can create a certain dissonance that hurts the meaning the advertising is trying to communicate. The next example was Target's experience regarding the flighting of different campaigns.

Flighting and sequencing is the process of determining when, at what level, and in what order (if there are multiple messages) advertising is running. For example, with some flighting patterns (as we'll see with this Target example), you might decide to run three weeks of advertising about apparel followed by a couple of weeks of advertising about housewares. Flighting patterns is a whole area and discipline of marketing that owes much to General Mills and its early research some decades ago, where they found that if they pulsed their advertising—that is, one week on, one week off, one week on again—they would save money and actually lose very little in terms of sales.[1] That discovery introduced this whole idea of flighting as a scientific way of stretching budgets farther. This flighting strategy is now used by many marketers who have multiple products to promote and limited budgets, which require trade-offs.

Consider the following questions:

1. How do you use the on-air then off-air flighting or timing of your advertising?
2. How much time should pass between ad exposures?
3. How should you alternate products under a single brand (as in the case of a retailer that has different departments)?
4. What's that optimal pattern?

As mentioned in Chapter 12, Target had a Fashion-for-All campaign, and it was a great campaign: It featured great music and great design—it really worked in influencing consumers and produced great ROI across all media we measured. The newspaper insert was brilliant—designed like a fashion catalog. The magazine ads were great, and the online ads carried the style into cyber space.

The first phase of the campaign focused on Target's clothing line, and the ads focused exclusively on the fashion image and on designers such as Isaac Mizrahi. Target ran television, magazine, newspaper, and online advertisements. These ads had a very big impact and increased consumers' positive perceptions that Target was relevant to them, that is, that Target sells clothing and apparel that consumers are interested in.

What was interesting is that the positive apparel perceptions didn't maintain and slowly decay (as is typical of all advertising) as they normally should, but instead, they dropped like a rock. What happened? The Target campaign about housewares, featuring coffeemakers, lamps, and Q-tips, kicked off the day after the apparel campaign ended. Psychographics suggests that the reason the impact of the apparel ads dropped so quickly was that consumers top-of-mind perceptions of Target were only as *either one* of these two things, either housewares or apparel, but *not both*. The idea that Target is the place to go for a coffeemaker and lamps and is also a good place to shop for trendy, fashion-oriented apparel simply isn't the way most consumers organize their thoughts about the brand.

FIGURE 14.2 Rabbit-and-Duck Phenomenon

From Mind Sights by Roger N. Shepard. Copyright © 1990 by Roger N. Shepard.
Reprinted by permission of Henry Holt and Company, LLC.

We call this *the rabbit-and-the-duck phenomenon.* Do you see a rabbit or a duck in Figure 14.2?[2] This type of optical illusion shows how, depending on how you look at it, you'll either see one image or you'll see the other, but very few people can mentally visualize both images simultaneously.

And that's exactly what was happening with the Target ad campaign. Target had so many different lines of vision that very few people could keep in mind the totality of everything that Target sells. Instead, the advertising will focus a consumer on one particular department that Target offers.

One strategy to overcome this problem would have been to wait a couple of weeks between when Target promoted its apparel and when it promoted its housewares, so that the advertising about housewares would not *erode* and *cannibalize* the company's positive gains in advertising about apparel. In this way, Target would let the ads naturally "decay," as consumers go through a natural "forgetting curve," and that way a marketer can get a longer-term ride for each ad dollar spent. Or, Target might research to see what products and departments are natural "cross-sells." Or, Target could segment consumers based on highest value to each department and target messages accordingly. Or, Target can investigate if an ad could effectively show both housewares and apparel. Each of these data-driven approaches should produce greater ROI than the existing flighting and sequencing of fashion and housewares running back to back.

> *Target could let the ads naturally "decay," as consumers go through a natural "forgetting curve."*

PSYCHOLOGICS PRINCIPLE #3: SURROUND-SOUND MARKETING

Principle #3 is about using media synergy to achieve better results within the same budget. Assuming that you got your consumers' motivations right and that you communicated those motivations with the right messaging for each medium, then optimizing the mix has great impact on the performance of your ad campaign.

We've referred to this media synergy concept as *surround-sound marketing*. Just as in stereo systems, one speaker doesn't do it all; instead, it's the combination of the woofer, tweeter, and mid-range that gives the sound a richness and quality. Throw in some rear speakers in a home-theater environment, and a big plasma screen synchronizing the visual image to the speakers, and you will have a great entertainment experience. The same thing applies to marketing.

For example, seeing an ad multiple times in the same medium can actually be *less* efficient than if people see a well-orchestrated advertisement in *different* media, say television, magazine, and online. Let's look at a couple examples: Dove Nutrium and AstraZeneca.

How Dove Optimized Its Media Mix—Beyond TV Only

We have examined Dove by using many of the principles of media mechanics and psychologics. We found that maximizing reach and managing frequency to reduce diminishing returns contributed to achieving better results within the same budget. But there is one other contributing factor, and that is the media synergy achieved when each of the components of the advertising plan reinforces one another.

As we analyzed the data on Dove we found that the results from a consumer who saw three TV ads had more diminishing returns than when a consumer saw a combination of three ads *across different media*. In other words, we found that an exposure to one TV ad, one magazine ad, and one online ad performed better than seeing three ads concentrated in any one media type.

> *Exposure to one TV ad, one magazine ad, and one online ad performed better than seeing three ads concentrated in any one media type.*

We touched on this idea in our discussion of messaging touchpoints in Chapter 12, and the psychological mechanism at work here is *imagery transfer*. It is a phenomenon that happens when a consumer sees a *prompt* (in this case, a visual prompt from the online or magazine ad) that causes the brain to connect to the *memory* of the TV ad. The memory is a *replay of* the TV ad in their minds while experiencing the magazine or online ad. The experience encodes a deeper, more meaningful impression in consumers' minds. There have been times when a radio ad that uses the same core *sound* as a television ad triggers consumers to *see* and recall the *visual imagery* of the TV ad, even when the TV ad hasn't run in more than a month. The radio ad triggers imagery transfer. In Dove's case, imagery transfer was clearly happening between online and magazines with television.

The implication to media planning is to recognize that our brains are naturally looking for patterns to create meaning; having advertisements in different environments that connect the dots to other media creates *synergy*. Just like the surround-sound stereo system, a more powerful effect is created when all the speakers are working together to create a consistent impression; therefore, media planning should emphasize the surround-sound effect.

How AstraZeneca Optimized Its Media Mix for The Purple Pill

AstraZeneca is reaching out to those who suffer from acid reflux, a condition that can erode the lining in the esophagus. Acid reflux is a serious condition that requires talking to a doctor to find out if Nexium is right for the consumer. Surround-sound marketing is important in a case like this because of the higher stakes involved in consumer decision making. This isn't buying soap—it's dealing with one's health and well-being.

Although *awareness* and *brand image* follow the diminishing-returns curve we discussed in Chapter 12 on media mechanics, *intent to talk to a doctor* (which we found corresponds to actual discussion with doctors) follows what is called an *S-shaped curve*. S-shaped curves in advertising are rare, in our experience. The S-shaped curve means that in the first few ad exposures, the consumer has little or no response, then, at some "inflection" point, the consumer begins to respond to the message, and from there on, the curve follows a natural diminishing-returns curve. It is the fact that the repetition of the messages takes some critical mass before it generates an effect that is unique. In nearly every case, advertising begins to have its biggest influence upon the very first impression. Not so with an S-shaped curve. By using *intent to talk to a doctor* for AstraZeneca's Nexium (The Purple Pill), the Nexium ad followed an S-shaped curve.

What we found, as we examined the data more carefully, was that the impact could be achieved faster when a combination of media was used to convey the message. Now this campaign for Nexium was extremely well done and used a consistent look and feel across a combination of TV, magazine, and online advertising, and that combination created meaning faster for the consumer, we theorize, because consumers' brains see patterns. Seeing a consistent message across media creates a more powerful pattern in consumers' brains than the mere repetition of the exact same message in the same media.

Until we discovered this surround-sound marketing effect at work with online and magazine ads, AstraZeneca was following a very logical approach based on the media-mechanics principle that says to "go for broad reach and minimize frequency duplication." It was steering away from buying ads from companies that had both a magazine and online for the same media (such as *Prevention* magazine and Prevention.com). The reasoning is that a marketer gets too much duplication. However, given the way that magazine and online advertising worked together, in concert, we found more value in using the combination of both.

Define and Refine Your Strategy

Many dynamics in optimizing media can be defined up front to achieve good ROI from the start of a media plan. These are observable, knowable dynamics that can be measured and acted on to optimize media mix. Marketers should begin with media mechanics and psychologics to build their media mix, but it is unrealistic, in our experience, to expect to get all the dynamics nailed right out of the gate. To know exactly how your brand is going to behave, you have to be in-market—measuring those dynamics, knowing what to look for, and setting up your organization to respond fairly quickly. That is the nature and value of the COP.

We call this aspect of the COP *Define and Refine,* where you *define* all the drivers up front so you know what to look for and take an informed guess at how the dynamics will work for your brand (ideally, leveraging a knowledge storehouse of success drivers). Then *refine* your strategies and tactics based on actual in-market observation of how consumers respond. Success in optimizing your media mix is about continuous improvement. In the define-and-refine way, marketers will achieve better results for the same budget.

If you are like most marketers we've talked to, you may be fairly overwhelmed by now with the multitude of dynamics. If motivations and messaging weren't tough enough to get right, now we have media mechanics (basic "laws" to take into consideration) and psychologics (which put the nuance and art back into the business). By this point, some readers may be thinking: "Oh my goodness, the cards are really stacked against me. It's an under-count to say that there are only ten decisions with ten choices resulting in a billion possible different directions my marketing plan can go. There are just too many variables to effectively manage them all. How can I ensure my advertising is successful?"

We can assure you that using measurement systems to build a knowledge storehouse of what works across the 4Ms will be a lot easier than going to your CFO for more marketing money to spend without answers to the ROI marketing questions. The measurement systems to get these ROI answers exist today and have been used by the companies we worked with to improve marketing effectiveness and ROI. If you use them, you will know exactly what you are doing with the company's money and what the value is of those efforts. Who knows, maybe the CFO will soon be calling *you* to tell you to spend *more* because the company needs to achieve growth and profit targets. Wouldn't that be a change?

> *Maybe the CFO will soon be calling* you *to tell you to spend* more *because the company needs to achieve growth and profit targets.*

In the next chapter we'll look at case studies on the economics of media that pull together both the media mechanics and psychologics to measure and improve marketing ROI.

CHAPTER FIFTEEN

Media Optimization

Getting More Bang for Your Buck

We argue, based on our experience, that the right research can make the difference between marketing success and failure. Most marketers recognize outright failure, such as the ill-fated Ford Edsel that cost Ford an estimated $2 billion in today's dollars.[1] The Edsel is a well-documented fiasco that John Brooks, writing a series chronicling the Edsel failure in the *New Yorker*, attributed to disregarded science and to organizational ego overriding listening to the consumer:

> Science was curtly discarded at the last minute and the Edsel was named for the father of the company's president. . . . As for the design, it was arrived at without even a pretense of consulting the polls. Instead it was arrived at by the method that has been standard for years in the designing of automobiles—that of simply pooling the hunches of sundry company committees. . . . Instead of spending millions on listening and learning about the market, it spent millions on a campaign to launch the product it had developed in isolation. In this sense, the Edsel story is a classic of what so often goes wrong in a silo-based enterprise: Organization and ego got in the way of sound decision making."[2]

Edsel is a reminder to marketers to listen to the consumer. Outright failure like the Edsel is rare. Ford today invests a lot of time and energy in listening to consumers. Their research effort is extensive and highly professional. It is hard to imagine another Edsel-scale failure from a leading marketer today. However, our experience is that there is a space between success and failure. That space is vaster than most realize. Living in that space are campaigns that look successful enough for marketers to claim victory, but in fact they are suboptimal and they cost companies billions of dollars. These seemingly successful campaigns are less productive than they could be. Each year, billions of dollars in lost productivity fall into this space between success and failure.

> *Living in the space between success and failure are campaigns that look successful enough for marketers to claim victory, when in fact they are suboptimal and costing companies billions.*

In this space are campaigns that look successful enough and maybe even received positive reviews from the marketing press, but a focus on productivity would help these campaigns produce a greater ROI. It is not unlike the focus on productivity that came to supply-chain management. If one considers a supply-chain's definition of success as getting the products to the customer, many could have claimed victory years ago. But those in supply chain recognized the space between success and failure held billions of dollars in lost productivity. They strove to fill the space with measurement. They improved the productivity of the supply chain by measuring the cost per delivery and strove to achieve greater efficiency. It wasn't enough to get the products to the customers. They wanted to achieve that goal in the most cost-effective way possible.

Marketing may very well be the next frontier for productivity. Productivity gains have already been squeezed out of design, engineering, manufacturing, and the supply chain. Two decades of focus on these areas have delivered tremendous gains, but there's still some question about how much more cost-cutting and productivity gains can be had. We believe that significant advances can be made in the area of marketing. When we look at a company's profitability and growth goals, we generally find that at least half of that goal could be met by making marketing more productive. We believe that top management's demand for better marketing ROI will make heroes out of those who deliver marketing productivity.

There are companies reaping the rewards of greater marketing productivity. Take Philips for example. Elwin de Valk, Philips' vice president of Marketing, is responsible for the Philips Norelco brand. De Valk and his lead researcher, John Carter, have changed the marketing model. The old model was as follows:

1. Plan campaign
2. Execute campaign
3. Wait for results, which arrived in Q1, long after the campaign was over, and apply to next year's plan

Because Philips Norelco achieves the bulk of its sales in the fourth quarter, during the holiday season, improving marketing productivity requires optimizing the campaign while it is running. Based on adopting the Communication Optimization Process—our COP, and our marketing measurement system—Philips was able to define and measure leading indicators of success and get the data and insights at key milestones throughout the holiday campaign and adapt accordingly. We helped Philips achieve faster feedback so that they could see how the campaign was performing *during* the campaign in order to make adjustments while it still mattered.

De Valk recognized that consumer-media consumption is changing and that more media choice for the consumer has meant more fragmentation for the marketing plan. In the past, television was always the cornerstone of Norelco's fourth quarter holiday campaigns. But television alone might not do the whole job anymore. This realization meant that he and his team needed to become experts at integrating marketing communications to achieve effective surround-sound communications and generate sales. Research feedback accelerated their learning curve and helped them become experts fast.

Measurement in real time empowered Philips to shift over $1 million during the campaign; adjust creative messaging in one of their media and the mix of messages in another; refocus their targeting; and make several other adjustments. As de Valk reported to the Advertising Research Foundation (ARF) at their annual conference in 2006, Philips saw a "dramatic market share increase: +5 points in Q4." At the same time, Philips saw "dramatic market growth: +3% in Q4 after four years of market decline."[3] Based on the market size and profit margin, we estimate the total value of the adjustments

Philips made at over $27 million in incremental bottom-line profit. Philips' de Valk calls this new approach "adaptive marketing." We call it successful optimization.

> Measurement in real time empowered Philips to shift over $1 million during the campaign; adjust creative messaging in one of their media and in the mix of messages in another; refocus their targeting; and make several other adjustments.

De Valk, Carter, and the team at Philips—and the media agency, Carat, that supports them—are heroes who are defining a new way forward for marketing. Elwin has been promoted to head up Philips DAP—the consumer electronics division in the United Kingdom—and our COP and the associated research is rolling out in additional pilot markets around the world. Philips is well ahead of the curve in achieving marketing productivity boosts.

How does this optimization work? Let's take a low-involvement product, Dove Nutrium bar, and a high involvement product, Ford F-150, and dig into the details of optimization. We will draw together various principles throughout the book and show how improved marketing productivity can be delivered.

OPTIMIZATION CASE STUDY: DOVE'S NUTRIUM SOAP BAR

Unilever is a great company with smart marketers. The Dove brand is particularly good and has a team open to innovation. When corporate said that they'd like to learn more about improving the marketing mix, and to see where online advertising fits in the mix (which included television and magazine), the Dove brand was quick to volunteer.

The COP approach suggests starting with an unambiguous definition of success. The Dove team selected purchase intent as the measure for their success of advertising. Unilever has found that this measure is a very good predictor of sales and demonstrates whether the advertising has increased the desire for the product among consumers. With a clear definition of success, the COP turns to the 4Ms. Because the 4Ms build on one another, the marketer must succeed in motivations to have effective messaging. And, the marketer must have effective messaging to have a chance at an effective media mix. So let's look at how Unilever performed.

In terms of motivations, Unilever had it nailed. In terms of message, the Dove team took advantage of surround-sound marketing. The ads showed pink and white stripes coming together to convey that Dove Nutrium had both cleansers and lotions to nourish the skin. The ads all leveraged a common creative concept—even though the television and magazine ads were developed by one advertising agency and the online ads by another. Kudos to the Dove team for ensuring integration of the message across media and agencies. The television and magazine messages worked well. The online message worked well enough, but we found that it would have benefited from adding the "Nutrium" text in a larger font persistently on each frame of the online animated ad—the online ad had the Dove logo and pink and white Nutrium bar in the ad at all times, but only had the word "Nutrium" in the last frame of the ad. We found the consumer was hearing "Dove" but not "Dove Nutrium" as demonstrated by comparison of exposed and control group that showed an increase in Dove awareness, but the flat levels on Nutrium awareness. Overall, the online ads were strong enough, especially in combination with television and magazine ads, to call them a success and to move on to the next two Ms: media mix and maximization. The Dove media mix is shown in Figure 15.1.

FIGURE 15.1 Dove Media Mix

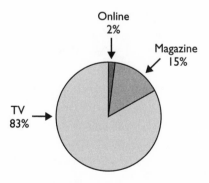

In terms of the last M, maximization, Dove was exploring online advertising's role in the media mix, specifically the ability of online ads to increase purchase intent. Dove asked: What is this the optimal mix of media for the brand across television, magazines, and online?

When we do our media mix optimization, we look at media mechanics and psychologics to quantitatively measure the ability to get better results from the same budget. Ultimately, because optimization is about achieving the highest return on the investment, we tie these principles back to a financial analysis and optimization. Let's start with psychologics.

> *Ultimately, optimization is about achieving the highest return on the investment.*

The first psychologics principle is that the media is part of the message. Because Dove is aiming for a new innovation in soap, with a premium product, this might suggest premium magazines focused on beauty, fashion, and lifestyle. Unilever selected magazines in the beauty and fashion segments, such as *Glamour* and *In Style*. They selected health and lifestyle magazines, such as *Self* and *Shape*. Dove bought a host of other targeted magazines as well. Online was focused primarily on MSN's Women Central and a few other women's content-focused Web sites.

In terms of the second psychologics principle, which states each media is diverse as with a Swiss army knife, magazines certainly took advantage of the fact. Dove used broad reach magazines, such as *People,* and more targeted women's magazines, such as Allure. But online did not appear to take advantage of this principle. Online was used narrowly for highly-targeted women-oriented content and used very little broad-reach sections of Web sites to reach the target audience of women aged 25 to 49. Expanding Online to include more reach oriented Web sites may be an opportunity, because if the television buy includes a broad cross section of content from the docudramas COPS, NYPD Blue, and X-Files to daytime soap operas, why not use a diversity of online to achieve broad reach too? Would broad reach Web sites be effective? Would they be cost-efficient? Unilever decided to test this as part of their *maximization* strategy and included a small element of broad reach, specifically the front page of one of the leading Web portals, MSN.

In terms of the third psychologics principle, surround-sound marketing, Dove bought certain coordinated programs such as *Oprah* and *Rosie,* which have both magazine and television advertising options. The timing of the TV and magazine ads was synchronized and messaging was well coordinated visually across media. In sum, Unilever and their media buying agency of record, MindShare, made extremely good use of the psychologics principles. Now let's turn to media mechanics.

To address the first media-mechanics principle, no see, no hear = no impact, Dove had a broad reach television schedule. They also used magazines such as *People,* which deliver one of the best reach numbers among magazines. We would rate Unilever's performance against the media-mechanics principle no see, no hear = no impact as very good. Unilever certainly did a good job in getting the message out using the traditional television and magazine media.

Media mechanics principle #2 warns to beware of diminishing returns; and principle #5 tells us to focus on the outcome metric, which in this case is purchase intent. So let's look at the diminishing returns in terms of the outcome metric.

Let's start with TV, because it's the largest portion of the budget (see Figure 15.2). Note that because some groups see more than the average 6 frequency, we are able to see what the curve looks like above that level. We see that the curve has really flattened at 7 to 8 and above.

FIGURE 15.2 Dove's Curves—Television

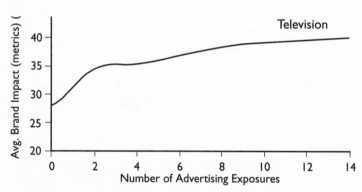

n = 12,990 | Analysis Date: 03/25/02

FIGURE 15.3 Dove's Diminishing-returns Curves—Television, Magazine, and Online

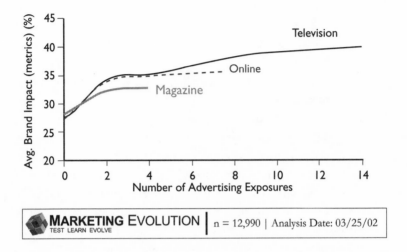

The benefit of buying more TV is limited because of diminishing returns. Magazines had a much smaller part of the budget. When we add the magazines' curve next to TV, in Figure 15.3, we see that the magazines curve flattens much faster than the TV curve. This suggests that in this six-week campaign, a magazine's impact occurs the first time the consumer sees the ad. Repetition of the ad does not increase the overall effect much. Magazines' current average frequency is 2.6. Online has its own curve too. It tracks very close to the TV curve, but the online curve flattens out sooner. Figure 15.3 gives a very clear idea of where there are diminishing returns. Online is currently at 1.6 frequency.

To conduct optimization using media-mechanics principles, we must take into this consideration the cost. We include the *cost* of each media to make allocation decisions. So let's look at this exact same data, but use cost per impact, rather than just impact on the vertical axis. For Dove, Figure 15.4 shows the cost per impact at different numbers of exposures. Cost per impact is the incremental cost per person impacted by the advertising. For example, TV starts out costing .30¢ per person on average to influence them to want to buy the product. You'll see that because the magazines' diminishing-returns curve showed that magazines' impact diminished faster than the other media, the cost of impact increases rapidly. In other words, increasing frequency just increases costs; it doesn't produce much incremental value. Therefore, although magazines completely make sense for this plan, magazines will probably not be used at higher frequency levels—the media category is optimal as is.

FIGURE 15.4 Dove's Cost per Impact

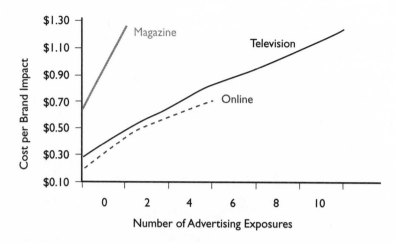

Draw a line at the price you are willing to pay for each person that you influence to buy your product. If the price you are willing to pay is .50¢ per person influenced, then any media that fall beneath this line will produce incremental purchase intent at that cost—and is therefore worth investing in.[4] The chart also shows the maximum frequency before diminishing returns makes the media too expensive.

> *Increasing the frequency of advertising just increases costs; it doesn't produce much incremental value.*

Knowing what the actual cost effectiveness of your brand is at different frequency levels for each medium is critical. There is no way you can optimize your plan without that information. And as we've hopefully demonstrated (and will continue to do in the next section), optimization is what separates the good from the great.

FIGURE 15.5 Optimization, Holding Budget Constant

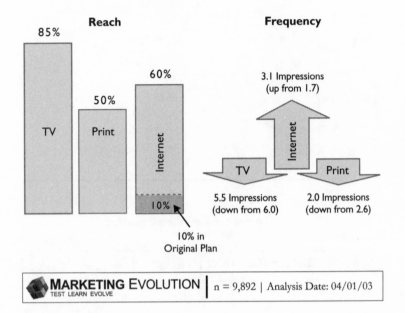

The Act of Optimization

Dove's results as is, without our optimization, were good. Purchase intent increased from 8.7 percent to 11.5 percent. Many would call this a success. But, there is room for optimization, and Unilever wanted to find it.

Looking at the cost per effect and diminishing returns, we can see that magazine advertising was at an optimal level, television was over-invested, and trimming it ever so slightly from an average of 6.0 frequency to 5.5 frequency and trimming magazine frequency slightly would free up enough dollars to expand online reach from 10 percent to 60 percent, and frequency from 1.6 to 3.0. The result of these changes would be that *the overall Dove purchase intent would increase +14 percent,* as shown in Figure 15.5, without spending a single dollar more: Same budget, better results!

It's hard to believe there is not a marketer around who wouldn't do all he or she could to get this kind of increased impact, given the very favorable economics that in this case was just the cost of research (which was under $250,000, as we recall).

OPTIMIZATION CASE STUDY:
FORD F-150

In the fall of 2003, Bill Ford, the Chairman of Ford, said that the F-150 was the most important vehicle launch in Ford's 100-year history.[5] Clearly, there was intense pressure on the marketing team to make sure it got everything right. Ford was planning to spend tens of millions of dollars on the media campaign for the F-150s over six months—and Rich Stoddart was the person in charge of this budget, working with Ford's ad agency, J. Walter Thompson (JWT), Detroit. They were looking for whatever edge they could get, and our approach to optimizing the media mix was embraced quickly as the way to squeeze the highest possible ROI from each media dollar spent.

The COP suggests starting with an unambiguous definition of success. The Ford team selected *purchase intention.* "Why not sales," we asked. "We can measure all the way to sales." The team responded that they'd certainly like to see the affect of advertising on sales, but the role of advertising is to make the F-150 the one vehicle a *consumer* would buy, if the consumer was to make the decision today. Other variables such as incentives and quality of the salesperson factor into sales. In addition, the team pointed out that advertising needs to influence a range of consumers at different points in the buying process (from a few days from purchase, to a few years from purchase). As a result, different media have different objectives and should be optimized accordingly. We discussed each and developed prioritization of the various goals. In our experience, Ford's more complex goals are typical of higher-involvement products, and those goals necessitate a more complex optimization.

With a clear definition of success, and prioritization of secondary objectives by media, the COP turns to the 4Ms. As with every marketer, the marketer must succeed in motivations to have effective messaging. And, the marketer must have effective messaging to have a chance at an effective media mix. Ford performs well on motivations and messaging, so let's look at the media mix and maximization.

The ad campaign kicked off on the opening National Football League (NFL) weekend during the first weekend of September 2004. On that single Sunday, JWT bought a ton of media during the opening football games because males between the ages of 25 and 49—which was the target market segment for the Ford F-150—scored pretty high in watching football.

JWT also bought ad space in more than 50 different magazines, ranging from the obvious car magazines (such as *Car & Driver* and *Motor Trend*) all the way to specific magazines such as *Truckin'* and outdoor lifestyle magazines such as *Western Horseman*.

Online also played a unique role. JWT chose to start the F-150 campaign on the Saturday of opening NFL weekend and bought the home-page ads on AOL/Netscape, MSN, and Yahoo. This is called a *roadblock* because the portals are the main on-ramps to the information superhighway for most consumers, and by entering the Internet, consumers would pass through the advertisement as if it was a roadblock. This was a fascinating strategy for an automotive brand because it was using online as it uses television, for *broad reach* rather than just for typical targeted, *in-market vehicle buyers* (which typically includes advertising on sites such as autos.msn, cars.com, yahoo autos, and others). What shocked us all was that Ford's online portal roadblock ads reached more than 43 percent of the target audience of males aged 25 to 54 in one day. Most didn't realize that online could be such a broad reach media tool.

> What shocked us all was that Ford's online portal roadblock ads reached more than 43 percent of the target audience in one day.

Ford was faced with the same questions all marketers deal with: Where's the best ROI in the mix? For Ford, this translated to questions such as the following:

- Would a dollar in magazine advertising do better than a dollar invested in displaying the F-150 truck at a rodeo?
- Would a dollar invested in the premiere of Fox's TV show *24* do better than buying an online home-page takeover advertisement on MSN?
- Because an online roadblock ad can cost much less than a TV ad, but TV ads are more effective, which provides the better ROI?

Given the importance of the launch, answering these questions and others were critical for Ford and were the focus of its cross-media optimization analysis.

Our research measured the F-150 campaign by surveying more than 10,000 consumers (different consumers were surveyed each day), and by grouping consumers based on our proprietary design of experiments, we analyzed impact across media. We also linked sales data to the analysis of attitudinal-branding metrics. In other words, we isolated the purchase intention and sales impact of magazine ads or online banners from that of TV advertisements, and much more. By separating these factors, we can report the individual and combined effects on key branding success metrics.

The advertising effect analysis is only a prelude to the key analysis that is central to improving marketing productivity. This analysis is a side-by-side comparison of the cost efficiency of each medium. We calculated the *return on marketing objective* (ROMO), which represents the relative cost efficiency of each marketing element against all the key advertising objectives, from awareness to brand imagery to sales. Although many marketers make their comparisons of media in terms of cost per impression or rating points, our approach goes a critical step further by looking at the consumer effect derived per dollar spent.

Results of the Ford F-150 Campaign

We measured every level of the "purchase funnel." The *purchase funnel* (Figure 15.6) is a standard way that most automotive brands think about marketing. At the upper end of the funnel, the brand just needs to get noticed among people that are months or years away from purchasing a new vehicle; here, *unaided awareness* and *aided awareness* are the key metrics. The lower funnel is about converting market shoppers to buyers; here, increasing *purchase consideration* and generating *shopping activity* are examples of success metrics.

FIGURE 15.6 Branding Metrics Purchase Funnel

Upper Funnel

• Ad Recall
• Familiarity
• Brand Image

Lower Funnel

• Purchase Consideration
• Shopping
• Purchase Intention

Media-specific results are shown in Figure 15.7. The results demonstrated variability in the advertising impact on brand metrics across the different media. Although Internet and magazine advertising had brand-metric improvements that were comparable with television advertising, due to the reach of television, TV is still the most successful at influencing large numbers of people, especially in terms of the so-called "upper-funnel" metrics.

So was cranking up the volume effective? Was it cost efficient? Are there ways to ensure each element of the surround-sound system is balanced?

To answer the first question, our research found each element of the mix was effective. To answer the second question, television advertising was significantly *less cost efficient* than advertising in magazines and on the Internet. Therefore, let's consider a third question: Could Ford cut back television volume and optimize results like we found with other brands, such as Dove? Actually, *no:* Due to the highly competitive nature of the auto category, we found that any significant cut to television resulted in a *drop* in purchase intention. As one Ford executive who saw the results put it, TV spending is like holding a bull by the horns: You're not at all happy to be holding on, but you're not about to let go for fear of what might happen.[6]

FIGURE 15.7 Individual Media Effects

	Overall	TV	Magazine	Roadblock	Online
Familiarity	+9	+3 pts	+11 pts	Not Sig.	+10 pts
Average Brand Image Attributes	+13	+12	+8	Not Sig.	+9
Purchase Consideration	+17	+6	+6	+4	+6
Shopping	+12	Not Sig.	+4	+6	+6
Purchase Intention (unaided)	+4	+2	+3	+5	+12

* Point difference observed is based on the Online over-sample, which has an average time difference from last ad exposure to survey intercept.

Web-wide sample finds the average time between online exposures in campaign is less than 24 hours.

MARKETING EVOLUTION | n = 9,892 | Analysis Date: 04/01/03
TEST LEARN EVOLVE

TV spending is like holding a bull by the horns: You're not at all happy to be holding on, but you're not about to let go for fear of what might happen.

As we looked at it more closely, though, we found room for optimization *within* television. The TV schedule that Ford bought was very premium priced. Ford was buying the *most expensive* areas of television, premium sporting events. This strategy was very effective. However, Ford could most likely have improved results further by mixing in some less-expensive cable advertising. The key question, though, is this: What is the marketing mix that will yield the best ROI?

Return on Marketing Objectives

Based on the standard brand metrics, the F-150 campaign appeared successful, but Ford was interested in *new measures* that would demonstrate marketing productivity and allow the company to determine the relative values of different media. The point of the analysis is not whether the campaign is a success or not—that's only part of the story. The more important part of the story is *cost efficiency.* In other words, how can Ford achieve the best marketing ROI?

Figure 15.8 presents the ROMO for each of the primary media Ford used. The ROMO is a cost-per-impact analysis that tells the marketer the average cost to influence each person on a particular branding metric. Although nearly 90 percent of the budget was spent on television advertising, it was clear that better ROMO was coming from magazine and online advertising. The ROMO analysis also indicates why using only the overall branding impact can be misleading. Whereas television and magazine advertising produced similar point gains (+6 points) in impact, magazine was *less than half the cost per person influenced.* And although the online roadblock was less effective on an absolute basis, it was *a better value in terms of cost per person impacted.*

Reallocating Media Dollars at Ford

As noted, TV is *very effective,* especially on the upper-funnel metrics. But compared to the three other advertising elements (magazines, online on auto

FIGURE 15.8 Ford F-150 Return on Marketing Objectives (ROMO) Table

Brand Metric: Purchase Consideration (top 2)	Impact	Relative Cost Index
TV	6.1	1104
Magazine	6.1	456
Online Portal Roadblock	3.8	100
Online	6.2	135

Impact = Point gain over baseline is calculated by measuring the post-branding level and subtracting the pre-campaign level. Costs per person impacted indexed against campaign as a whole.

Index = Relative cost efficiency (cost per impact) based on campaign as a whole.

Volume = Total number of people affected by the campaign.

Max Potential Volume = Total number of people that could have been affected had the reach potential been maximized for the media used. For example, Online reach was 34 percent, but could have been as high as 60% among this particular target audience.

Cost per Impact = Total advertising spend divided by total volume of branding effect.

MARKETING EVOLUTION | n = 9,892 | Analysis Date: 04/01/03
TEST LEARN EVOLVE

sites, and online roadblock on more general-interest sites), TV is *not very cost efficient*. The implication of this finding is a rethinking of the marketing mix.

Ford extended its branding analysis to examine the impact of online advertising on *sales* of the all-new 2004 F-150. We examined the incremental impact of online advertising (both the roadblock and the display ads) by comparing a control group and the exposed group against the F-150 buyer list in the first three months of the ad campaign. The results showed that those in the exposed group bought 20 percent more than the control group. We found that there was surround-sound marketing synergy at play. If Ford advertised only in television, it would have missed the power of television, magazine, and online advertising to reinforce one another and create a more powerful experience for consumers.

In summary, this incremental impact caused by online advertisements accounted for 6 percent of total vehicle sales. This application of an experimental design allowed us *to precisely quantify the impact of online ads*. The ROMO analysis of sales confirmed the branding analysis, and it suggested that Ford could improve its overall sales by as much as 5 percent through reallocation of media. How much does that add up to? A reallocation based on our estimates results in $625 million in incremental sales and somewhere around $90 million in incremental profit—without spending a single dollar more. That's a very powerful optimization.

ADDITIONAL IMPLICATIONS FOR FORD'S MEDIA MIX

Our analysis also showed that media plans must methodically *diversify* the advertising mix to simultaneously transfer media weight to magazine and online media, while exploring and measuring alternative strategies for purchasing television to improve TV's price/value ratio. Many managers question the value of placing ads in magazines, pointing out that magazines charge as much as a 30-second television spot for a spread, and more for a gatefold ad. They point out that the average time spent looking at a full-page magazine ad is a couple of seconds on average—and that many consumers read magazines in planes, trains, and bathrooms. However, the analysis done in this campaign showed otherwise: The Ford F-150 magazine ads performed exceptionally well—in fact, the effect was generally *greater* than the very effective television ad. The magazine ads featured the best-practice use of a white background, with plenty of white space around an interesting visual of the truck and strong, clear copy (judiciously limited in word count)—all of which translated into a strong ROMO performance for magazines.

Many managers question the value of placing ads in magazines. . . .
However, the analysis done in this campaign showed otherwise:
The Ford F-150 magazine ads performed exceptionally well.

Ford's results really highlighted the value of *creatively experimenting* with new advertising models. Ford bought out all the ad time on the Fox premiere of the TV program *24*. It was an expensive proposition, but the results demonstrated that it was effective, and Ford now knows much more about the ROI of such programs. Online roadblocks were a meaningful budget item, too, but they were also well worth it. Ford also used Spanish-language advertising developed by Zubi, which we measured and found quite effective. In each case, Ford knows both the effectiveness and the cost efficiency—and you need to know both to optimize your ROI. Ford now has tools that its competition doesn't. And Ford knows that there is value in exploring and experimenting with other ways to make television advertising work harder and smarter.

Based on the results, Ford not only learned that its F-150 campaign was successful across the board, it also learned valuable insights into how to increase marketing productivity. And in a competitive category like autos, *every edge helps.*

Companies have made major strides in improving the ROI in areas such as production, supply chain, and services. However, examining the productivity of marketing has long been ignored, and that has led many companies to view marketing as an expenditure that can be cut at any moment, especially in difficult economic times. Calculating ROI for marketing expenditures—such as media—can help marketers in all of the following ways:

- It can help them allocate limited resources the most profitably.
- It can help them defend their marketing and media decisions.
- It might even help them obtain larger budgets.

Examining the productivity of marketing has long been ignored, and that has led many companies to view it as an expenditure that can be cut at any moment—and cut first in difficult economic times.

In the studies discussed in this chapter, Philips, Dove, and Ford used ROMO cross-media analysis to improve their resource allocations to optimize the productivity from their media expenditures. In the final two chapters, we look at maximization and how innovation can be a source of continuous improvement in marketing ROI. We can feel CFOs licking their chops at finally being able to use marketing as a revenue *generator,* instead of just as a *cost* they have to accept. And we have seen that the marketers who deliver improved marketing productivity are rightly rewarded.

CHAPTER SIXTEEN

Marketing as a True
Competitive Weapon

Ever wonder why it took some companies so long to recognize the value
of the Internet to marketing? The answer is that many marketers work with
blinders on: They seldom spend on ideas or media they haven't validated, but
they can't validate what they haven't tried yet! In our experience, as innovative
as advertising is perceived, advertisers don't do innovation very well.

In contrast, a few savvy marketers are really determined to drive their business, and they know to do that, they have to push the boundaries. They do this
from either amazing foresight, or luck, or the best ones do it through systematic, rapid *experimentation and applied learning.* We've found two distinct
types of innovation "drivers of success," and these are the last two facets of our
measurement map, as follows:

1. *Intra-media optimization.* Can you fine-tune your spending within
   your existing marketing channels? Can you stretch the dollars you
   spend now and get more out of each one?
2. *Extra-media optimization.* Do you know what the next breakaway
   opportunity might be, and are you getting there faster than your competition? Have you considered doing something you haven't yet tried
   or conducted any advertising just for experimentation?

Of course, nearly every company does systematic product or service inno-vation, with lots of experimentation. But what about marketing innovation? What's your marketing research and development (R&D) budget? We're not talking about the budget for researching the advertisements you're already doing; instead, we're asking about your R&D to push the boundaries of your marketing. If your company has a commitment to innovation and major R&D budgets for *other* parts of the business—such as product development or operational improvement—but *not* for marketing, that should raise a red flag. Can you imagine a drug company doing well without trying to develop new drugs all the time? Or a toy company that doesn't come out with new products every year? Or a car company that never develops new concept cars? Marketing innovations are every bit as important.

> *If your company has a commitment to innovation and major R&D budgets for other parts of the business but not for marketing, that should raise a red flag.*

By applying both intra-media and extra-media optimization, leading mar-keters are leaving in the dust their competitors that resist change and continue with business as usual. How much is marketing innovation worth? Although it's easy to identify the marketing losses that missteps in motivations, message, and media cost the company, maximization (the 4th M) is the path to gains in marketing return on investment (ROI). This chapter shows how to innovate marketing, and it provides tangible examples of the power of maximization. We'll give you a process and a direction for making it happen.

THE PROBLEM OF TRADITIONAL MARKETING "OPTIMIZATION"

Our use of the term *maximization* is very purposeful: You'll often hear marketing people talk about *optimization* (as we have in previous chapters). But our experience with optimization is that it creates the classic Catch-22 where marketers spend only on what has been proven to work in the past, and therefore they have little room to try new things, nor do they have a process to systematically access and improve on past efforts. *Optimization* might be fine for business processes where all factors of success are very well understood and little changes over time, but that's not the case with marketing. In contrast, *maximization* acknowledges that marketers must adapt to the changing landscape by constantly learning—and by building on that learning with systematic experimentation.

MARKETING RESEARCH GOT STUCK IN THE 1970s

Market-mix modeling (also known as *econometric modeling*) grew out of 1970s marketing that was centered on a mass-media marketing model. This model used statistical analysis of sales and marketing data over the past two or more years. For example, it correlated

- *sales* per week, per market,
- with how much *advertising* weight was delivered per week, per market,
- along with *pricing and promotion* details, also organized by week and by market.

Here's an example of the correlations market-mix modelers look for: If sales increase in cities *A*, *B*, and *C*, compared to decreasing sales in cities *D*, *E*, and *F*, market-mix modelers search for a statistical relationship between the *media rating points* and those *sales fluctuations*. The researchers would also look to see if any certain factors (such as pricing) could have affected the difference in sales. If not, then the changes would be assumed to have been from *advertising*.

In the 1970s, when the delivery of media was more random than targeted, and marketers were content to gather several years of data before making decisions about effectiveness. This analysis for products such as those sold in grocery stores (i.e., mass-market products) was beneficial to those brands. Market-mix models apply science to marketing, which we of course applaud.

But the media landscape has changed. It's no longer a mass-marketing landscape, and the use of marketing-mix models, which relied on mass-media marketing data, can therefore have the following two limitations:

1. The first challenge is that marketers began to optimize things that worked in the past and not try new things. The reason for this was that the analysis was designed for "mass" marketing programs. To be

specific, the scale of a new program had to be very large; for example, 40 percent reach of the audience and typically $1 million or more in spending. Given this size, most marketers couldn't afford to try new things and measure a new program in the marketing-mix model. Instead, these marketers worked themselves into fewer and fewer marketing tools in the tool box. Again, marketers found themselves in a classic Catch-22 situation, where they couldn't get funding for something that they couldn't prove with data worked in the market-mix modeling, and they couldn't get the data for the new marketing program in the market-mix model because the new program didn't get funded.

2. Compounding this, marketing-mix modeling was challenged to measure new programs because a marketer needs to have two or three years of quality sales data by market. Aside from packaged-goods companies (selling in grocery stores), many marketers don't have that level of detail for sales. And, as marketing programs moved to consumer-targeted programs, such as customer magazines printed and delivered to a database of valuable customers, or television programs bought because they had a very high percent of brand purchasers, the mix model wasn't designed for that type of data. So most modeling companies ignored the consumer-targeted programs in the model, and many marketers either cancelled their programs because there was no evidence that the programs worked, or they accepted that these other programs "fly under the radar" and therefore are funded based on *hunch* rather than *proof.*

So, this approach to optimization put companies in the position of doing more and more of the "same old, same old," when, in fact, what companies *really* need to be doing is finding new ways to measure their marketing and advertising campaigns. Especially as marketing has fragmented and consumers' media habits change, marketers need to be looking at their strategies and asking, "How do we not only capitalize on what we know works, but how do we also expand our marketing and look for new ideas and new concepts? And if we find that those new approaches could also work, then how quickly can we assess those and capitalize on the opportunity to actually maximize results so that we're getting the full value out of our marketing investment?"

Kraft Foods Inc. (Kraft) was the first marketer to bring this conundrum to our attention. Kraft was early to recognize the potential of the Internet. Kraft created a recipe database and made it available on their Web site. They had also been early to use the Internet for advertising and, being a great marketing organization, had approached it with a significant amount of research around messaging. But Kraft needed more than messaging research. Kraft marketers embraced disciplined budgeting based on marketing-mix data, but the Internet doesn't generate the same data, so the mix model had the potential of stifling innovation. Kraft recognized the importance of marketing innovation and approached us for help to update market-mix models to include online advertising. The engagement encouraged us to solve both the immediate issue of getting online into market-mix models, but also to consider how to have a disciplined budgeting process that was data driven and at the same time embraced innovation. We looked far and wide and found the 70/20/10 solution.

APPLYING THE 70/20/10 SOLUTION FOR MARKETING

MSN invited Eric Schmidt, chief executive officer of Google, to address several hundred marketers who make a pilgrimage to Redmond, Washington, each spring to hear industry experts discuss the current dynamics of Internet advertising. Schmidt's talk focused on how analytical Google is when it comes to approaching product innovation. He shared the classic Silicon Valley mix of spending 70 percent of their time supporting existing products, 20 percent extending their existing products with "sustaining" innovations, and 10 percent working on "wild skunks-work" ideas for new products.

As we looked closer we found that this is what the fast-changing categories like high-tech use to keep competitive in an ever-changing environment and the rapidly changing world of consumer tastes. We investigated to see if this 70/20/10 approach could work in the new world order of marketing. After all, the marketing and media landscape are changing every bit as fast as technology (in fact, it's changing *because of* technology).

Through our research studies, we've found that this organizing principle of 70/20/10 works quite well to guide marketers to better manage their investments of resources.

The basic 70/20/10 idea is

- 70 percent of your budget should go toward marketing strategies and tactics that are *proven to work,* that you *know* work;
- 20 percent should go for *sustaining innovations*—that is, marketing efforts that are similar enough to what you've done in the past, yet they're *different enough* that you say, "Okay, we're going a little bit out on a limb here, but it's worth doing that to figure out if there are opportunities to improve our ROI"; and
- 10 percent is speculative, that is, *disruptive innovation*—trying new models of advertising and marketing, and systematically learning from the experiments.

How Ford Used the 70/20/10 Approach

Recall from the Ford example, discussed in Chapter 15, that TV was a cornerstone that had been a proven part of Ford's campaign for its F-150 truck—so Ford's use of TV is part of what we'll call the 70 percent. For 20 percent of the marketing budget that would go toward *sustaining innovations,* Ford looked at its magazine advertising and said, "Well, we know that in-market magazines—car magazines and truck magazines—work for launching a car like the F-150 truck. But let's go out on limb a little bit more and buy lifestyle magazines. Instead of just car and truck magazines, we'll buy *Cabela's* (a hunting and outdoor lifestyle catalog), and we'll buy *Western Horseman,* or we'll maybe even buy *Town & Country* because this is a luxury truck."

Who knows if *Town & Country* will work? But what if it does? If Ford didn't explore advertising in this magazine, it would be a loss of opportunity if the magazine did work better than the alternatives. The key is not in the *spending,* but in the *exploring*—remember that the "R" in R&D is *research.* To develop and try new things without capturing learning that can be applied to maximize your marketing ROI is worthless.

Remember that the "R" in R&D is research. To develop and try new things without capturing learning that can be applied to maximize your marketing ROI is worthless.

The final 10 percent of the budget should be allocated to marketing that's completely different—marketing that pushes new boundaries and helps determine whether greater effectiveness and a greater ROI can be achieved with alternative approaches. For example, for the F-150 truck, Ford's marketers knew that online advertising worked in-market (*in-market* is defined as media where the consumer is looking to buy at this time, such as Cars.com, Edmunds.com, KBB.com [Kelly Blue Book], and the auto sections of AOL, MSN, and Yahoo!). What Ford did not have any idea of was whether or not the Internet could be used as a *broad-reach* advertising tool to influence new-product *awareness and interest* in the same way that television is a broad-reach media tool. So they developed a program and researched it.

> *10 percent of your budget should be allocated to marketing that's completely different—that pushes new boundaries and helps determine whether greater effectiveness and a higher ROI can be achieved with alternative approaches.*

We believe the marketers who will win battles in marketing are the marketers who are able to learn faster and deploy that knowledge effectively. Therefore, we devote the final chapter of this book to the 10 percent innovations. Let's look more at the 20 percent sustaining innovations.

INVEST 20 PERCENT OF YOUR RESOURCES IN SUSTAINING INNOVATIONS

For the moment we're going to assume that you're clear on the 70 percent of your advertising that is working in a tried-and-true manner. You've done the research and stored it in a knowledge storehouse. Let's now address the 20 percent of sustaining innovations. With any given medium or advertising concept, you can drill into it and ask, "How can we buy this media differently, or execute this media differently to generate greater learning?" For example, for television, you might ask the question, "What's the differential value between 15-second and 30-second TV ads? Or between 30-second ads and 60-second ads? Or what's the delta (or difference) in impact between highly-targeted cable TV programs or broader-reach TV programs, such as *The Oscars?* Or, what if we are a company that has traditionally targeted men, and we suddenly realize we should be targeting women?" What are the strategies and tactics that can boost marketing ROI?

David Poltrack, the head of research at CBS, told us he remembers when one of the big three auto makers realized that women where major influencers, if not the outright purchasers of automobiles, and so the marketer started buying ads on daytime television to reach women. They had never done that before. Two things are interesting about this example. One is that this "revolutionary" idea to target women came as late as the early 1990s; the other is that there was a study from Chilton Research back in the mid-1980s that showed that women were responsible for about 75 percent of the purchase influence on automobiles! In other words, it took about a decade for an auto maker to act on a documented consumer trend.

Many believe that the bigger ad budget will always beat the smaller one. We believe there has been a shift: It's no longer true that *big crushes small,* but it is true that *fast defeats slow.* Therefore, the goal of our 70/20/10 principle is to dramatically shorten the cycle time to capitalize on trends in the landscape to develop better ROI and competitive advantage. The 20 percent devoted to sustaining innovation is very much in line with our previous discussion in Chapter 15 of "optimizing within a media." The 20 percent provides a funding framework to force innovation and learning on how to optimize within a media type. If you organize your budget this way, you'll find that it enforces a discipline to specifically identify

- what new marketing approach you'll try,
- how you'll measure it,
- and how you'll apply it to future programs if it works.

> *It's no longer true that* big crushes small, *but it is true that* fast defeats slow.

Therefore, we suggest integrating the 70/20/10 discipline into your COP discussions and establishing quarterly learning reviews.

Following are four examples of areas marketers might explore for the 20 percent:

1. The content and focus of your creative message
2. Opportunities in how you target your audience or who you target

3. Whether you should alter the reach or frequency of your advertising messages
4. Whether you should change the size or type of your ads

There are certainly many other areas you should brainstorm and measure, but let's take a closer look at these four, to demonstrate the concept of the 20 percent.

Sustaining Innovations by Maximizing the Creative

We once heard a famous creative director say that there's no greater ROI for advertising than improving the creative work. While that may be perceived as a self-serving statement for a creative director to make, we'd wholeheartedly agree. Even at $500 per hour for top creative talent to develop new messages or new advertisements, communicating your brand's motivations in an even clearer or more compelling way has a huge lift on the impact of your advertising.

But what works and what doesn't can be tricky to guess at without systematic experimentation. One example is from Colgate Total toothpaste, where a simple change was made to the ad shown in Figure 16.1. Note that in ad A the company extended the presence of the brand product shot to more frames of this online animated ad.

Ad A performed 27 percent better on brand image and was ten times better on the more important measure of consumers' intent to purchase. Yes, *ten times better.* Colgate came to this learning because it forced a change to its process. Instead of developing one ad, Colgate insisted on developing multiple creative concepts, sometimes with subtle differences, and some with radically different approaches. And it paid off.

FIGURE 16.1 Improvement of Colgate Total Ad

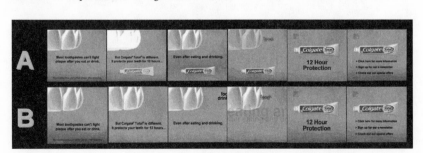

ET the Extraterrestrial DVD Example

When the DVD for *ET the Extraterrestrial* was launched, marketers at Universal Studios decided to put some of its ads in rich-media format, meaning that the online ads became more video-like. The ads featured a picture of Elliott (the boy ET befriends) flying across the moon, and this image extended over the page on the AOL Web site so it was very eye-catching. That ad actually cost three times more for the media than a traditional banner ad, and it was more expensive to produce, too. The question the marketers asked themselves was: "Well, that's a good innovation. We have a strong belief that the online banner should work, but would this new, more eye-catching ad, format work better and would it justify paying three times more?"

It turns out the more expensive ad was more effective. It actually was *five times* more effective. Also, the ad didn't need nearly as much frequency. Universal really only needed to show consumers the more eye-catching rich-media ad once, as opposed to needing to show the consumers the banner three times to have similar impact. This finding provided direction on how Universal could boost marketing ROI through new creative formats and different media-buying strategies (which emphasized reach and minimized repetition of the message frequency). Dedicating part of the 20 percent to creative A/B split tests across different media is key to increasing marketing ROI.

Adjusting creative or trying different approaches to media buying can have some of the most high-value impact. Yet in our experience, not many brands really look at the broad range of options available to them and systematically experiment. Much of the learning is serendipitous.

> *Not many brands really look at the broad range of options available to them and systematically experiment. Much of the learning is serendipitous.*

Sustaining Innovation through Targeting

As we mentioned, targeting women for automotive advertising was, at one point, unexplored, but now it is common practice. Coming up with new approaches to segmenting their audience has been high value for some advertisers. For example, independently AOL, MSN, and Yahoo! developed approaches that allowed each to identify actual product or category purchasers. Yahoo!, for example, does this by matching the behavior of certain consumers with the Nielsen HomeScan database that captures consumers' actual buying habits (thus making advertising more relevant, and Yahoo! does this with the full permission of these consumers). Yahoo! is then able to look for that Web-user behavioral pattern online, and it serves ads to those anonymous consumers. There is a high enough correlation with the Web behavior and the purchasing of certain products.

For example, a shampoo brand we measured used targeting to find consumers who are heavy purchasers of competitive brands. The company's goal for targeting these consumers was to get them to switch brands. Because this company measured this innovation, it learned that the effectiveness of each ad is *less* than if they were targeting a cross-section of consumers because competitive buyers have some degree of loyalty to their existing brands. It's still worth targeting these consumers, but it's less efficient (i.e., more costly) to get them to purchase a new brand. The company also learned that it requires a different frequency level to influence a competitive buyer as opposed to one of its current consumers. Applying this learning improves effectiveness and makes the difference between success and failure at influencing consumers—in other words, between *positive* ROI and *no* ROI.

Sustaining Innovation through Altering Reach or Frequency

Maybe a sustaining innovation is the altering of the reach and/or frequency of your campaign. Many marketers we worked with tackled this question, as seen in the following examples:

- Universal's *ET the Extraterrestrial* campaign found that the rich-media ad required *much lower frequency* than the other online ads.
- The shampoo brand using targeting of competitive buyers also experimented with optimal frequency within different contexts, and the company found that certain contexts required a *much higher frequency* in order to create change.
- Some of our work with Microsoft advertising measured different levels of frequency in TV advertising to see the points of diminishing returns for its advertising of a Microsoft product. This helped them determine how much they could increase the TV budget.
- Our work with Philips looked at different reach and frequency strategies for gift givers and those who buy consumer electronics for themselves.

Our findings suggest a wide range of optimal frequency by product, target, and context. With too little frequency, consumers will be unaffected. With too much frequency, the marketer wastes money and cuts into business profitability.

Sustaining Innovation through Changing the Size or Type of Ad

Sustaining innovation is just as important when it comes to options about the size or type of ads. Think about the following questions:

- Should you consider 15-second ads in TV if you have mostly used 30-second ads?
- Should you consider 60-second ads or maybe 2-minute ads, as the direct response industry has found them to be very beneficial?
- Would flooding a TV break (called a *pod*) with multiple ads work?
- What about the 30-minute infomercial format that has worked well for complicated products or those benefiting from a longer, story format?

For Ford-150, we measured the impact of buying out all the TV ads as the exclusive advertisers on the Fox *24* premier. Although we can say the findings on ROI were very interesting, you'll have to measure your own experiment with flooding a pod or buying out a program because data was part of the private research we conducted for Ford. The company is keeping this learning to itself.

In magazines, stretching to spreads or gatefolds can be done in addition to changing categories of magazines. For example, many years ago, Bounty paper towels did a special magazine insert. The brand picked a heavy paper stock that really made the ad stick out to consumers. Bounty resold the back of that insert to another Procter & Gamble brand for 75 percent of the cost of the whole insert program. So Bounty's advertising had a much better ROI at 25 percent of the cost of a regular magazine ad. Similarly, AstraZeneca measured glued-in business reply cards for a seven-day free trial within magazines; attached to its magazine ads, the cards produced great effect.

With respect to online, the options for different sizes and types of ads are numerous. For example, ads that expand when a mouse brushes over them, new larger half-page ads, and home-page intro ads have been very popular. Because online is so new, there are a huge number of arbitrage-type opportunities where we've seen marketers double their payback from advertising by taking advantage of learning the value of different ad formats that much of the market hasn't really figured out.

Now that you have some examples of how you can increase ROI by using 20 percent of the budget as an extension of your existing strategies and tactics, and going slightly out on a limb with similar but new approaches, let's take a look in the next and final chapter at how you might invest the remaining 10 percent of your budget in truly innovative marketing strategies.

CHAPTER SEVENTEEN

The Critical 10-Percent Factor

How does a weight lifter get stronger? Imagine a weight lifter who just kept lifting an empty bar without adding any additional weight to it. That wouldn't do much good. A weight lifter gets stronger through *resistance training*—using progressively heavier weights on the bar.

The same idea applies to marketers. Marketers won't get any stronger by simply lifting the same empty bar again and again. Marketers need to challenge themselves by increasing the weight on the bar, trying new things, and systematically learning from experience. Our advice to marketers: Make a list of the marketing ideas that have merit but haven't been executed yet. Challenge yourself and your team to try new ideas. Go outside your comfort zone with an open mind about at least one new program per financial quarter. Most marketers and advertising agencies we've met have a dozen or more programs that they just don't do because they don't know for sure if they would work. Maybe there are new strategies or marketing approaches that you've never tried before but that could improve your marketing results by a significant margin.

How a brand handles the 10 percent in the 70/20/10 allocation strategy is really where your big opportunity occurs to accelerate growth and really begin to shift your market share and fortunes (assuming your competition

How a brand handles the 10 percent in the 70/20/10 allocation strategy is really where the big opportunity occurs to accelerate growth and really begin to shift market share and fortunes.

hasn't already read this book and acted on it). Certainly, it's a top priority to get the first three of the 4Ms right by

1. getting the consumers' motivations right,
2. delivering messaging that sticks, and
3. optimizing the media mix.

Don't put off the 4th M, maximization, until the first three are perfect. Instead, use maximization today. We would probably even start with maximization because an emphasis on maximization brings the DNA of continuous investigation and improvement into the marketing department. Measurement is a key ally of innovation and should be used to extend the effectiveness and scope of all marketing programs with the 20 percent you're investing in sustaining innovations and 10 percent to disruptive innovations. The innovations may be trying new media, better tapping into motivations, or developing superior messages.

Maximization is the new battleground for marketing. It will be the research and development (R&D) in marketing and advertising that provide the necessary competitive advantage, separating the great brands from the not so great. This 10 percent in particular is just like the R&D that separates great technology, packaged goods, consumer electronics, and others around the new product innovations that they develop and release.

INNOVATING WITH 10 PERCENT IS BETTER THAN BETTING 100 PERCENT ON THE UNKNOWN

When we first introduced the 70/20/10 maximization principle, we were confronted by a marketer who said, "I spend half a billion dollars a year on advertising. Are you saying I should just blow $50 million on the unknown?" No, maximization is *not* simply "blowing" 10 percent on the unknown; it's systematically *learning* how new approaches to marketing and advertising can improve your ROI. As we said, it's about R&D and building a better foundation for tomorrow, and taking advantage of that learning today.

Every new program that comes out of the 10 percent fund should have a research and learning component to the investment that translates into action (as Johnson & Johnson calls it: "Test, Learn, Deploy"). This research ensures that marketers can determine if the new concept has merit and act accordingly. If the program isn't contributing to learning for the marketing organization because research and action plans are absent, then, yes, this is an investment that is "blown," and that's not what we'd advocate. In fact, we pressed the person who asked us this question on what he knew about the effectiveness and detailed ROI of the $500 million his company was currently spending. As it turns out, the basis of the half a billion dollars in spending was, "We think this works." The evidence was intuition and a typical, old-fashioned brand-tracking survey that provided little more than broad-brush trends in consumer preferences and ad recall but no insight on advertising ROI. This approach suggested that this marketer was actually spending the *full* 100 percent of his budget on the unknown and unproven. So to have 10 percent carefully measured as part of a maximization learning effort would have been a vast improvement for his company.

> *Every new program that comes out of the 10 percent fund should have a research and learning component to the investment that translates into action.*

BECAUSE THE FUTURE AIN'T WHAT IT USED TO BE, BE DISRUPTIVE . . .

The media landscape is changing significantly and marketers need to keep pace. Devote one day a month to disrupt the marketing status quo. Assume the persona of a consumer segment—do something that gets you into the skin of your consumers, and then explore what untapped marketing opportunities are part of the consumers' lives.

Let's say you learn that your consumers are extremely mobile and heavily into podcasts. You learn that *podcasts* are audio or video content downloaded to an iPod (hence the name) or other similar device such as a "smart phone." The consumer listens to or watches the content on the go. From this perspective, consider spending some of the 10 percent of your budget in this area.

Devote one day a month to disrupt. Do something that gets you out of your protective marketer role and pushes you into the skin of your consumers.

Example of Innovation through Podcasting

Advertising can be radio-like ads inserted into podcast content, or announcers plugging sponsors' products, or all the content could be the ad, like an audio brochure. As of the writing of this book, an estimated 12 percent of U.S. adults have an MP3-type device, and the number continues to grow at a rapid pace,[1] indicating that podcasting could be an influential medium within a very short time.

Given that portable MP3-type devices were introduced only a few years ago, there's very little knowledge about the effectiveness of them as a new ad medium. It's currently unknown what the pricing between content providers and marketers should be, and thus what would be the ROI from podcast advertising. In other words, some is known, but much is not.

Also, what about taking advantage of the fact that podcasts are individually addressable? (*Individually addressable* means each podcast can have different ads inserted in them, which is a big deal for targeting.) Because of this addressable nature, an experiment can be executed to try different creative formats for ads, and, by using a control group, a brand could easily quantify the precise effectiveness of podcasting and could try lots of different creative messages, ad lengths, etc., to really understand the dynamics of effectiveness and consumer acceptance of the advertising. You could know within a month or two whether podcasting can move sales or brand attitudes for your product.

Part of the 10-percent budget should be spent piloting podcasting strategies. Don't just pick one podcasting tactic; try a broad range of ideas. Remember, this isn't the 20 percent of where you already know what works and are extending a proven concept into new territory. This is the 10 percent disruptive innovation. Look for *scalable ideas,* that is, ideas that are easily expandable on demand. Don't narrow your options or assume you know what works. Instead, approach with open-minded experimentation. Don't be afraid to use a very different marketing strategy, or new creative messaging, or very different media.

Let's say you decide to try podcasting. Maybe you do a talk show about your product that people can download onto their MP3 players to take with them and listen to whenever they choose. Or maybe your idea is to embed your ads into a podcast program that is somewhat related to your product. Maybe you try the video podcasts. Try all of these ideas. And most important: *measure them.*

As we've shown through our research and described in this book, marketers and agencies don't often have good metrics for measuring success. They often undervalue all new media (just as they did with the Internet). Therefore, podcasting presents an opportunity for the marketers who figure out its value and dynamics first. How much value? Who knows?

Podcasting is one example. There are many others, such as interactive video, mobile advertising, blue-casting, consumer-created content advertising, various forms of game advertising, numerous sponsorship programs, community sites, social networks, and many more. Each is a relative unknown in terms of ROI. Each potentially holds competitive advantage. So, what are you waiting for?

Knowledge Is Power

Remember that for the majority of 10 percent programs, most of the value comes to your organization from learning what and how something new works (or doesn't work) so that it can be done better the next time. If you did find that podcasting (or any of the other ideas you test) was a successful strategy, all of a sudden you have a new insight in your knowledge storehouse and a new tool in your marketing toolbox that your competition may not have. You'd know how much you should pay for it, and what the ROI is, and how to optimize it—that's a significant advantage. That's true marketing maximization. When marketers begin to systematically look at the new things that they can do that will broaden the effectiveness of ROI for their marketing campaigns, marketing effectiveness begins to accelerate!

Most companies don't have any systematic approach to marketing innovation. In 1997 or 1998, just on the cusp of the whole dot-com explosion, one of the authors was in a top packaged-goods company's boardroom with the company's top marketers after they had just signed a deal to spend $100 million advertising on two Web sites. "That's amazing that you're going to spend that amount," the author remarked. "I'd love to know about your measurement plans or programs that you'll use to learn from this investment. Because this is such a new area of marketing, what a golden opportunity to figure out how this media works. What are your measurement and learning plans?" And, in this room of top executives, the most senior people from the advertising agencies and the marketer, you could have heard a pin drop. The silence spoke volumes in terms of R&D, the $100 million was all "D" with no "R."

TIME AND MONEY

On the other end of the spectrum is a company such as Johnson & Johnson; it is really taking this idea of measured innovation to heart. When Johnson & Johnson makes an investment in new marketing ideas, it typically measures that investment. Johnson & Johnson has a special innovation fund to encourage marketers to try new approaches. Their *Test, Learn, Deploy* approach ensures that learning is captured and action follows insights. The litmus tests to see whether you are maximizing is to ask yourself this: How do you set your budgets and how do you allocate time? If you set your budgets by looking at what you did last year and making only minor tweaks, it would suggest that you may be missing a major opportunity for breakaway innovations that can contribute to the future success of your brand.

> *When Johnson & Johnson makes and investment in new marketing ideas, it typically measures it. Johnson & Johnson has a special innovation fund to encourage marketers trying new approaches. Their Test, Learn, Deploy approach ensures that learning is captured and action follows insights.*

Your time should also follow a commitment to innovation. For example, as we understand it, all Google employees devote 20 percent of their time to innovation. Fridays are devoted to innovation. Employees are not to work on their regular jobs on Fridays; instead, they are to invest their time on innovation, either working on their own project or contributing as a team member to someone else's innovation projects. What if you did the same in your marketing department? What if every Wednesday, instead of answering e-mails and doing your regular job, you devoted your time and focus to an innovation project?

Discontinuous innovation ideas can come from a lot of sources. They may come from media owners pitching new ways of using their media. Or they might come from the ad agency. Or maybe they're in the marketers' own minds. We've observed that marketers often have great ideas but are often afraid to implement them because they have only a hunch that their ideas might work and they are concerned about failure if the ideas don't work. Johnson & Johnson's David Adelman remarked, "We'd rather see our marketers try 100 new ideas and have 80 fail then to see no innovating. In fact, we'd rather see marketers try lots of ideas now than to wait for the 'perfect idea.' Waiting for the perfect idea can too often act as an excuse for not innovating."[2] List your ideas, spend on them, invest in them, and apply the learning. As Johnson & Johnson teaches us, ideas must be backed with a learning measurement plan like their Test, Learn, Deploy system or our COP.

> *List your ideas, spend on them, invest in them, and apply the learning. Ideas must be backed with a learning measurement plan.*

Innovation without measurement is worthless. The two most important questions for any innovation are these: "What is success?" and "What are the action standards if the new program achieves success?" Following are additional questions to ask the marketing team:

- What strategies are you putting in your innovation fund?
- What type of marketing and advertising are you testing to make sure you've truly maximized your results?
- Now that you've tried all the things that have a decent chance of success, what have you learned from these trials?
- What haven't you tried?

The idea of an innovation budget is that it would guarantee that you have a certain amount to spend on pursuing new ideas. When you go about measuring these new marketing or advertising approaches, the idea is to start with the following two simple dimensions, in this order:

1. Can it be effective?
2. Can it be cost efficient?

The reason we separate these two questions is that you may find a great idea that's effective, but it isn't cost efficient. And those are the ideas that we encourage spending more time on because when you try something entirely new, it is highly unlikely that you're going to get all the dynamics exactly right the first time out of the gate. So find ideas that are effective and then work to make them *cost efficient.*

Example of the Innovation Cycle

Earlier, in Chapter 13, we told about Procter & Gamble's (P&G's) first forays into online marketing for the Olay brand. First and foremost, P&G's marketers wanted to understand if online advertising could influence sales in stores. They knew that the Internet was changing their consumers' media habits dramatically. But they wondered whether the payback was on par or better than their other media choices in terms of influencing sales.

We advised them to first focus on effectiveness in absolute terms—that is, does online advertising affect sales? If it did, then how can the marketer achieve sales in the most cost-efficient manner, and that might include learning more about the best frequency, targeting, and other dynamics we've covered in previous chapters.

So P&G started with an ample frequency of 40 ads per consumer over 8 weeks. Because this was way past the point of diminishing returns, it wasn't at all cost efficient. However, it *was effective*—and therefore, the next step was to make it efficient. We found that P&G could refine frequency by cutting it back, and in fact P&G made online the #1 ROI in the mix. If P&G's marketers had expected any new marketing element to be both effective and have superior ROI out of the gate, they might have really missed that opportunity.

We have found that by separating effectiveness and cost efficiency in the analysis, the savvy marketer will learn about the dynamics and tactics that best lead to success. Success, in terms of improved ROI, will likely come in a second phase—after the research has illuminated the underlying media dynamics regarding how consumers' use of the new media creates meaning and how that translates into sales (or any other marketing goal).

Some of the examples that we have today of discontinuous innovations in media are podcasting, interactive video, mobile advertising, various forms of game advertising, and consumer-created content or ads to name a few. And for some marketers, out-of-home, radio, or other traditional media might even be discontinuous innovations. Or, maybe the discontinuous innovation is advertising to an entirely different segment, such as using Spanish-language advertising. It really depends on what you've done before and proven as a marketer for your brand. The best marketers use innovation research to add information to their knowledge storehouse, and they work to quickly apply the learning. To explore making innovation a reality, let's look at the best-practice work of Johnson & Johnson in more depth.

Johnson & Johnson's Best-Practice Innovations

Johnson & Johnson has quickly become one of the world's leaders in marketing communications innovation. Johnson & Johnson's marketers have set up an "innovation fund." They figured out that because brand managers move from brand to brand, they might be less interested in taking funds from today's budget to invest for the future. These brand managers didn't want to be responsible for trying something new that might fail. In addition, because innovation can take a longer horizon to pay off, the brand manager's short-term tenure might mean he or she could try something new but not be around to see it working and not be rewarded for the benefit of the advertising innovation. This situation led to the aphorism translated to marketing as "no one ever got fired for running television" as an advertising medium. But what if TV is a middle-of-the-road performer and much better results could be achieved with new approaches? Or, what if new approaches to television could boost ROI substantially? So how did Johnson & Johnson encourage innovation?

> *Innovation can take a longer horizon to pay off, so the brand manager could try something new, but not be around to see it working and not be rewarded for the benefit of the innovation.*

Johnson & Johnson's solution was simple and brilliant. At the corporate level, the company set up an innovation fund to provide incentive for brand managers in all of Johnson & Johnson's different brands to try new marketing and advertising strategies and build in measurement and action standards with scenario planning. This encourages brand teams to seek out new innovations, measure them, turn the learning into best practices and, most important, act on the learning.

For example, let's look at what Johnson & Johnson has done with respect to media optimization. In measuring Johnson & Johnson's Neutrogena acne product, we analyzed television, radio, magazines, and the Internet. The learning led to changes in media allocation for Johnson & Johnson and to millions of dollars in increased sales and thus increased profit—without spending a dollar more in advertising or marketing.

With respect to Johnson & Johnson's *extra-media* optimization, the company learned about leveraging online advertising, and noted that they hadn't tried out-of-home ads, particularly in malls and schools, which are increasingly taking digital advertising. So the ad agency OMD suggested putting 2 percent in the out-of-home ad area, and measuring how it worked for their Neutrogena acne brand as part of another innovation cycle to see if it made a difference.

This is the essence of innovation and measurement: You put your toe in the water; you measure if it's warm; and if it is, you dive in. And then, to continue the innovation, you look for another pool to dip your toe in. Sometimes you'll find deep, warm hot springs of opportunity. Other times, you find shallow puddles that you can dip your toe in, and then move on. If you only continue with what you've already done, you'll miss innovations; you'll miss things that are outside of the box of what you've already done. In fact, we think you'll miss the reasons you got into the cutting-edge, exciting world of marketing to begin with.

Example of Foster's Group Budgeting Innovation

Innovation isn't just the message, or the media mix; it might be the underlying budgeting process and rules. Foster's Group has the largest selling beer brands in Australia. The company buys lots of advertising space at events that it sponsors on TV, in magazines, and online. Normally, ads are bought from each media separately. But what if Foster's Group encouraged their media partners who own properties across media to provide a single, consolidated dollar figure across all media and to allow the media partner to manage the allocation across media within their portfolio such that Foster's marketing ROI is optimized? Could such an innovation change the structure from parochial silos organized by media to more of a surround-sound marketing strategy that took advantage of cross-media synergy?

Or what about managing brand budgets differently? Foster's is innovating budget silos for sponsorships. Because ad spending is often determined as a percent of sales, the two powerhouse brands, VB and Carlton Drought, are the only brands large enough to afford premium sponsorship for high-profile sports and music events. But what if Foster's managed the brands as a financial portfolio manager might, and it took "dividends" from one "stock" with slow growth (but good returns) and instead invested in fast-growth brands that couldn't afford the sponsorship because of the smaller size of the brand? Foster's is using VB's budget to fund smaller, high-growth brands to maximize the return of Foster's overall portfolio of brands. Now, that's the type of innovative approaches that makes Foster's Group world class.

Example of Business Model Innovation

In addition to innovation in marketing communication and marketing budget practices, there is innovation in products and business models. Product and business model innovation takes more discipline than innovation in marketing communication because the investments, time horizons, and stakes can be much more significant. Consider the case of Intel Celeron. Taddy Hall, the Advertising Research Foundation's chief strategy officer, and Harvard professor Clay Christensen addressed the challenge that marketers face by pointing to Intel. Intel has had tremendous success, but business model and product innovation in a fast changing technology field is always a challenge and potential threat. But innovation in terms of business models and product is much harder than innovation of a media plan. While innovating a media plan simply requires the discipline to examine where consumer's behaviors are changing, and experimentation to see how to effectively communicate with consumers in these new media, product and business model innovation requires, according to Hall, "Pursuing disruptive opportunities from the context of an established business (extremely hard) and differentiating between a bold idea and a bad idea (difficult)."

It's on this last point that the theory developed in *The Innovators Dilemma* is so helpful. "After the fact, bad ideas are easy to spot! Looking forward, though, a crummy idea and a potential game-changing master stroke look kind of similar. That's why it is so important to get the theory of innovation right," according to Hall. The theory suggests looking at five characteristics of successful disruptive product and business model innovations. Innovations:

- Target small or ill-defined markets
- Take root in the least profitable, low-end segments of existing markets or . . . target "nonconsumers"
- Are technologically unsophisticated
- Often establish a new basis for competition from the established leaders
- Target marketers that are generally unattractive for established leaders

Almost always, established leaders win when innovations simply *sustain* the forward march along the prevailing performance trajectory. More often than not, though, established leaders *lose* share to entrepreneurial companies that *disrupt* the prevailing business model by introducing a new model that targets customers that either are at the low end or are excluded entirely from the current marketplace.

Many of America's greatest companies began as disruptors—think Dell, Southwest, Google, Sony, FedEx, Enterprise Rent-A-Care, Wal-Mart. What is exceedingly rare, however, are those successful at repeat disruptions. In fact, Intel stands virtually alone among large companies to have performed this feat. With Celeron, Intel's low-end processors, they set-up an independent group within the company that developed a less-sophisticated chip, targeted at a smaller, but growing market segment with lower margins, and successfully grew the business. Had they not taken this action, Christensen and Hall argue, they would have been disrupted and undercut by a new entrant that would have disrupted the market for them.

YOUR 70/20/10 ALLOCATIONS SHOULD CHANGE OVER TIME

A good litmus test for how well your brand or company might be doing to maximize your marketing is to assess whether your media plans have changed in the past five years. If your media plans today are not much different than they were five years ago, especially given all the changes in consumers' media habits (the Internet, iPods, TiVo, game systems, and more), then you can pretty much be assured your plans are suboptimal, and probably even fuddy-duddy, old-fashioned, money wasting programs.

> *If your media plans today are not much different than they were five years ago, especially given all the changes in consumers' media habits (the Internet, iPods, TiVo, mobile, game systems, and more), then you can pretty much be assured your plans are suboptimal, and probably even fuddy-duddy, old-fashioned, money wastingly suboptimal.*

Perhaps someday, allocations based on limited research, or on no research, will be considered criminal. It may take a COP to intervene. It's disconcerting (if not outright insane) for people to think that intuition alone can deliver effective marketing plans and systematic innovation. Look at the complexity of marketing (recall the "10 to the 10" decision-making process that we described in Chapter 5, where ten major marketing decisions with ten different options leads to 1 billion unique combinations of marketing plans). Finding the optimal ROI with a billion possible marketing plans is daunting.

But as we've shown, gold-standard measurement and a COP can help tremendously. Most of the companies we've worked with are on a *journey* for better marketing ROI. Few have arrived, but they are climbing the mountain. Join them. Join us. And, as you embark on your journey, remember the following three things:

1. *Bring a compass and aim it toward better marketing ROI.* Just spending on new ideas *isn't* maximization; it's running aimlessly in circles in the wilderness. Understanding what the spending is *doing* for you in a *systematic* way is how you get to your destination of maximized results.
2. *Bring a flashlight and illuminate your path with research.* With no vision into where you're going, getting there is that much harder and usually unlikely. Great measurement will light your path.
3. *Bring a map and be sure to lay out a plan and a path for where you are going.* Make the 70/20/10 principle become part of your organization's culture, because *there has to be a bottom-line orientation* regarding how your budgets should be organized.

And, finally, if you need a guide, measurement tools, COP, or examples and more case studies, you can find us at *www.whatsticks.NET.*

Guaranteeing Your Advertising Works With the 4Ms

1. The 4Ms: motivations, message, media mix, and maximization are a powerful way of organizing and measuring marketing communications. If you're not perfecting the 4Ms, your marketing is likely suboptimal. The communication optimization process (COP) ensures that learning translates into action.

2. Motivations is the cornerstone of effective marketing. Get consumers' motivations wrong and it is very likely that your campaign will not succeed. To get consumers' motivations right, consider why consumers hire your brand. Consider the functional, emotional, and social benefits of the brand. Also, consider how different segments of your consumer market may be motivated by different needs. At the same time, consider the financial opportunity each segment represents to your company. Focus your message accordingly.

3. Message is an area where most marketers use intuition, or out-of-date assumptions of how consumers process advertising, but advances in neuroscience and design of experiments reveal why so many marketing messages fail to resonate with consumers. Consumers typically process advertising in low-attention mode, while marketers generally experience their own advertising in high-attention mode. This disconnect in perspective can make it hard for marketers to use their own judgment as to whether an advertisement will work or not. A better approach is to use A/B Split testing to arrive at an accurate understanding of message effectiveness.

4. Media-mix analysis is only useful if the marketer has successfully aligned strategy to match consumer motivations and developed messages that effectively communicate with the consumer. If these first two Ms are right, then optimizing the media mix can significantly improve marketing return on investment. Media mechanics are the principles related to diminishing returns and other aspects of how media works. Psychologics, such as the media is the message, looks at the way in which meaning is created through different strategies of media planning.

5. Maximization involves pushing marketing beyond its current boundaries. An approach to continuous improvement in marketing is the 70/20/10 principle, which suggests that marketers invest their time and energy around both sustaining innovations (innovations that are fairly similar to what they have currently found successful) and disruptive innovations (marketing ideas that are radically different from current approaches). Innovation without measurement is worthless, therefore, when engaging in innovation research and development (R&D), it is critical to invest in the "R" so that learning is captured and acted upon.

Explanation of Scenario Planning

The firm Marketing Evolution has developed and refined a rigorous scenario planning process over the past three years. Scenario planning is a consensus process that a senior marketing expert facilitates. By working with advertisers in many different industries, we have found that often when they first approach Marketing Evolution they ask to "measure marketing return on investment (ROI)." This marketing ROI is sometimes focused just on direct marketing efforts and at other times it spans many different budgets. We have found that the first step to achieving an understanding of how to define or how to measure marketing ROI is to execute the following scenario planning process, wherein the output is

1. a shared, unambiguous definition of success;
2. identification of key success drivers;
3. action standards based on agreed upon metrics; and
4. milestones identifying opportunities to modify and improve a campaign if needed.

The process first defines success and then links the shared definition of success for the marketing to the success drivers. The drivers of success typically fall into the following categories:

- Strategy

- Understanding of motivations for selecting one brand, product, or company over another
- Message
- Media mix and media use
- Competitive activities
- Pricing, availability, and product quality
- Media sequencing and layering
- Role of individual media to the purchase decision process

WHY IS SCENARIO PLANNING IMPORTANT?

People often have different theories of how a campaign will work, and, therefore, they have different expectations and definitions of success. These theories of success need to be formally stated, discussed, and prioritized so that there is a consensus on what the campaign can achieve.

From a common set of beliefs about how the advertising is intended to work, the group can map appropriate action plans based on the potential outcomes of the advertising measurement. This is the decision tree process.

Scenario Planning in Essence

- Works across company silos and achieves the teamwork and preplanning that is critical to the continuous improvement of marketing
- Cuts down on the Monday-morning quarterbacking (the "If I had my way, we wouldn't have made that mistake" politics) that occurs when the group fails to define expectations and action plans up front, prior to campaign launch.
- Provides—perhaps most importantly—a process to ensure that the results are acted upon to improve marketing ROI. ROI research that isn't applied is worthless.

Marketing Evolution's philosophy is that accountability isn't measurement, it is doing something about the measurement and the scenario-planning process is the approach to delivering action according to this marketing philosophy.

Building Decision Trees

Marketing Evolution's process to help improve advertising ROI is based on the development of decision trees. A decision tree begins with the key business questions and branches out to the possible outcomes and action plans related to the key business questions and research findings. These decision trees allow for an in-depth scenario-planning exercise where all key stakeholders in the advertising develop consensus on the actions to be taken based on different outcomes from the analysis of *return on marketing objectives* (ROMO), described in more detail in Appendix B.

Step one: Define the mechanisms that the marketing campaign plans to use to communicate with consumers. We start by reviewing both theories of how the marketing team expects the advertising to work. These theories are not mutually exclusive. Each may be at work with a different segment of the consumer base. The value in defining the theories is that the ROMO analysis will specifically focus on accessing the degree to which success is achieved as defined by each theory. This then helps a marketer to refine their understanding of how advertising works with their consumers.

Step two: Prioritize the mechanisms. The group might consider this question: Is it more important to drive existing customers to a new brand or to influence underlying beliefs among a new target? The ad campaign may do both, but if there was a trade-off between one or the other, which is more important? These questions allow the marketer to make critical strategic choices about the role of advertising.

If the overarching priority is to drive market share, we may additionally look at a secondary priority of examining how core benefits are driving purchase intents. This examination can help focus messaging to ensure it is on strategy. With this strategic prioritization complete, the decision trees are developed.

Step three: Develop decision trees based on the advertising mechanisms. With consensus around the priorities and mechanisms of advertising effectiveness, scenario planning digs deeper into defining success metrics. In parallel, the decision trees require the marketer to think through the action they will take depending on different outcomes of the in-market ROMO measurement.

The marketing team brainstorms ways to respond to possible scenarios. For example, if the question is, "Does the advertising communicate the message most closely linked to purchase intent?" then a "no" answer to this question leads to the following five-part plan based on the "miss" on the core message:

1. Determine if current advertising should be halted:
   a. If advertising is addressing a secondary motivator and having a positive influence on consumer behavior, advertising should be continued.
   b. If advertising is addressing a motivation that has little or no influence on consumer behavior, and the campaign is having little to no influence on behavior, it is better to conserve budget until ad creative can be refocused.
2. Identify the core motivators most highly correlated with the product purchase:
   a. Assess if the brand can deliver against these core motivators. If the brand's advertising does not currently speak to these highly motivating attributes, explore the development plan and analyze cost/benefit of developing a new message to meet these consumer needs.
   b. Brainstorm advertising ideas to illustrate how the brand delivers against these core motivators.
   c. Evaluate timing for new campaign creative to be relaunched.

Step four: Finalize consensus. Prior to any ROMO data presentation, the client receives the summary report of the scenario-planning exercise. This report is circulated (and amended if necessary) so that everyone in the marketing group can sign off on the scenario-planning premises, decision trees, and action plans.

Step five: Receive ROMO results and take agreed-on action. The final step is the presentation of ROMO data and the application of this data in future marketing actions. We have found that this scenario-planning process has improved marketing significantly. Marketers who have used the scenario-planning process may provide better perspective. As the brand manager for Neutrogena's Acne Division, Salini Bowen, put it in a recent public forum, "Marketing Evolution's Scenario Planning was excellent. It made a huge difference in our business." Echoing those sentiments, David Adelman, from Johnson & Johnson's advertising group said, "We learned so much from the ROMO research, and it is Marketing Evolution's scenario-planning process that is helping us apply this great learning."[1]

Research
Methodology

The basis of this book is Marketing Evolution's Return on Marketing Objectives (ROMO) proprietary Methodology for analyzing marketing campaigns. This Methodology has been independently reviewed by the Advertising Research Foundation (ARF), and this Appendix draws heavily from that independent review.

OBJECTIVES

The objective of analyzing marketing campaigns is to provide accurate and rapid feedback on marketing effectiveness and ROI. Marketing Evolutions ROMO service advances cross-media planning by measuring each medium on a common measure of advertising response and/or sales response. This cross-media measurement is a departure from the traditional planning that focuses on one-medium-at-a-time. Instead, ROMO looks at all media holistically and is necessary to address today's demands for marketing accountability in the complex environment of marketing.

ROMO

The ROMO process accomplishes the following:

- Provides a real-time system to evaluate sales and a full range of attitudinal performance that is focused on in-market conditions as they are now . . .
- Delivers the ability to measure new media and integrate them into a current media plan.
- Analyzes marketing efforts in context of a Communication Optimization Process (COP) in order to link data to decision making.

METHODOLOGY

ROMO is designed to measure the impact of advertising campaigns over a period from as little as several weeks to continuing long-term campaigns.

In ROMO research, Marketing Evolution uses a patent pending media and data collection approach based on design of experiments (also known as exposed and control group or randomized controlled experiments) and surveys conducted online to assess the impact of traditional and online media on the attitudes of the people surveyed. Where the target audience is judged not to be well represented by the online population, telephone surveys are conducted to supplement the online surveys.

EXPERIMENTAL DESIGN

According to the independent review conducted by the Advertising Research Foundation (ARF) of the ROMO methodology;

Marketing Evolution pairs the media and interviewing design with randomized-controlled designs that are widely recognized as offering valuable accuracy and power, or efficiency, particularly in complex settings such as those found in marketing. The use of randomized-controlled designs enables the researcher to establish causality with greater assurance than by any other research technique.

Randomly determining which individual, group, or market receives advertising exposure or not can eliminate the effects of uncontrolled influences—such as a change in competitive spending—that often contaminate and bias studies comparing exposed and unexposed consumers, or simple marketing mix analyses. ROMO is one of the few advertising measurement approaches that uses experimental design to isolate the effect of media in the advertising mix.

The survey design uses continuous tracking to capture the overall effects of the advertising together with experimental design to isolate the effects of each individual media channel. Where media exposure can be affordably controlled on a market-by-market basis, markets are randomly assigned to advertising-exposed and randomly matched advertising-unexposed (control) treatments. Surveys are administered in both sets of markets. This method allows marketers to achieve cross-media insights without having to make changes to their national TV plan. Alternatively, marketers can experiment with TV to achieve a richer set of insights from the ROMO research. The effect of TV has been estimated by comparing the measures of impact during and following the campaign with measures obtained prior to the campaign launch (when TV advertising was not on air), after the combined impact of the other media has been subtracted out.

Starting measurement is straightforward and takes about six hours spread over three meetings. The first meeting kicks off planning for the measurement by gathering basic brand and competition information and discussing the media to be used in upcoming marketing campaigns. Marketing Evolution uses this information to design data collection, media experiments, and survey instruments.

The next two meetings with marketers focus on scenario planning. Typically, these meetings are two hours long and are conducted by Marketing Evolution leaders along with the marketer and agency partners to formalize the definition of success and expectations of the advertising campaign under study. A list of key business questions that must be answered by the research is developed and agreed on. Decision trees are used to clarify the marketing options, and action plans are drafted as to how the marketer will respond to a range of potential research outcomes. The data collection and measurement then begins.

SURVEY DESIGN

Continuous tracking is used with surveys administered throughout the course of the campaign. Ideally, data collection begins prior to the start of the campaign to provide a pre-campaign baseline for pre-post comparison. Surveys taken are primarily through online surveys, but telephone surveys are used when necessary to achieve good representation of the campaign's target. Surveys gather attitudinal and behavioral measures related to the campaign objectives and marketing needs. Measures of purchase intention and reported purchases have become the prevalent factors in the ROMO tracking and baseline surveys as the emphasis on sales response has grown. In situations where category logistics make it possible, separate surveys of media behavior are conducted on any verified buyers of the test brand.

CAMPAIGN MEASURES

To provide fair comparisons across various media and to aid analytic transparency, Marketing Evolution uses a straightforward cost-per-impact measure of media effectiveness. The analysis has been designated *return-on-marketing-objectives (ROMO) analysis*. Depending on the marketing campaign objectives, one or more measures are selected for the ROMO analysis to assess the impact of the campaign. For each medium the difference in the metric is calculated between exposed and control respondents. The gain in the impact measure between exposed and control is divided into the cost of the media buy to calculate the "cost per impact," or "return on marketing objectives."

$$\text{Cost per branding effect} = \frac{\text{Total cost of media}}{\text{Total Effect}}$$

$$\text{Total effect} = \frac{\text{Number of people exhibiting effect}}{\text{post(branding \% – baseline branding \%)} \times \text{target population size}}$$

EXPERIMENTAL DESIGN

ROMO studies apply experimental designs as a core approach to isolating individual media effects. The population base for the experimental design ranges from the comparisons of exposed and control geographics (or cities) to comparisons of individuals assigned to control or exposed groups.

For example, radio advertising is randomized among a list of markets where 80 percent to 90 percent receive the advertising and 20 percent of the markets are held out as control. The frame of reference is the entire market—ROMO avoids trying to determine who within the market is exposed and who is not (because measuring radio response with self-reported data is less reliable). By analyzing the entire exposed market compared to the control markets, a proper experimental design is achieved. ROMO projects the results to arrive at the total incremental impact of radio across the United States. The following equation is useful:

$$\text{Total number of people impacted} = \frac{(\text{branding \% exposed} - \text{branding \% control}) \times}{\text{population (entire exposed markets)}}$$

Online advertising uses individuals rather than markets as the units of experimental control. The moment before the ad is delivered, the individual is assigned to an exposed or control cell based on a random number generator. If the individual has already been assigned to the exposed or control group, that assignment is maintained. A cookie is placed and that person is designated to receive the advertising for the brand under study (exposed) or a placebo ad such as a public service announcement (control). When individuals are selected for the survey, the presence of the cookie and its numeric value are noted, the responses from "ad-exposed" individuals are assigned to the "ad-exposed" cell, and the responses from the public service placebo ad are assigned to the "control" cell. Those individuals not exposed to either are assigned to the "not reached" cell.

In evaluating online campaigns, the random assignment of "exposure" or "control" is made at the individual respondent level, while for radio or newspaper the control is exercised at the market level. When using an individual-level design, adjustments must be made to the individual data to match the level of reach that was achieved in a market, while the reach level is measured directly in the market-level design. This adjustment modifies the statisticians T-test to accommodate for mixing market-level and individual-level experiments.

Magazine measurement uses a respondent-level calculation of exposed and control groups. While "selective binding" (experimental design among subscribers or regions) is offered in ROMO, only one of the public studies has used this approach. The rest have opted for a less costly quasi-experimental design. For each magazine used in the advertising campaign, Marketing Evolution compares the effects of (potential) exposure to the campaign among readers of the issue or issues in which the campaign ad or ads are placed with readers of issues in which the ad or ads did not occur.

Marketing Evolution measures magazine ad impact using the following method:

1. All those who read *any* issue of the magazine are classified as *readers*. (Consumers are shown the cover of the current issue and the covers of the two previous months' issues, or the covers of five previous weeks' issues in the case of weeklies—using the actual magazine covers.)
2. The number of issues read is counted in order to arrive at a total number of issues read.
3. The media-plan data is then overlaid, and readers are divided into an "exposed" or "control" group based on whether they happened to read an issue containing an advertisement or not.
4. "Exposed" and "control" respondents are balanced, based on total number of issues read, demographics, and median date of survey completion, to ensure accurate comparison.

Because many people read or look through some but not all issues of a magazine, and because marketers buy ad insertions in some but not all issues of a magazines, the respondents grouped into "exposed" and "control" can be compared with a low likelihood of bias or contamination.

The accumulation of reach and frequency is not explicitly modeled in the ROMO analysis because the pre-post, repeated-survey design captures the majority of the cumulative print impact as well as it does with TV. Therefore, modeling reach and frequency is unnecessary.

TELEVISION

Television is measured in much the same way that a continuous tracking study measures the impact of a TV campaign. Wherever possible, a baseline measure is gathered prior to the launch of a brand or a new campaign for a brand. This allows for pre-advertising and post-advertising comparisons, as well as analysis of "flighting," the change in creative effort and competitive spending effects.

To separate out the effects of television, other media that can be isolated through experimental design are subtracted, leaving the underlying effect of television to be assessed.

COMPETITIVE SPENDING

If competitive media spending changes during the course of the campaign, the ROMO estimates are adjusted by means of a share-of-voice-by-medium factor. This method requires the tracking of competitive media spending from the pre-campaign survey through the campaign measurement period.

REPORTING

ROMO reports the overall effectiveness of the campaign and, where effects can be separated by the research design and/or analysis, ROMO uses the cost-per-impact analysis to measure the effectiveness of each media channel used in the campaign and to compare the relative cost effectiveness with the other media, and with nonmedia marketing activities such as public relations (PR) efforts, events, etc. The result is an optimization recommendation that recommends an optimal media mix and estimates the gain in core metrics the client can expect to receive as a result of the optimization.

ROMO reports also give recommendations based on the findings of the study for future marketing campaigns. These recommendations typically require analysis beyond the ROMO modeling. Based on regression analysis of the tracking results, advertising spending effectiveness curves are estimated, and optimum spending levels calculated and reported for each media channel.

ROMO provides the following:

- Full marketing optimization
- Optimization of media for maximum brand *and* sales impact (long-term and short-term competitive advantage)
- Complete competitive spend analysis and competitive brand tracking, resulting in actionable analysis of the impact of competition on brand performance

■ Full assessment of how to improve performance of creative, targeting, reach and frequency, messaging, and media usage to maximize campaign performance

■ Consultation and direction on how to interpret and employ results.

This methodology appendix draws heavily from the independent review by the Advertising Research Foundation (ARF) and the ESOMAR best-practices chapter on Marketing Evolution's ROMO Methodology. Links to these documents can be found at *www.whatsticks.NET.*

A Brief Review of
Motivation Research

As is the case of most research about advertising, the results of motivations research are only as good as the questions asked. Broadly, following are the two components to research consumer motivations:

1. The *qualitative* up-front work done that should be used to guide strategy explorations
2. The *quantitative* work that confirms that you hit the mark and that your "mark" is financially optimal

Let's look at these in brief detail.

QUALITATIVE RESEARCH

Qualitative research is often used up front to define a structure of consumer needs and is not statistically based or analyzed. It is used to define a problem, generate theories, identify important issues, and often used to design the quantitative research. It is used to begin to understand the framework under which a consumer experiences your brand.

Because there are many variations on qualitative research, and entire books have been written on the subject, take this appendix as a brief and incomplete overview. Plenty of good approaches exist to generate motivation insights. To give just two examples, consider the use of trade-off techniques (i.e., discrete choice and conjoint[1] in technical speak) where you ask the consumer to choose between alternatives while considering different situations. This approach allows the interviewer to probe the choices consumers make.

Another useful approach is the ZMET metaphor elicitation. ZMET is a qualitative approach to finding the underlying consumer motivations. It is based on the insight that consumers think in metaphors; therefore, marketers can best understand consumer motivations by probing for consumers' metaphors as to why they choose a brand, or the role the brand plays in their lives, etc. A marketer might ask a consumer to make a collage related to the product, and then have the consumer explain the collage, listening carefully for the metaphors and the underlying meaning to better understand consumer motivations.

There are several other techniques that can be used to gain insights into motivation. The category of qualitative research includes traditional focus groups that should include a representative group of your consumers that you gather into a room in order to have a dialogue with them about what they think and feel about your brand and the communications they may respond to. Generally you gather groups of 10 to 15 people who often are led by a professional moderator capable of teasing out consumers' perspectives. Focus groups tend to be the research technique of choice for most ad agencies to economically begin the ad campaign development process.

But focus groups are only as good as the people that you invite (most agencies tend to do multiple groups in multiple cities) and as good as the group itself is in letting divergent views emerge. Given the ability of a focus group to be derailed by one compelling or outspoken personality, many researchers are concerned that too much emphasis is put on the group conclusions. As in all research, success depends on how representative the group is, the way in which the questions are asked of them, and the way the discussion is moderated.

Another technique that agencies and marketers use is "one-on-ones" or "individual in-depths." These are structured like focus groups, except with this technique you talk to only one consumer at a time. The technique avoids the bias of the "groupthink" that can occur in focus groups. It is commonly used where there is a short list of key customers or buyers for the product. However, it can be expensive and take a lot of time. Plus, only one interviewer actually gets the consumer's perspective directly; others must rely on the interviewers interpretation of consumers' motivations.

Another approach in the right situations is to watch consumers interact with the product itself and then interview them during that process. All of these approaches are about building a framework for what motivates consumer behavior. We suggest mapping the functional, emotional, and social reasons consumers hire a brand. Given the sampling bias inherent in each qualitative approach, they are not meant to be used to extrapolate from your entire customer base. That's what *quantitative research* is for.

QUANTITATIVE RESEARCH

After doing qualitative research, you should be able to map out a structure of needs and begin to understand the basic segmentations of your customer base. Quantitative research, often called "survey research," can then be used to assess the prevalence and relationships of the various attitudes and needs with a sense of importance or weakness against each. Remember, too, that consumer needs can be very functional or they can be purely emotional, and they are most often some combination of both. Other motivations research, such as problem detection, focuses on making sure that marketers solve a real problem that consumers have. And pure needs research looks at consumer aspirations.

If your research is done well, you can begin to better understand the size and value of various segmentations. In sum, what is the size, value profile, and motivation of the various segments?

For example, let's assume you believe you should be marketing only to heavy users of your product. Quantitative research would help you figure out what percentage heavy users are of your total audience and, if the questions are asked well, some sense of how much volume in sales they represent. Additionally, this will give you a sense of how their attitudes and profiles differ from your other customers, a learning that will be important to you in both developing messaging or in targeting your media.

The final goal here is to determine that you have identified a motivation that will push your consumers to actually buy and to confirm that the attributes you have focused on will not only change consumers' beliefs about your brand but that they will take action. The research should correlate to purchases. Don't ask the consumer directly why they bought. Consumers can't introspect completely on the emotional trigger and development of meaning that led to their preference for a brand and purchase. Instead, the research must observe the connection between seller and brand perceptions (which is related to motivations) without relying on directly asking the consumer.

A Quick Primer
on Pretesting
Messaging Research

Doing research for messaging prior to the launch of a message is generally referred to as *creative pretesting,* or sometimes *concept testing.* It is the art of assessing consumer impact against various advertising messages or strategies before the ads enter the *real world.* As pointed out in this book, this part is critical to ensure that consumers hear the messaging in the way it was intended and that it has the expected impact on consumers. The best way to know the impact is to measure it in the real world using A/B split tests, as in the backbone of our research presented here. But because putting the message in the real world without confidence in its effectiveness is a risk, many marketers look to minimize that risk by pretesting the messages while the messages are in development.

A number of different forms can be used, and most occur in a laboratory of sorts. Generally the research puts the advertisement into a traditional, often cluttered, media environment by sending a consumer a DVD of a TV pilot or a magazine—or uses some other pretense to simulate the normal media environment—and then surveys the consumers for their awareness, communication, brand image takeaway, and/or their intent to purchase the brand based on that pretense. Other techniques dispense with the pretense and have consumers use dials to indicate their feelings as they observe a message. These *dial tests,* as they are called, are used extensively in testing political messaging. Some marketers are experimenting with new brain imaging and eye tracking systems. The technique of *neuroimaging* requires a consumer to watch an ad while their brain blood flows are monitored. This blood flow measurement can indicate at what point the ad draws consumers in and at what point it loses engagement. A host of other mental activities can help the marketer to determine how consumers are processing the message. Another technique is eye tracking that not only helps marketers see where consumers are looking while an ad plays, it provides a path for how the eyes navigate the message, where the gaze holds, and where it bounces back and forth quickly (which can indicate confusion). Some marketers even suggest that monitoring the different rate of pupil dilation and minor fluctuation differences between right pupil and left pupil provide answers to whether the brain is experiencing a more emotional response or a more rational response.

The goal of all this research varies from study to study and technique to technique, but in general the point is to determine if the brand was recognized and whether the messaging had impact with consumers and therefore will work in the real world. The better research should confirm if the ad communicates the motivations intended to be addressed, specifically, if the key messages had any impact on consumer beliefs in some way that matters. And finally, critically, the pretest should provide a measure of propensity to purchase or act. This is where a lot of ads in our experience fall down. The ads might get noticed, the consumer may even like the ads, but the consumer is not any more likely to believe that the product is aligned with a motivation nor is the consumer any more likely to act.

Creative testing is available for most media. The most popular is creative testing for TV. This testing can be done in various stages from concept to finished commercial. Magazine testing is done very similarly: The consumers are tested via Starch or other services. Print ads can be pretested by tipping them into a magazine. The Internet introduced a new testing option. The Internet can be measured in the real world using one to two million impressions and A/B split tests. A/B split tests can be done in most media for creative tests, but usually are not due to expense. But with the Internet, the cost of A/B split tests are much more affordable. This removes the artificial conditions of a laboratory, and, therefore, we've seen more and more marketers start with their ads online, test them live, in-market, and then take that concept and messaging into other media. Finally, radio ads can also be tested, but they very seldom are.

Some agencies don't believe in creative testing. This is foolish behavior and should not be tolerated by marketers. Research will not kill a good idea, but it can decimate bad ideas and it should. Doing the research the wrong way, though, can filter out the good ideas. And therefore it is important for the marketing team to understand the way the research is conducted (in the lab or in the real world) and the assumptions of the research.

Notes

Introduction

1. *www.thearf.org/about/index.html*

2. Advertising spending is $450 billion worldwide and nearly $300 billion in the United States alone, Robert Cohen's Insider's Report on Advertising Expenditure 12/05.

3. *Untold Millions,* Lukenbill, Grant; Harper Business, New York, NY 1995; *The Advertising Business: Operations, Creativity, Media Planning, Integrated Communications,* edited by John Philip Jones, Sage Publishing, Inc. "Net Results," Bruner, Rick, Hayden Book Company, Excellence in International Research 2002, ESOMAR Publications, etc.

4. This is a partial list of the companies that agreed to make their research results public.

Chapter 1

1. Universal McCann, Advertising spending is $450 billion worldwide and nearly $300 billion in the United States alone, Robert Cohen's Insider's Report on Advertising Expenditure 12/05.

2. David C. Court, Jonathan W. Gordon, and Jesko Perrey, "Boosting Returns on Marketing Investment," *The McKinsey Quarterly.* McKinsey and Company, Dusseldorf 2005, vol. 2.

3. Jim Stengel, AAAA Media Conference and Trade Show, Universal, Orlando, FL, 11 February 2004.

4. ANA Conference. "Survey Finds Senior-Level Marketers Not Focusing on Important Aspects of Return-On-Investments," New York, NY, 6 July 2006.

5. Barbara Bacci-Mirque, Marketing Evolution Client Conference, Napa, CA, 2–4 November 2005.

6. Deutsch allocates $3 billion in advertisers' money and hosts the CNBC show *Big Idea.*

7. Donny Deutsch, Video-taped presentation, Redmond, WA, 3 March 2005.

8. *Wall Street Journal,* "Putting a Value on Marketing Dollars," 27 July 2005; *Wall Street Journal,* Econometrics Buzzes Ad World As a Way of Measuring Results, 16 August 2005.

9. Rex Briggs, "How the Internet Is Reshaping Advertising," *Admap,* April 2005, Issue 460, 59–61.

10. Meta analysis of each study totaling $1 billion in advertising spent across 30 top marketers, projected to the $250 billion spent annually in the United States on advertising.

11. Rex Briggs, "Quantifying Marketing ROI: The Philips Journey," *Admap,* February 2006, 8.

12. Richard Grammier, Marketing Evolution Client Conference, Napa, CA, 2–4 November 2005.

Chapter 2

1. iMedia Brand Summit, Park City, UT, Fall 2004.

2. Jim Nail, "Dove Cleans Up Online Advertising's Image," Forrester Tech Strategy Brief, 15 February 2002.

3. ESOMAR's Best International Research Paper Award, The John & Mary Goodyear Award.

Chapter 3

1. *dictionary.com*

2. Jim Nail, "Dove Cleans Up Online Advertising's Image," Forrester Tech Strategy Brief, 15 February 2002.

3. Patti Wakeling, Unilever and Brian Murphy, Information Resources, Inc., "e-AdWorks Internet Advertising Effectiveness Consortium," ARF Proceedings, 2002.

4. Robert Heath, "The Hidden Power of Advertising," *Admap,* Monograph No. 7, August 2001.

5. Erwin Ephron, "Gotterdammerung, Baby," p. 2, *www.eppronmedia.com*, 2 January 1999.

6. Jon Howard-Spink, "Does Invisible Mean Ineffective?" *Admap*, December 2005, No. 467, 41–43.

7. Greg Welch, "CMO Tenure: Slowing Down the Revolving Door," Spencer Stuart Blue Paper, July 2004.

Chapter 4

1. Donny Deutsch, Video-taped presentation, Redmond, WA, 3 March 2005.

2. Rex Briggs, Marketing as a Supply Chain, Working Paper, *www.market ingrevolution.com*, 2005.

3. Author interview with Dawn Jacobs and David Adelman, Johnson & Johnson, 12 April 2006.

Chapter 5

1. *Business Week*, Interbrand 2004 Brand Value Scorecard.

2. Chad Terhane, "Recharging Coke," *Wall Street Journal*, 17 April 2006.

3. Mike Hess and Gregg Ambach, "Short- and Long-Term Effects of Advertising and Promotion," AAAA series on Value of Advertising, 2002.

4. Rex Briggs, "Integrated Multichannel Communication Strategies: Evaluating the Return on Marketing Objectives—The Case of the 2004 Ford F-150 Launch," *Journal of Interactive Marketing*, Volume 19, Number 3, Summer 2005.

5. Jack Neff, "P&G Eyes the Influencer," *Advertising Age*, 17 November 2003.

Chapter 6

1. Clay Christiansen and Taddy Hall, "Marketing Malpractice," *Harvard Business Review*, December 2005.

2. Gerald Zaltman. *How Customers Think: Essential Insights into the Mind of the Market*. Harvard Business School Press, 2003, 9.

Chapter 7

1. Barbara Bacci-Mirque, ANA, Interview in New York, NY, 9 March 2006.

Chapter 8

1. According to a simple analysis on *Cockeyed.com*, Target's prices were only 4 percent higher in an analysis of 20 products.

2. Don Gher, an analyst with Coldstream Capital Management in Associated Press as Reported on MSNBC, "Wal-Mart Turns Attention to Upscale Shoppers," 23 March 2006.

3. Christine Bittar, "Getting Totaled," *Brandweek*, 12 October 1998, 36.

4. Ibid, 37–38.

5. Kim Cleland, "The Marketing 100," *Advertising Age*, 29 June 1998.

6. George Peterson, president of AutoPacific Inc., "Minivan or SUV: Which Is Right for Your Family?" Reported by Carol Traeger in *Parenthood.com*.

Chapter 9

1. Garth Hallberg, *All Consumers Are Not Created Equal*, New York/London, John Wiley & Sons, 1995.

2. Don Peppers and Martha Rogers, *The One to One Future*, New York, Currency Doubleday, 1996.

3. *www.imdb.com*

4. Max Southerland, *Advertising and the Mind of the Consumer*, Allen & Unwin, 2000

5. Mintel, The Hair Styling Products Market, U.S. Consumer Intelligence, *www.marketresearch.com*, November 2002.

6. Rex Briggs, "Integrated Multichannel Communication Strategies: Evaluating the Return on Marketing Objectives, The case of the 2004 Ford F-150 Launch," *Journal of Interactive Marketing*, Volume 19, Number 3, Summer 2005.

Chapter 10

1. Rex Briggs, "The Role of Creative Execution in Online Advertising Success," Volume 1, No. 4, Interactive Advertising Bureau monthly newsletter, *www.iab.net*, New York, NY, 2002.

2. WGBH Educational Foundation, 2000–2001, *www.pbs.org/wgbh/building big/wonder/structure/citicorp.html*.

3. St. Lewis's theory is drawn from his experience in face-to-face sales in the 1890s. He brought the theory to advertising, which at the time was print advertising characterized by substantially more copy compared to modern print advertising. These print ads, he suggested, needed to first get the consumer's attention, then build interest, and then desire so that the advertising could lead to action. The theory is called *awareness, interest, desire, action* (AIDA). The theory does not address the process consumers go through in dealing with lower-attention cognitive behavior when processing media such as radio or TV because the media didn't exist at the time the theory was developed.

4. Jon Howard-Spink, "Does Invisible Mean Ineffective?" *Admap*, Issue 467, December 2005, 41–43.

5. Ibid, 41–43.

6. Robert Heath, "The Hidden Power of Advertising," *Admap*, Monograph No. 7, August 2001.

7. Gerald Zaltman, *How Customers Think: Essential Insights into the Mind of the Mark.* Harvard Business School Publishing, Boston, Mass., 2003, 9.

8. George Lowenstein, "The Creative Destruction of Decision Research," University of Chicago Press, Volume 28(3), 503, December.

9. Rex Briggs, "Quantifying Marketing ROI: The Philips Journey," *Admap*, Februry 2006, 18–22.

Chapter 11

1. Robert M. Lee quoted in, "Behind the Headlight," Ferrari Barchetta, SpeedTV.
Matt Stone, executive editor, *Motor Trend* Magazine as quoted in "Behind the Headlights," Ferrari Barchetta, SpeedTV.

2. Ibid, 41–43.

3. We call this a field experiment because consumers are measured in the real world, or *field*, as economists would call it, not in an artificial setting of the laboratory.

4. Claude C. Hopkins, *Scientific Advertising*, NTC/Contemporary Publishing Company, Chicago, IL, 1923.

5. Rex Briggs and Horst Stipp, "Excellence in International Research," *How Internet Advertising Works*, 2000, 217.

6. Rex Briggs, "The Role of Creative Execution in Online Advertising Success," *Measuring Success*, Volume 1, No. 4, *www.iab.net* or *www.marketingevolution.com*.

7. IAB New Formats Study 2001. *See www.iab.net*.

8. Rex Briggs, Sullivan and Webster, Hong Kong Online Advertising Effectiveness Study, 2001.

9. Artie Bulgrin, *Measuring Effectiveness When Sales Aren't the Goal: ESPN's Dream Job*, 19 July 2004. New York.

10. Tuchman Coffin, " TV without Pix." *Mediascope,* February, 1968. See also Statistical Research, Inc. "Imagery Transfer Study," a presentation to Radio and Television Research Council, 18 October 1993.

Chapter 12

1. Anne Saunders, CMO, Starbucks, Boston Globe's 2nd Annual Ad Club Symposium, Boston, Mass., Brand Now, 10 March 2005.

2. Mixx Conference and Awards Expo, New York, NY, 26–27 September 2005.

3. "Smelling the Brand Opportunity," *Adweek,* 14 March 2005.

4. Martin Lindstrom, The 51st Annual Research Foundation Convention, New York, NY, 17–19 April 2005.

5. Rex Briggs, "How the Internet Is Reshaping Advertising," *Admap,* April 2005, p 2–4.

Chapter 13

1. The author, Greg Stuart, would like to offer his apologies to the brands that he advised over that decade of media allocation deceit, including AT&T, American Express, Rockport, Frito-Lay, Ethan Allen, Minolta, Nabisco, Apple Computer, Cars.com, Sony Online Ventures, Kraft, Lucent, Quaker Oats, Sears, Prodigy, U.S. Postal Service, Viacom, and Welch's. It wasn't your fault or the agency's teams that did their best to help you; we lacked the measurement tools that exist today. As a way of setting right past errors, I would be happy to come share some of these insights with any of these companies.

2. Monitoring Advertising Performance Conference, London, United Kingdom, 25 January 2005.

3. Krysten Crawford, "A Sneak Peak at Super Bowl Ads," *cnnmoney.com*, Feb. 4, 2005.

4. Erwin Ephron, "Gotterdammerung, Baby," p. 2, *www.epprononme dia.com,* 2 January 1999.

5. In most European countries, the TV measurement is superior to that of the United States in that the reported reach reflects the average audience tuning in during the minute in which the ad was aired.

Chapter 14

1. Gerard J. Tellis, *Effective Advertising*, Sage Publications, 2004, 125–127.

2. *www.naute.com/illusions/rabduck.phtml.*

Chapter 15

1. *www.hi.is/~joner/eaps/cq_strp2.htm.*

2. John Brooks, The Edsel, Rubic Annals of Business, New Yorker Magazine, Part I, Nov. 26, 1960 & Part II, Dec. 23, 1960.

3. The 52nd Annual ARF Convention, Re:think!2006—March 20–22, New York, NY.

4. Rex Briggs, Excellence in International Research 2003, Cross Media Measurement, ESOMAR, Amsterdam, The Netherlands, 2003.

5. Rex Briggs, "Integrated Multichannel Communication Strategies: Evaluating the Return on Marketing Objectives, The case of the 2004 Ford F-150 Launch," *Journal of Interactive Marketing*, Volume 19, Number 3, Summer 2005.

6. Tom Greene, AHAA Conference, Miami, FL, 21–23 April 2004.

Chapter 17

1. *www.gigaom.com/2005/04/13/sunny-skies-forecast-for-ipod/.*

2. Interview with author, April 2006.

Appendix A

1. SAS Conference, Seattle, WA, April 2005.

Index